KINGS

OF

SHANGHAI

KINGS
OF
SHANGHAI

Two rival dynasties and
the creation of modern China

JONATHAN
KAUFMAN

Little, Brown

LITTLE, BROWN

First published in the United States in 2020 by Viking
First published in Great Britain in 2020 by Little, Brown

1 3 5 7 9 10 8 6 4 2

A CIP catalogue record for this book
is available from the British Library.

Hardback ISBN 978-1-4087-1004-3
Trade paperback ISBN 978-1-4087-1003-6

Designed by Meighan Cavanaugh
Printed and bound in Great Britain by Clays Ltd, Elcograf S.p.A.

Papers used by Little, Brown are from well-managed forests
and other responsible sources.

MIX
Paper from
responsible sources
FSC® C104740

Little, Brown
An imprint of
Little, Brown Book Group
Carmelite House
50 Victoria Embankment
London EC4Y 0DZ

An Hachette UK Company
www.hachette.co.uk

www.littlebrown.co.uk

For Barbara, and for Molly, Ben, and Nick—
who shared the adventure, with love and laughter

Contents

Cast of Characters

THE SASSOON FAMILY

David Sassoon (1792–1864). The patriarch. Scion of a prominent Jewish family from Baghdad, he and his eight sons built a business empire across Asia. Though he never learned Chinese or English, he piloted his family to dominate the China trade, subdue and shape Shanghai, control the opium business, bankroll the future king of England, and advise prime ministers.

Elias Sassoon (1820–1880). A loner, thin and bespectacled, Elias established the Sassoons' business in Shanghai and eventually across China. Not even a bitter falling-out with his elder brother that split the family could slow his business success.

Flora Sassoon (1859–1936). The wife of one of David's eight sons. A brilliant scholar and businesswoman, Flora took over the Sassoon business in Bombay and Shanghai when her husband died, working from her home because women in India at the time weren't allowed to even visit business offices. She succeeded beyond all expectations until her brothers-in-law threw her out in a family coup.

Rachel Sassoon Beer (1858–1927). One of a string of talented Sassoon women, she was socially progressive and an early feminist who crusaded against anti-Semitism and rose to become the most powerful female journalist in England, editing *The Observer* and *The Sunday Times*. Yet she was scorned by her family and died alone of depression after being declared insane.

Victor Sassoon (1881–1961). Billionaire playboy, crippled at age thirty, Victor transformed Shanghai into a world-class city, bankrolled the Nationalist government, defied the Japanese, and saved thousands of Jewish refugees fleeing Nazism. Yet a friend said about him, "Victor always made the wrong decision at the wrong time in the wrong place."

Emily Hahn (1905–1997). An American writer for *The New Yorker*, based in Shanghai. She became Victor Sassoon's lover and companion and saw before he did the rise of the Communists and the inequalities of colonial Shanghai. Victor, jealous of Hahn's affair with a Chinese writer, didn't listen to her.

THE KADOORIE FAMILY

Elly Kadoorie (1865–1944). Elly started out as a student and employee of the Sassoons, but he quickly set out to seek his own fortune. Always an outsider, he built alliances with Chinese revolutionaries like Sun Yat-sen, immigrants like himself, and local Chinese, accumulating a fortune that made him one of the richest and most powerful men in Asia.

Laura Kadoorie (1859–1919). Born into a rich and powerful British family, Laura left it all behind to marry Elly and move to China. In Shanghai, she survived wars, was witness to the poverty and the transformation of Shanghai, and became the most emancipated woman in the city. Her death shattered the family and turned her into a figure of fascination and reverence for the Chinese.

Lawrence Kadoorie (1899–1993). Elly and Laura's eldest son. Sturdy, with powerful shoulders and a love for fast cars, Lawrence had dreams of becoming a lawyer but was forced into the family business by his father. Refusing to abandon China after the Communists seized Shanghai, he rebuilt the family fortune in Hong Kong and was embraced by Deng Xiaoping and the Chinese when China emerged from isolation in the 1970s.

Horace Kadoorie (1902–1995). Lawrence's younger brother. Shy where his brother was gregarious; tall and thin where his brother was five-foot-nine and built like a boxer. A lifelong bachelor, Horace lived with his father in Shanghai's largest mansion and then in a country house away from the center of Hong Kong. He and his brother shared an extraordinary bond, and together they saved 18,000 Jewish refugees who fled Nazism and later helped 360,000 Chinese who fled communism rebuild their lives in Hong Kong.

IN CHINA

Jardine, Matheson & Co. (1832–). A great British trading house created to trade opium with China. Its leaders persuaded Great Britain to invade China and open Shanghai to foreigners. Outmaneuvered by the better business tactics and technology of the Sassoons, the company abandoned the opium trade in the 1870s and resented the Sassoons for the next half century.

Robert Hotung (1862–1956). The richest man in early twentieth-century Hong Kong. He became a business ally and friend of Elly Kadoorie. The two outsiders launched a series of corporate raids on the British establishment in Shanghai that gave them control of vast parts of the city.

Silas Hardoon (1851–1931). A Baghdad expatriate like the Sassoons, Hardoon was hired by the family to work for the Sassoon company in Shanghai. He quit in 1920 and became a real estate magnate.

Sun Yat-sen (1866–1925). China's George Washington, Sun led the revolution that overthrew the Chinese empire. He formed an early alliance with Elly Kadoorie that benefited both, and the relationship between the families persisted into the twenty-first century, cementing the relationship between the Kadoories and China.

Madame Sun Yat-sen, also known as Soong Qing-ling (1893–1981). Wife of Sun Yat-sen, educated in the United States, a convert to communism, an agile diplomat. Madame Sun rose to become vice president of Communist China and China's liaison to many in the West—including the Kadoories.

Ho Feng-Shan (1901–1997). A Chinese diplomat stationed in Vienna during World War II, Ho issued thousands of exit visas to Jews fleeing the Nazis, many of whom escaped to Shanghai.

Rong Family (1873–). China's most successful businessmen, they learned from the Sassoons and the Kadoories starting in the nineteenth century and rode the waves of politics in China from capitalism to communism and back to capitalism. Their connections with the Kadoories helped transform Hong Kong, but their rise also threatened the power of the Kadoories as China became more assertive in the twenty-first century.

Koreshige Inuzuka (1890–1965). An anti-Semitic Japanese captain, Inuzuka was flattered and wooed by Victor Sassoon into protecting 18,000 Jewish refugees who fled to Shanghai during World War II.

Chiang Kai-Shek (1887–1975). Leader of the anticommunist Nationalist Chinese, Chiang manipulated Western businessmen, American politicians, and public opinion to support his crackdowns on dissidents and his civil war against Mao Zedong. His army was forced to flee Shanghai and abandon the mainland in 1949 and establish a new government on the island of Taiwan.

Mao Zedong (1893–1976). The Chinese Communist revolutionary was a tenant of Silas Hardoon. Mao Zedong loved Shanghai for its radicalism and hated it for its capitalism, and the city played a pivotal role for him and his wife, Jiang Qing, as they transformed China. His death paved the way for the return of the Kadoories to Shanghai and the city's reevaluation of the Sassoons.

Deng Xiaoping (1904–1997). The leader of China from 1978 to 1992, he was determined to modernize China. He ordered officials to reach out to Lawrence Kadoorie to build China's first nuclear plant and welcomed the Kadoories back into the circle of power at the Great Hall of the People.

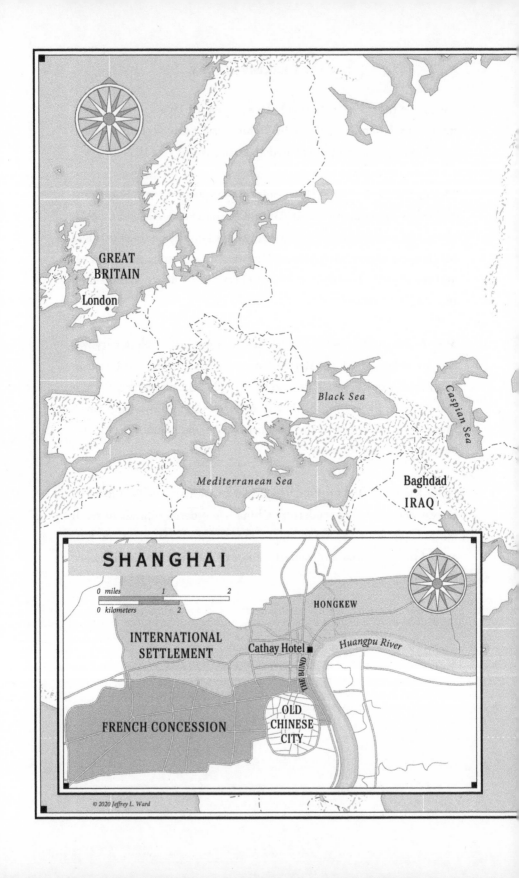

GREAT
BRITAIN

London

Black Sea

Caspian Sea

Mediterranean Sea

Baghdad
IRAQ

SHANGHAI

0 miles   1   2
0 kilometers   2

HONGKEW

INTERNATIONAL
SETTLEMENT

Cathay Hotel

Huangpu River

THE BUND

FRENCH CONCESSION

OLD
CHINESE
CITY

© 2020 Jeffrey L. Ward

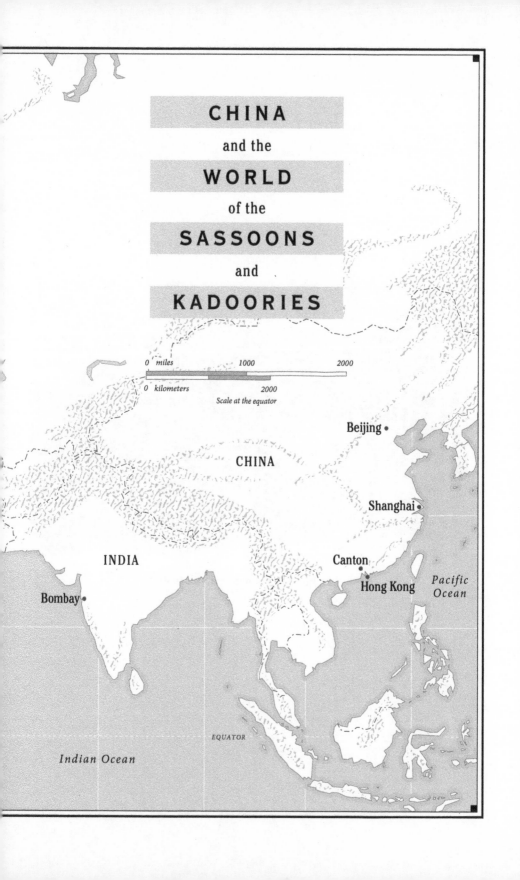

CHINA
and the
WORLD
of the
SASSOONS
and
KADOORIES

0 miles 1000 2000
0 kilometers 2000
Scale at the equator

Beijing •

CHINA

Shanghai •

INDIA

Canton •

Bombay • Hong Kong

Pacific Ocean

EQUATOR

Indian Ocean

The Bund in Shanghai in the 1930s

Introduction

I t was a muggy late-summer day in 1979 when I stepped out of the Shanghai heat into the cool marble lobby of the Peace Hotel.

I was twenty-three years old, a fledgling foreign correspondent on assignment. The United States had just established diplomatic relations with China after thirty years of the Cold War. China had begun opening itself to the world. The hotel sat on a curve of the Bund, the pedestrian promenade that runs along the busy Huangpu River waterfront. Its façade, like the prow of a mighty ship, jutted toward the sea, anchoring a skyline of art deco buildings that overlooked the river below. China was preserved in amber, circa 1949, the year the Communists seized power and "liberated" the country from capitalism and foreign invasions. Everything was cast in black and white. No billboards or advertising or colorful storefronts enlivened the streets. Sturdy, thick, black-framed bicycles thronged the roadways, interrupted occasionally by boxy black roadsters. White lace curtains on the passenger windows of limousines hid the Communist

Party officials inside. Chinese men and women alike wore white shirts and stiff dark-blue Mao suits draped over their frames. All the clothes looked one size too big. For thirty years, China had been cut off from the world, certainly from most Americans. "Red China" had fought the United States in the Korean War, sided with the North Vietnamese in the Vietnam War, denounced the United States as "running dogs" and "imperialists," threatened nuclear war. Richard Nixon had broken China's isolation seven years earlier with his presidential visit, but the country still felt alien and menacing. The Communist Chinese leader Mao Zedong had died three years earlier, in his final decade having presided over the chaos and near–civil war of the Cultural Revolution. His successors, led by Deng Xiaoping, had quickly arrested and jailed the radical "Gang of Four" headed by Mao's widow, Jiang Qing, and her leftist Cultural Revolution followers, many of them from Shanghai.

Every conversation—with "ordinary" farmers and factory workers trotted out by government officials, with Communist Party bureaucrats, even with taxi drivers—began with a programmed denunciation of the toppled Gang of Four:

"Under the Gang of Four our cows never met their milk quota, but since the arrest of the Gang of Four, milk production is up 30 percent."

"Under the Gang of Four our factory failed to meet our quota for textiles. Since the overthrow of the Gang of Four, our workers are more efficient, and we have tripled production."

The meetings were so rote that at one point my fellow journalists and I donned Mao jackets and caps and staged sophomoric skits in our hotel rooms, away from the prying eyes of our official Chinese minders: "Under the Gang of Four my husband never had sex with me. Since the overthrow of the Gang of Four, we have sex three, four times a week!" More than twenty years later, when I returned to live in China as bureau chief of *The Wall Street Journal*, I talked to a Beijing taxi driver about this bizarre time. He laughed. "I was driving a taxi back then, and they told us what to tell the foreigners: 'Under the Gang of Four, blah-blah-blah.'"

If Shanghai back in 1979 was a black-and-white movie with stilted dialogue, stepping into the Peace Hotel was like entering a 1940s movie. In color. With French subtitles.

Chandeliers hung from the vaulted ceilings. Wall sconces ran along corridors leading from the lobby, illuminating the path to marble and carpeted stairways. Off in a corner, a poster advertised a nightly jazz band.

I walked toward the bank of elevators. An elderly bellhop, dressed in white pants, a cropped white jacket, and a small white cap, stepped up to me.

"*Puis-je vous aider? Que voulez-vous voir?*" Can I help you? What would you like to see?

"*Je ne parle pas français,*" I stammered back in long-forgotten high-school French.

"*Quel dommage,*" he said with a smile. What a pity.

What was this place? What was this relic of European luxury— even hedonism—embalmed in a city, and a country, that thirty years of Communist totalitarianism had turned drab, egalitarian, regimented, and a little kooky?

A decade passed before I visited Shanghai again. It was 1989, a few days after the Tiananmen Square massacre that killed hundreds of students in Beijing and sent the rest of China into shock and armed lockdown. I spent much of my time speaking furtively to students and other Chinese. One of the few official visits I was allowed was a tour of the "Children's Palace." I knew it would be an innocuous and obviously staged contrast to the anger that was seething outside: Chinese children playing piano and taking ballet lessons—a forced normalcy.

I was right about the propaganda, but the "palace" overwhelmed me. It was a European-style mansion, a "great house" that wouldn't have been out of place on the outskirts of Paris or London. There was marble everywhere; there were soaring ceilings and elaborate chandeliers, sumptuous room after sumptuous room with inlaid wooden floors, elegant wainscoting, and fireplaces. A sweeping staircase led to a second floor. It felt like the home of a British noble family. That's not surprising, my Chinese guide told me earnestly. For twenty-five years, from 1924 until the Communist takeover in 1949, it had been home to a rich British capitalist family—the Kadoories. I stopped. The Kadoories? I knew from my time in Hong Kong that the Kadoories—led by Sir Lawrence Kadoorie—were one of the city's richest and most powerful families, owners of the legendary Peninsula Hotel with its elegant lobby, extravagant afternoon teas, and exquisite—and expensive—rooms. The Kadoories also owned Hong Kong's largest electric company. And a stake in its cross-harbor tunnel. And the tram that ran up the Peak. They were "taipans"—a leftover colonial term that conveyed power and money and roots that stretched back to the Opium Wars.

They weren't Chinese. I knew, in fact, that they were Jewish. The Kadoories had helped fund programs at the synagogue I had gone to in Hong Kong while I lived there as a reporter.

I didn't have a chance to learn more about the Kadoories then. My reporting took me to Berlin, where I covered the fall of the Berlin

Wall and the collapse of communism in Russia and Eastern Europe. I didn't return to China for almost fifteen years, even as it reemerged and twitched back to life.

In 2002, I found myself back in Shanghai to cover China's rise as a global economic power for *The Wall Street Journal*. My reporting took me to a neighborhood away from the waterfront and away from the hustle and bustle of the business districts. China had begun to understand the virtues of tourism and had reopened a synagogue built by another Jewish family, the Sassoons, in the 1920s. The Communist government had turned the synagogue into a museum. Hebrew letters were carved over the entrance, but inside it was stripped bare of any signs of what it had once been. On the second floor was a small library with an elderly Chinese attendant. We sat down and chatted about his memories. He remembered that Jewish families had lived in Shanghai in 1949, before the revolution. He had worked for some of them, lighting their stoves, because, he said, they couldn't do it for some reason on Saturdays. He had been, I realized, a "Shabbos goy," a non-Jew hired by observant Jews to do certain tasks that Jewish law prevents them from doing on the Sabbath.

I asked him if he knew the name Sassoon. They were, I learned, the rich family that had built and owned the Peace Hotel before the Communists seized power.

"Of course," he said. "The Cathay Hotel." He was using the name the hotel was given when it first opened, in the 1930s, before the Communists renamed it. "Everyone knew the name Sassoon," he said, nodding emphatically.

The Communist Party had been founded in Shanghai, and the wealth enjoyed by the Sassoons was in stark contrast to the poverty, hunger, and desperation that had fueled the Communist victory.

"Did you hate them, their wealth?" I asked. He nodded. That wasn't surprising.

With memories still fresh of conversations I had had with elderly Germans and Czechs and Poles still poisoned by anti-Semitism, I asked gingerly, "Did you hate them because they were Jewish?"

He paused thoughtfully.

"No," he said. "We hated them because they were British imperialists."

Outside, as I left, I spotted two elderly Chinese women picking over fruit at a nearby market. They looked old enough that they might, like the caretaker, remember Shanghai before the Communists conquered the city in 1949.

I went up to them and, with the help of my Chinese assistant, explained that I was visiting the old synagogue building. Before "Liberation," as the Chinese called the Communists' 1949 victory, Jews might have lived in this neighborhood. Did they remember that?

"Have you come back for the furniture?" one of the women asked brightly.

"What do you mean?" I asked, baffled.

She heaved two sacks of groceries into her arms and, declining my offer to help carry them, brusquely directed us across the street and up a flight of stairs to the one room where she lived. It had clearly been part of a larger apartment at one time. Now the original apartment was chopped up into a series of rooms with dividers of plywood and fabric to accommodate a half-dozen families. A mahogany double bed predating World War II took up one corner of the room, a companion chest of drawers next to it.

"The Jewish people, they lived here," she said. "Then they left. They left the furniture." I quickly conferred with my Chinese assistant. Did she mean the Jews had been taken away, deported by the Chinese or the Japanese? Taken to camps or made to disappear or killed?

No, no, the woman explained. "They lived here during the war. After Liberation, the Jews stayed for a while, then they left. For Israel, for Palestine. Far away." She pointed again at the mahogany bed and chest.

"Have you come back for the furniture?"

In a sense, I guess I had.

FOR DECADES, China's Communist rulers have obscured the stories of the Sassoons and the Kadoories, two rival foreign families who journeyed to China in the nineteenth century and became dynasties. They painted the century these families shaped—from the end of the First Opium War in 1842 that opened China to the West to the Communist takeover in 1949—with the broad brush of propaganda. They erased history, and, like politicians the world over, mobilized support by invoking national myths and stories. In elementary school classrooms across China there is a poster that declares WU WANG GUO CHI—NEVER FORGET NATIONAL HUMILIATION. The Communist leadership wants schoolchildren to remember how foreigners like the Kadoories and the Sassoons lived in splendor, exploiting the Chinese working class and imprisoning Chinese citizens in squalor, ignorance, and a haze of opium. Only when Mao and his devoted army of Communist guerrillas toppled these rapacious capitalists did China stand on its feet again. As China's power grows and its rivalry with the United States intensifies, understanding the stories that it tells itself matters. They can help us understand what makes China tick.

Digging out the truth behind them also may suggest different ways of dealing with China, and of China dealing with the world.

There is much truth in the Chinese Communist version of history. But there are other truths as well. Shanghai was China's melting pot, the crucible in which all the forces that shaped China—capitalism, communism, imperialism, foreigners, and nationalism—came together. By 1895, Shanghai had a modern tram system and gas works that rivaled London's. By the 1930s, led by taipan Victor Sassoon, it had skyscrapers and a skyline that rivaled Chicago's. It was the fourth-largest city in the world. While the rest of the world sank into the Great Depression, Chiang Kai-shek's government worked with the Sassoons to stabilize the currency and create an export boom. Shanghai became China's New York, the capital of finance, commerce, and industry. It also became China's Los Angeles, the capital of popular culture. In the 1920s and 1930s, Shanghai's publishing houses produced more than 10,000 pamphlets, newspapers, and magazines. Its film studios churned out hundreds of films, many of them set in the westernized city. Colleges flourished. So did politics. The International Concession of Shanghai was governed like a republic of business. A seven-member council made up of businessmen, including representatives of the Sassoons, ran the city independent of Chinese law. Paradoxically, that meant a relatively liberal political atmosphere—protecting Chinese activists, reformers, and radicals from heavy-handed Nationalist Chinese-government restrictions on free speech, communism, and protests. What would become Mao Zedong's Communist Party held its first meeting in Shanghai, just a few miles from the business headquarters and mansions of the Sassoons and the Kadoories.

Together the Sassoons and the Kadoories helped shape a city that made them billionaires—and inspired and enabled a generation of

Chinese businessmen to be successful capitalists and entrepreneurs. They helped create a thriving entrepreneurial culture, which the Communists wiped out in 1949. Victor Sassoon made Shanghai part of the "Grand Tour" that opened China to the world's elites. His masked balls and his Cathay Hotel ballroom attracted Noël Coward, Charlie Chaplin, and American socialite Wallis Simpson, who reportedly learned in Shanghai the sexual techniques that would entice a king to leave his throne a few years later.

In the Roaring Twenties and the 1930s, middle-class and wealthy Chinese flocked to Shanghai, drawn by its economic opportunity and a life unavailable anywhere else in China: glamorous department stores, hotels, nightclubs, gambling casinos. After decades of stagnation and retreat before the British, Americans, French, and others, many Chinese believed that Shanghai was forging a new, dynamic Chinese culture—outward looking, cosmopolitan, prepared to embrace the twentieth century. The Sassoons and the Kadoories helped open the world to China—and opened China to the world.

When the Japanese invaded China and joined Germany as an Axis power, the Sassoons and the Kadoories joined forces and achieved one of the miracles of World War II. As 18,000 European Jews traveled 5,000 miles from Berlin and Vienna and streamed into Shanghai fleeing Nazism, Victor Sassoon negotiated secretly with the Japanese while Nazi representatives urged the Japanese occupiers to pile Jewish refugees onto barges and sink them in the middle of the Huangpu River. Together, the Sassoons and the Kadoories did something that Jews in Europe and Palestine and even the United States couldn't do: they protected every Jewish refugee who set foot in their city, among them thousands of children—including Michael Blumenthal, who would grow up to be U.S. treasury secretary; the artist

Peter Max; Hollywood executive Michael Medavoy; and Harvard Law School professor Laurence Tribe.

When the Communists conquered Shanghai and seized the Kadoories' and the Sassoons' hotels and mansions and factories, the Kadoories retreated to the British colony of Hong Kong on China's southern tip. The Sassoons fled to London and the Bahamas and even Dallas, Texas. But they never stopped thinking about Shanghai.

The world of this book, much like our world today, was defined by innovation and globalization, growing inequality and political turmoil. Long before Mark Zuckerberg, Steve Jobs, Microsoft, and Google grappled with how to deal with China and political pressures in the United States, the Sassoons and the Kadoories, with their offices in Shanghai, Hong Kong, Bombay, and London, mastered the global economy and struggled with the moral and political dilemmas of working with China. Both the Sassoons and the Kadoories showed the great things that business, especially enlightened business, could do. They went where governments wouldn't, or couldn't, go. Their decisions changed the lives of hundreds of millions of people. The Sassoons helped stabilize China's economy in the 1930s when the rest of the world was falling into depression. They trained a generation of Chinese in global capitalism, paving the way for China's astonishing success today. The Kadoories brought electricity to millions of people in Hong Kong, transforming regions where the pace of life hadn't changed in hundreds of years. The Kadoorie family's decision after 1949 to partner in Hong Kong with Chinese factory owners from Shanghai who were fleeing communism opened global markets, ignited Hong Kong's growth, and helped set the stage for the export boom that in the twenty-first century would make China the world's factory floor.

And yet, for all their political and economic acumen, the Sassoons and the Kadoories missed the Communist revolution that was brewing right outside their offices and lush living rooms in Shanghai. When, to their astonishment, the Communists triumphed in 1949, the Sassoons and the Kadoories lost almost everything. They left behind a legacy that haunts China's relations with the United States and the rest of the world to this day. Not a museum visit or tour of China or business meeting or diplomatic negotiation ends without a reference to the history of foreign exploitation and imperialism in China, the humiliation China endured, the determination that it will never happen again. From the anger over the opium trade to the dramatic skyline of Shanghai's Bund and the tensions over the future of Hong Kong, the history and legacy of these families hang over nearly every decision China makes today.

Readers may note that while China stands at the center of this narrative, Chinese characters often stand at the periphery. This reflects the peculiar colonial world these families inhabited. Even while living in Shanghai they dealt with the Chinese at a distance, separated by language, wealth, and colonial stereotypes. It is revealing that no Chinese ever penetrated the inner circle of either family and, in almost two hundred years of living in China, none of the Sassoons or the Kadoories bothered to learn Chinese. At the same time, their distance from most Chinese made it easy for China and especially Communist leaders and historians to dismiss or caricature these families and minimize their impact and influence. One of the goals of this book is to embrace this complexity and help us understand the choices the Kadoories and the Sassoons made. Many of their actions were in keeping with the times, or were more progressive than the times, even when driven by profit or paternalism. In other cases, they were blind to the consequences and accepted the colonial assumptions of the time. Their own Jewish background complicated how they navigated among these different worlds. The story that follows isn't the story of China since 1840; rather, it restores part of the mosaic of Chinese history.

As China embarks on what many consider to be the Chinese century, sending students and businesses and visitors abroad, its leaders shun the complexity of history. They like portraying China, even as it rises, as a historical victim. Had China remained poor, weak, and isolated, the story of Shanghai and the Sassoons and the Kadoories might be a curiosity, an alternative history of what might have been. But the issues China faces today—working with foreigners; inequality and corruption; finding a place in the world; balancing nationalism and openness, democracy and political control, diversity and change—were the issues that shaped Shanghai and confronted the Kadoories and the Sassoons every day. As much as the Kadoories and the Sassoons, Shanghai—its growth, its development, its struggles and contradictions—is a character in this book.

Few countries are given a second chance. The story of China in the twentieth century, and the twenty-first, is of a great power that fell, driven into decline by internal corruption, Western colonialism, and Japanese imperialism, and then fought to rise again. If China succeeds, it will not be just because it emulates the spirit of Beijing, center of China's political power, with a leadership that embraces a repressive state and quashes dissent. It will be because it also emulates Shanghai, the elegant, industrious, sophisticated, outward looking, and cosmopolitan city, and the merchant princes—now forgotten—who helped yank China into the modern era. For more than sixty years, Shanghai—and China—hid that history away in closets and cupboards, in the yellowing papers of old office safes, and in stories whispered over tea in shuttered rooms and at kitchen tables.

In 2014, the Fairmont hotel chain was hired by a Chinese hotel company to restore Victor Sassoon's once-elegant Cathay Hotel overlooking the Bund. Returning there soon after, I was taken up a narrow flight of stairs off the lobby to a room filled with glass cabinets and display cases. Soon after buying the hotel, the new owners had placed a small advertisement in a local Chinese newspaper seeking antiques and artifacts from the hotel's glory days in the 1930s. They expected a couple of old menus, perhaps, or a souvenir ashtray. Hundreds of Shanghainese responded. They deluged the hotel with embossed dishes, crystal glasses, and elegantly printed menus. They sent in photographs of Chinese women in floor-length, formfitting cheongsams and Chinese men in Western suits celebrating weddings and birthdays in the hotel dining room—Sir Victor Sassoon, every inch the British aristocrat, hovering with his monocle and walking stick in the background. Fifty years of communism had put China through revolution, famine, and the Cultural Revolution. Yet, like the woman I met at the food stall who slept in a Western bed every night, hundreds of Chinese families had saved these pieces of the past in apartment closets scattered across Shanghai—a memory, a dream of Shanghai that once promised a different China.

This is their furniture, too.

PART ONE

Shanghai Calling

David Sassoon

1

The Patriarch

Through the darkened streets, the richest man in Baghdad fled for his life.

Just hours earlier, David Sassoon's father had ransomed him from the jail where Baghdad's Turkish rulers had imprisoned him, threatening to hang him if the family did not pay an exorbitant tax bill. Now a boat lay waiting to take thirty-seven-year-old David to safety. He tied a money belt around his waist and donned a cloak. Servants had sewn pearls inside the lining. "Only his eyes showed between the turban and a high-muffled cloak as he slipped through the gates of the city where generations of his kin had once been honored," a family historian wrote. It was 1829. His family had lived in Baghdad as virtual royalty for more than eight hundred years.

Jews fleeing oppressive rulers was a common historical theme even by the nineteenth century. Jews had been expelled from Britain in 1290, from Spain in 1492. Venice had ordered them confined to ghettos starting in 1516. The horrors of the Holocaust were yet to come.

The flight of David Sassoon was different. Jews had always lived at the margins of society in Europe. But for more than a thousand years, Jews had flourished in Baghdad, known in the Bible as Babylon. More than any city in Europe, more than Jerusalem, Baghdad was a crossroads of cultures from A.D. 70 to the 1400s. When Europe was mired in the darkness of the Middle Ages, Baghdad was one of the most cosmopolitan cities in the world. It was home to some of the world's leading mathematicians, theologians, poets, and doctors. Raw wool, copper, and spices traveled along caravan routes across the desert. Pearls and silverware filled the bazaars. Merchants, doctors, and artists gathered in Baghdad's coffeehouses. The ruler's palace sat surrounded by three square miles of wooded parkland, with fountains and lakes stocked with fish.

Within this world, Jews flourished. They first arrived in 587 B.C., when Babylon's King Nebuchadnezzar laid siege to Jerusalem and, upon victory, carried 10,000 Jewish artisans, scholars, and leaders—Judaism's best and brightest—to Baghdad into what the Bible dubbed "the Babylonian Captivity." The book of Psalms famously documented the despair of these displaced Jews:

> By the rivers of Babylon, there we sat down
> Yea, we wept, when we remembered Zion.

In fact, "the Babylonian Captivity" changed the course of Jewish history. Jewish learning and religious innovation blossomed, giving Jews the religious, political, and economic tools—and a way of thinking—they would use to survive and thrive around the world over the next millennia and through to today. It marked the start of the Jewish diaspora: the dispersal—and survival—of Jews around the world, even when they made up just a small sliver of the population. Rabbis modified Jewish ritual practices to accommodate Judaism to modern life and enable Jews to participate in business. Though he had kidnapped the Jews into captivity, Nebuchadnezzar didn't treat them as slaves. He turned to the Jews to strengthen Baghdad's economy. He encouraged them to become merchants and trade between the different parts of his sprawling kingdom. So important were Jews to Baghdad's business life that many non-Jews working in trade and finance didn't go to the office on Saturdays, the Jewish Sabbath. When the Persians conquered Baghdad and offered the Jews the chance to return to Jerusalem, only a few accepted. Most decided to stay. Baghdad's Jews considered themselves the Jewish aristocracy. Like Jews in London and New York centuries later, Baghdad's Jews may have yearned to return to Jerusalem in their Saturday prayers at their local synagogue, but the other six days a week, they grasped the opportunities around them and built a thriving metropolis.

Presiding over this dynamic, self-confident community—leading it and nurturing it—stood the Sassoons. Trading gold and silk, spices and wool across the Middle East, the Sassoons became Baghdad's richest merchants. Starting in the late 1700s, the Ottoman Turks appointed the leader of the Sassoon family as "Nasi," or "Prince of the Jews"—their intermediary in dealing with Baghdad's influential Jewish population. Preserved among the Sassoon family papers are memoranda in Turkish and Arabic that testify to the sweep of the Nasi's power. The Nasi Sassoon blessed marriages and resolved religious disputes. The Nasi also played a key role in advising the Ottoman ruler, especially in economic matters. He negotiated loans, planned budgets, devised and collected new taxes. He was the de facto secretary of the treasury, charged with building a modern financial system. When the Nasi traveled to meet Baghdad's Turkish ruler at the royal palace, he was carried on a throne through the streets; Jews and non-Jews alike respectfully bowed their heads.

Buoyed by these connections, the Sassoons built a multinational economic empire that extended from Baghdad across the Persian Gulf and Asia. The family stocked Baghdad's bazaars with a rich cornucopia of products and sent members of their extended family to travel among the Bedouin tribes to buy their wool in exchange for cotton garments, shoes, and spices. Merchants from across the Middle East and from India and China passed through the Nasi's luxurious home and compound. They lounged in his walled courtyard, shaded by orange trees, to escape the 120-degree heat. Underground storerooms held the family's gold.

In the nineteenth and twentieth centuries, as their wealth and fortune expanded, the Sassoons became accustomed to business allies and rivals calling them "the Rothschilds of Asia" for the rapid way their wealth and influence spread across China, India, and Europe. But privately they considered the comparison misleading—and a little demeaning. In the Sassoons' minds, the Rothschilds were arrivistes— a poor family that in one generation had leapt from the ghettos of Europe to business prominence and political influence. The Sassoons may have been unknown to the Chinese emperor, the Indian raj, or the British royal family, but they had been rich, prominent, and powerful for centuries.

David Sassoon was born in 1792 and trained from childhood to become the future Nasi. He was a business prodigy with an extraordinary gift for languages. At thirteen, he started accompanying his father to the "counting houses"—the forerunners of banks and accounting firms—where the Sassoon revenues were calculated. When the bazaars opened in the morning, his father sent him down to learn how to calculate in different currencies and master disparate systems of weights and measures. He was tutored at home in Hebrew (the language of religion), Turkish (the language of government), Arabic (the language of Baghdad), and Persian (the language of Middle Eastern trade). He sat in on evening visits from representatives of the British East India Company newly arrived from Bombay, who encouraged the Sassoons to expand their trade to India—though he never bothered to learn English. Six feet tall, David stood head and shoulders over his family and the people he would one day lead. His community approved of David's planned elevation; he radiated trust and authority and, as was the custom, he entered an arranged marriage with the daughter of a prosperous merchant when he was fifteen. His wife swiftly gave birth to four sons.

As David was preparing to assume his vaunted role as Nasi, the comfortable position the Sassoons and the Jews of Baghdad had enjoyed for centuries collapsed. A power struggle among the Ottoman rulers of Baghdad put a faction hostile to the Jews in power. Desperate for money to boost a collapsing economy, the Turks began harassing and imprisoning the Sassoons and other wealthy Jews, demanding ransom. One wealthy Jewish merchant was strangled to death outside his cell. As conditions worsened, some Jewish merchants fled to India, seeking British colonial protection.

Frightened by the volatile political situation, David's father made the unusual decision to step down as Nasi and hand power over to David, who would traditionally have had to wait until his father's death. But David refused, correctly sensing that the position no longer held much power. Instead, against his father's advice, David sought the help of the Turkish sultan in Constantinople on behalf of the Jews and Sassoons of Baghdad, accusing the city's rulers of corruption. But he was wrong to put his trust in the imperial government, and word of his betrayal quickly reached Baghdad. He was arrested; the Turkish pasha ordered him hanged unless the family paid for his release. Taking matters into his own hands, his elderly father bribed his son out of prison, hustled him through the city in disguise, and chartered a boat to get him to safety.

David left Baghdad in a state of rage and helplessness. He had just remarried following the death of his first wife. He was abandoning his new bride and his children. All the glory of the Sassoons, their wealth and position, had been promised to him and was now snatched away. As the ship sailed away, he turned toward the disappearing shore and wept.

DAVID LANDED AT BUSHIRE, a port city controlled by Iran beyond the reach of the Turks. Many of the refugees who had left Baghdad as conditions deteriorated had settled there. But while the stories they sent back home were of great riches and success, in fact they were struggling, crammed into poor neighborhoods, foraging a small living. Disoriented and despondent, David spent his first night away from Baghdad sleeping on the floor of a warehouse by the waterfront, which had been lent to him by a seaman. He kept a gun by his side to shoot rats that skittered across the floor.

As he gathered himself in the first few weeks, his mood improved. The traders in Bushire all knew the name Sassoon and had heard of the campaign being waged against the Jews. Several who had

previously dealt with the family lent him money, so he could establish credit. His father, still in Baghdad, arranged caravans of goods
and currency to be smuggled out of the city and delivered to his son.
Like many immigrants forced to flee, David faced a choice: succumb
to the anger and depression that surely consumed him or, at thirty-
seven, reinvent himself. In those first few months, he received word
from Baghdad that encouraged him. The campaign against the Jews
in Baghdad was easing and his father was beginning to pay bribes to
enable the family to join him in Bushire. The man who had once
planned to become the Nasi of Baghdad became the peddler of Bushire. He put his fluency in multiple languages to work, talking in Arabic to Arab sea captains and Hebrew to his fellow Jewish refugees. He
began exporting Arab and Asian horses, dates, carpets, and pearls.
Careful to wear his expensive Arab robes and turban, he met the
British representatives of the East India Company, reminding them
how their colleagues had met with the Sassoons in Baghdad. The
British wrote that they admired the heightened "dignity of his
appearance" and urged him to consider moving to Bombay to set up
a company there. A friend and fellow Middle Eastern trader, Samuel
Zacharia, offered him an interest-free loan to start in Bombay.

What Zacharia saw—and the British saw, too—was a man very
different from the other immigrants and refugees washing up in
Bushire. He was better educated than most traders—more knowl-
edgeable and experienced than even most government officials and
British officers. He was driven by something almost Shakespearean—
not a poor refugee struggling to seek a better life but a royal scion
who had his birthright ripped from him and was now determined to
win it back, if not in Baghdad then elsewhere. He had been raised to
command a commercial empire and advise royalty. He wasn't seeking

an ascent from poverty and obscurity to wealth and influence; he was pursuing a restoration.

In 1830, a year after David's flight from Baghdad, the rest of his family joined him in Bushire. The long journey proved too exhausting for his elderly father, who died in David's arms shortly after arrival. Reunited with his wife and children, David thought more about the opportunities that lay in Bombay. After a few years, with his wife newly pregnant, David finally decided to make the move, seeking the protection, and opportunity, of British rule.

Landing in Bombay, David Sassoon joined the British Empire at the height of its political and economic power. Almost one-third of the world was under British control, including parts of India, Australia, Malaysia, Syria, and Egypt. The British had crushed Napoleon in Europe and commanded the world's largest navy. Power and money flowed through London, the world's largest city. Some countries built empires primarily to capture slaves or natural resources, or to build a barrier between themselves and their enemies. Great Britain built an empire to fuel trade, finance, and business. "The great object of the Government in every quarter of the world," British prime minister Lord Palmerston told Parliament in 1839, is to "extend the commerce of the country." For decades, the British East India Company had held a state-sanctioned monopoly on trade within India and Asia. In 1832—the year David arrived in Bombay—the British government ended that monopoly, opening trade throughout Asia to private companies and individuals. A new laissez-faire era had begun.

From the moment he and his family arrived in Bombay, David allied himself with the British and the expansion of the British Empire. Though dark skinned and an immigrant, he chose to support imperialism. That wasn't surprising. David saw himself as part of the elite; the Sassoons in Baghdad had risen in part by advising and serving their Turkish rulers. The defining issue of his life—his flight from Baghdad—had been triggered by his misreading the politics of Baghdad and believing the sultan would side with him against Baghdad's rulers. He was determined that he and his family would never make that mistake again.

David arrived in India at a fortunate time. The expanding British Empire wasn't opening just trade routes, it was opening the British mind. Britain itself remained a stratified society, with clubs and landed aristocrats looking down on "outsiders." But business and politics were displaying more tolerance. In India, the British needed ambitious entrepreneurs to extend trade to the frontiers of a growing empire. Before leaving London for India, the new British governor-general of Bombay, Sir Robert Grant, had twice proposed in Parliament bills to end all discrimination against Great Britain's Jews. The bills were initially defeated, but soon official discrimination against British Jews came to an end. Jews might never be accepted in Bombay's British clubs, but their property and businesses were now legally protected—more than had ever been the case, even in Baghdad. And the new British ruler of the city was a proven friend to the Jews.

David was genuinely impressed by the British. He called the British government, in Hebrew, *malka chased*—a just and kind government. "I believe in the British because they are on the right side of history," David told his family. There was no bribery; Britain was a country of laws. In Baghdad, by contrast, bribery was the way business got done. The British colonial authorities welcomed a man they saw as intelligent, cultured, and a useful ally. Speaking through a translator, David began meeting with Bombay's British governor-general and with a British archaeologist to discuss the Old Testament.

David became an Anglophile. He commissioned a scholar to translate the lyrics to "God Save the Queen" into his native Judeo-Arabic and hired tutors to teach his sons the English language and British history. On a summer afternoon five years after landing in Bombay, he brought his two eldest sons, Abdullah, nineteen, and Elias, seventeen, to join a throng on the city's waterfront to hear the proclamation announcing the accession in London of Queen Victoria. His sons wanted to wear British waistcoats and ties. David forbade it. All three of the Sassoons wore the clothes of Baghdad—white muslin shirts with billowing white trousers bound at the ankle. David wore his embroidered turban and dark robes. As a British military band played, the three joined the crowd shouting in English, "God Save the Queen!"

David never lost his immigrant's perspective, the sensibility of an outsider. Even in cosmopolitan Bombay, with people of many backgrounds jostling along the wharves and narrow alleyways of the city, David appeared strikingly foreign and intimidating to many who met him—"tall, spare, hard of muscle, with an El Greco face the color of light cinnamon and fringed by a beard already flecked with grey," a family biographer wrote. Despite his social friendship with the governor, being an outsider meant that he was cut off from the British companies and banks that dominated the India trade, which wouldn't deal with a Baghdadi or a Jew.

He needed to think creatively. It took five months, for example, for ships to sail from England to India. David heard about an innovation—steamships—that would cut the travel time down to weeks. He invested his profits into buying more dock space, betting that more ships would soon be arriving in Bombay with greater frequency. That meant that when a ship tied up at a Sassoon dock, David got the first pick of goods before they reached the city's bazaars. When the ships sailed away, half their cargo holds were filled with Sassoon merchandise destined for England. Mingling with sea captains on the docks, talking with them in Arabic and Persian and Turkish, gave him key bits of commercial intelligence. Through the sea captains, David learned that the growth of industrial cotton mills in England was likely to boost the demand for raw Indian cotton. Realizing the value of being able to negotiate with local businessmen, he learned Hindustani and became close friends with one of India's biggest cotton traders. From him, David learned that British brokers were complaining that the bales bought from India contained too many stones. Using this information, David imported new cotton gins that solved this problem and produced more marketable cotton. When he was turned away from the old-boy network of British banks, he helped found the Bank of Bombay, which enabled him to finance new railway lines to ship cotton from the countryside more quickly. Two decades later, when the North blockaded the South in the American Civil War, cutting off the biggest supplier of cotton to Britain, David was perfectly situated to step into the breach—and to make millions.

David became a bridge between the traditional trading practices of the Middle East and the new global system developing under the British Empire. Doing business in Asia meant dealing with a hodgepodge of different weights and measures, different currencies, different languages. David imposed standardization. Inside his company, Sassoon employees conducted business in Judeo-Arabic—Arabic words written with Hebrew letters—the language they brought with them from Baghdad. But when it came to business correspondence, David ordered that letters to customers, suppliers, and other companies be written in precise English script, even though he himself barely read or spoke the language. He ordered that the Sassoon branding be on office stationery and that company checks be printed in both Hebrew and English letters. He switched to the more formal accounting system of ledgers and bookkeeping entries used by the major British firms. He frowned on haggling, which was the typical way traders did business on the docks and in the bazaars. He admired instead the British model of decorum. In times of crisis, he reckoned, appearing calm would be good for business.

David recognized that he needed to be flexible to succeed, and to preserve his own identity and values even as he navigated a new and powerful empire. He swore loyalty to the British Empire and prepared his sons and businesses to serve it. But his Judaism and outsider status softened some of the harder edges of his embrace of British colonialism. In Baghdad, the Sassoons had supported charity extensively and continued to do so in Bombay, building synagogues and supporting Jews who fell into poverty. Like many of his class, David owned a slave in India, but he freed him and recorded the manumission in an official document to assure that he wouldn't be re-enslaved. He endowed and built the first hospital that accepted Indian patients. Looking back, it is easy to criticize David's embrace of colonialism and imperialism. In Europe, Russia, and, later, the United States, many Jews faced with similar moral choices presented by colonialism and the excesses of capitalism embraced socialism and revolution. David was pioneering what would be a familiar figure as industrialization and modern finance swept across the world: the liberal Jewish businessman whose skills and talents led to fabulous financial success, but whose history of personal hardship and commitment to Jewish values made him more socially and politically progressive.

IN BAGHDAD, the Sassoons had relied on centuries of connections and relationships that stretched across the Middle East. Now David was starting in a new country without an established network. How to manage it? How to develop a loyal workforce trained in his techniques and prepared to take advantage of the opportunities being created by new communication, industrialization, and transport?

He came up with the idea of the Sassoon schools.

David set up the equivalent of a Sassoon company town, designed to attract Jewish refugees, first from Baghdad and then from across the Ottoman Empire, and turn them into loyal employees. Poor and striving families sent their teenage sons from Baghdad, Syria, Iran, and Afghanistan. They enrolled in the David Sassoon Benevolent Institution, where, using textbooks David commissioned, the teenagers were taught Arabic, geography, arithmetic, bookkeeping, and Hebrew. They were then hired as clerks to keep track of purchases and sales in the Sassoon warehouses, or sent to negotiate the sale of bales of cotton with British buyers. On Saturdays, the Jewish Sabbath, the Sassoon warehouses would shut down. Employees would gather for religious services at David Sassoon's house and, later, at Bombay's first synagogue, which he built. If employees became ill, they could seek care at the Sassoon General Hospital in nearby Poona, built and endowed by David. If they wanted to continue their studies, they could attend lectures or use the library at the David Sassoon Mechanics Institute, which featured mechanical models and lectures on science and technology. Employees who retired and lacked family to look after them were given money for food. When they died, they were buried in the Sassoon-endowed Jewish cemetery. David's school-to-grave social network enticed a growing stream of workers to his warehouses and offices. It cost him about $300,000 a year in today's money—and bought him ambition, talent, and loyalty.

Less than a decade after arriving in Bombay, David Sassoon was one of the richest men in India. The British governor of Bombay hailed him as "the first of our non-European merchants in wealth and responsibility." He was just getting started.

As GREAT BRITAIN EXPANDED across the globe through conquest, aggressive trade policies, rapid technological innovation, and harnessing the ambition and acumen of foreigners and outsiders like David Sassoon, China was becoming more closed, sclerotic, inward looking, and arrogant. Its weakness stemmed from its success. As late as 1800, China was a dominant world power whose rule and influence extended throughout Asia. Ships traded with Southeast Asia, and visiting traders and diplomatic delegations signaled their respect by approaching Chinese rulers with deference—the well-known ritual "kowtow," or bowing until their foreheads touched the ground, when approaching the emperor. Relations with non-Chinese people were conducted by officials who emphasized the cultural inferiority of foreigners.

The British, with their own arrogance, refused to play by those rules—British diplomats and military officials refused to kowtow. Starting in the late eighteenth century, just a few years after the American Revolution dealt the first blow to British imperial expansionism, Britain and China clashed in an escalating series of diplomatic and military confrontations. Britain sent emissaries to China demanding that China open its cities and ports to trade and the sale of British goods. They proposed that a British ambassador take up residence in Beijing, and they sent along, as gifts, examples of the best of British technology: clocks, telescopes, weapons, and textiles. In an oft-quoted letter to King George III in 1793, the Chinese emperor Qianlong rebuffed British efforts and expressed astonishment that the king could be so ignorant of China's superiority: "We possess all things," the emperor wrote to King George. "I set no value on objects strange or ingenious and have no use for your country's manufactures." But the balance of global power was shifting. As he left China after being dismissed by the emperor, the humiliated British ambassador told his superiors that China was bluffing. Its military was weak and wouldn't be able to withstand British pressure. China, he wrote, was like a leaky boat, "an old, crazy, first-rate Man of War, which a fortunate succession of able and vigilant officers has contrived to keep afloat for these hundred and fifty years past, and to overawe their neighbors merely by her bulk and appearance." In fact, the British ambassador predicted, China was listing and soon would be "dashed to pieces on the shore."

The opium trade became the flashpoint. In nineteenth-century Europe and Great Britain, opium was the best medicine available to treat pain and calm anxiety; aspirin wasn't patented as a medicine until 1899. Opium was also addictive and produced hallucinations and a feeling of well-being. "I sometimes seemed to have lived for 70 or 100 years in one night," a nineteenth-century British opium smoker wrote. Opium turned out to be one commodity that the Chinese did have need of. In the seventeenth and eighteenth centuries, the demand for Chinese goods in Europe, particularly silk, porcelain, and tea, created a classic trade imbalance. Britain was paying for all these goods with silver, but China wasn't buying anything in return. To counter this, the British East India Company encouraged the sale of opium even though a succession of Chinese emperors worried about the dangers of addiction and tried to restrict the drug or ban it. The British grew opium in India and sold it to middlemen, who then made massive profits selling the drug inside China, working with corrupt Chinese officials and evading efforts to sink their ships and seize their drugs. Nearly one-third of Bombay's trade was tied to the state-sanctioned opium business. The smuggling of opium into China was dominated by a British company—Jardine, Matheson & Co., founded by two Scottish traders. Even as the British pressed the emperor to let ships in to sell watches, clocks, and weapons, opium addiction had become a massive social problem. By the early nineteenth century, one out of every ten Chinese was addicted. (By contrast, about 3 percent of Americans misused or were addicted to hard drugs such as prescription opioids, cocaine, and heroin at the height of public concern over the opioid crisis and the "war on drugs" in the United States.) The Chinese official charged with eliminating the opium trade appealed directly to one of King George's successors, Queen Victoria. "Where is your conscience?" Lin Zexu asked in an impassioned official letter. The products China exported to Great Britain—tea, silk, handicrafts—were all beneficial, he declared. But Queen Victoria's subjects were "selling products injurious to others in order to fulfill your insatiable desire. . . . Suppose there were people from another country who carried opium for sale to England and seduced your people into buying and smoking it; certainly, your honorable ruler would deeply hate it and be bitterly aroused." Queen Victoria never responded. When Lin, at the emperor's direction, dumped chests of opium into the sea and began holding British officials hostage, Jardine, Matheson & Co. provided the British military with detailed maps and strategies and offered the assistance of company sea captains who knew the best routes into China and the weak points of China's navy.

Britain invaded China in 1839 in what became known as the First Opium War. As the British ambassador rebuffed by the Chinese emperor fifty years earlier had predicted, China was overmatched and easily defeated. The Treaty of Nanjing, signed in 1842, ceded the island of Hong Kong to Great Britain and opened five cities to Western trade, including a previously little-known city called Shanghai. Foreign traders doing business in China would pay no taxes. They wouldn't be subject to Chinese law—a status known as "extraterritoriality." Any commercial or legal disputes would go before British judges and be decided based on British law. The opium trade remained technically illegal, but the Chinese were unlikely to directly challenge British traders again so soon after a devastating military defeat. It was the start of what Chinese historians would call "one hundred years of humiliation." Lin Zexu, who had appealed fruitlessly to Queen Victoria's conscience and failed to blunt the British invasion, was sent into exile.

David Sassoon supported the British invasion of China. He had begun dabbling in the sale of opium. From his warehouses and office in Bombay, he purchased a ship and began loading it with opium and hiring captains to sail it to China. It was a hazardous journey. Since the Chinese considered opium illegal, the Sassoon ship had to offload the drugs onto small islands near the southern port of Canton and then bribe Chinese officials and pay Chinese dealers to distribute it. Still, every chest of opium shipped to China netted a profit of about £100, or $10,000 in today's money. David regularly attended the Calcutta Opium Exchange to bid on opium. In what was becoming a familiar strategy, he bought land and built warehouses to house opium bought by other merchants and supplied credit to opium merchants and traders. He was too small to compete with larger companies—he owned one steamer that smuggled opium, compared with Jardine, Matheson & Co., which owned twelve large steamers supplemented by hundreds of smaller boats—but he had established a foothold in a lucrative business.

India made David Sassoon rich, and it made him British. He moved his family to a mansion on Malabar Hill in Bombay, an exclusive area with cooling breezes, high above the filth and noise of the city. He modeled his new home on the design of an Italian palazzo and named it "Sans Souci" after the Prussian palace of Frederick the Great in Potsdam. In 1853, he took an oath and became a British citizen, writing his name in Hebrew script because he still didn't know how to write in English. Four years later, the British faced the gravest threat to their control of India when local Indian mercenaries employed by the British East India Company rose up in the Sepoy Mutiny; David allied himself wholeheartedly with Britain, contributing money and raising funds from other Baghdad families who had settled in Bombay. In a dramatic gesture, David went to British officials in Bombay's Government House and offered to assemble and equip a Jewish legion to fight for the British in the event the Indian rebellion spread. The volunteers weren't needed, but David bought government bonds to fund the British deployment of troops and invested heavily in the Bombay stock market to show his confidence in British rule. He also announced that his family and all his employees would be "permitted to wear western clothes as often as they wished, so that it may be known on which side you are." When British troops suppressed the rebellion, David led a torchlight procession in celebration and held a banquet and ball at Sans Souci. A military band greeted the arrival of the new colonial governor, Lord Elphinstone. He toasted David Sassoon: "We must not forget that at the time of the Mutiny, when threatened with danger and whilst some were panic-stricken, Mr. Sassoon and his family were the first to come forward in support of the British Government." Abdullah, David's eldest son, started calling himself "Albert," in honor of the Prince of Wales, whose full name was Albert Edward. The Anglophiles had become fully anglicized.

With Britain victorious in the 1841 Opium War, Bombay was now abuzz with the prospects of trade with China. The British were actively encouraging businesses to follow the Union Jack and promising the protection of British troops and gunboats. A dozen years had passed since David had scurried along the streets of Baghdad and fled in the night. He had succeeded in Baghdad. He had succeeded in Bushire. He had succeeded in Bombay. New opportunity beckoned. He turned his entrepreneurial gaze north, to China—and to Shanghai.

David Sassoon (seated) with three of
his sons in Bombay in 1858

2

Empire of the Sons—
and Opium

The daotai sat in his office in the walled city of Shanghai await-
ing word of the foreigners' arrival. He was China's equivalent
to a mayor—the imperial Chinese official sent by the palace in
Beijing to oversee Shanghai's courts, police, transportation, and tax
collection. The job paid reasonably well and, more important, was a
springboard to higher office. The previous daotais had presided over
a period of growing prosperity for Shanghai. Marco Polo hadn't even
bothered to visit the city several hundred years earlier, bypassing it
for Hangzhou to the south. But Shanghai had grown and prospered.
It sat near the wide mouth of the Yangtze River, which flowed into
central China, and its proximity to the Pacific was crucial. Trade
with Japan and Southeast Asia had turned Shanghai into a vibrant
city of more than 200,000 residents, even though the Chinese still
limited European trade. On any given day, harbormasters directed
hundreds of Chinese sailing ships called junks to unload their cargo
into large stone warehouses on the shore. Behind the thick brick walls

that ran for several miles enclosing the city—initially built as protection against pirates—shopkeepers sold merchandise and food from storefronts festooned with bright red signs adorned with gold Chinese characters. Street peddlers, tea sellers, barbers, tailors, and shoemakers jostled along the streets and alleyways. Librarians lent books from mobile pushcarts. Acrobats performed on street corners. Shanghai hummed with a dozen different dialects and smelled of a dozen different kinds of food. It vibrated with an energy and openness that contrasted with the staid capital of Beijing, where the emperor had rebuffed British emissaries years before, and foreigners were not welcome. The people in Shanghai were "always civil and affable, greeting us with smiles and polite salutations," a foreign visitor wrote.

Now, however, the daotai knew that change was coming. Eighteen months earlier, the British had invaded the empire. It was now 1843, and the Chinese had been forced to sign a treaty that opened five cities to British trade, including Shanghai. In Canton, a city in the south, the people had resisted the arrival of British merchants. Europeans were attacked in the streets, forcing the British to retreat to their rented homes for safety. Shanghai wouldn't be like that, the daotai hoped. Shanghai was a mercantile city, one accustomed to trade and money. It would treat the foreigners properly, if not warmly.

On this November evening, word reached the daotai in his office inside the walled city that a small British steamer had dropped anchor on the shore of Shanghai. The first British had arrived. The daotai didn't go down to the shore to welcome them. He decided to make them wait.

As morning dawned, the daotai sent two old sedan chairs down to the docks with porters to carry the British delegation to his office. Crowds of Chinese onlookers gathered and laughed at how bushy the

"Britishers" seemed with their beards and muttonchop sideburns in contrast to the smooth-faced Chinese. The foreigners' "legs and feet stretched out and bent with difficulty," one Chinese man wrote. They reminded him of "prancing Manchu ponies" and "water buffaloes." A British diplomat wrote that the Chinese "were always surprised, not to say astonished, to learn that we have surnames, and understand the family distinctions of father, brother, wife, sister, etc.—in short, that we live otherwise than as a herd of cattle."

The "Britishers" came with a translator, which was good, because neither the daotai nor any of his officials spoke English. They demanded a place to open an office and house their men, but the daotai politely refused. There was simply no place available.

Then a Shanghai merchant spoke up and offered to rent the British merchants a fifty-two-room house in the city. They stayed there for a time, but soon the daotai became uneasy with their presence inside the walled city. He worried that their strange habits might infect the harmony of Shanghai. He sent them instead to a vacant swampy area along the river outside the walls of the old Chinese city. The land was dotted with mulberry trees and ancestral graves, and the Chinese believed it was haunted by ghosts. Residents upriver dumped feces into the waterway that ran alongside the swamp. The daotai assumed the new arrivals would leave in a few years. Shanghai needed only to outlast them.

SEVEN YEARS LATER, Elias Sassoon, David Sassoon's second oldest son, landed on Shanghai's shore. His arrival marked the next stage of the Sassoons' expansion into a truly global enterprise. While Jardine, Matheson relied on British gunboats and cannons to open China and extend its empire, David Sassoon deployed his sons. They became his ambassadors and intelligence agents, his salesmen and advisers. In a time before telephones or telegraphs, when messages took months to get from India to Shanghai or London, the eight brothers would function as a team, intuiting the right business moves and supporting one another—and their demanding father—from outposts that stretched along the China coast, up to Japan, and, ultimately, across the seas to London. A global business required a globalized family. To familiarize them with every country and every aspect of the business, David rotated his sons from city to city for several months and sometimes many years at a time, accompanied and aided by a trained staff educated in the Sassoon schools and bound to the family by a common religion and culture. The elder Sassoon showed a shrewd ability both to keep his global family empire together and to keep his sons loyal. He paid each of them a generous salary and encouraged them to invest on their own. But none of them could become partners in the firm. The patriarch ruled alone. He drew up a detailed will that laid out his expectations for the future of his family, his children and grandchildren—that the boys marry Jewish women from Baghdad and continue attending orthodox synagogue.

When his sons were still teenagers, David brought them to Bombay's ports to practice bargaining with sea captains, just as he had been trained by his father in Baghdad. He showed them bookkeeping and explained the varied systems of weights and measures and the quality of different products. He insisted they learn English and familiarize themselves with new technologies—steamships and railways— that were transforming commerce and creating opportunities to trade in international markets. When the time came for them to set out into the world, David decided that their wives and children would remain in Bombay under the supervision of his wife. He hired servants for the families and tutors for his son's wives—a remarkably progressive move in a country where women rarely received an education. David anticipated that at some point they might need to live permanently overseas with their husbands—ultimately maybe even in London—and he wanted them to be prepared.

When it was time to set his global efforts in motion, David chose his second-oldest son, twenty-four-year-old Elias, to go to China. Elias was more withdrawn and reserved than his brothers. Unlike his siblings who embraced Western styles, Elias continued to wear his traditional Baghdad clothes, the only modern touch being a pair of eyeglasses to correct his nearsightedness. The glasses gave him the look of an aloof and studious academic. David reckoned that quiet and sensitive Elias, a bit of a loner, would be best suited to the rigors and loneliness of living far from family in an unfamiliar country.

Leaving his wife and newborn son at home, as his father required, Elias started the dangerous seventy-day sailing voyage from Bombay up to the China coast. The voyage often left ships becalmed for days. Passengers sat awake through the night brandishing guns, preparing for pirate attacks. Elias's first stop in China was Canton, where he followed his father's strategy of financing shipments of opium and textiles, offering loans to smaller merchants, and sending his own products up the coast to be sold and distributed. After a year, leaving a deputy trained in the Sassoon school in charge in Canton, Elias sailed seventy miles south to the new British colony of Hong Kong, where Jardine, Matheson & Co.'s opium trade was booming. Elias noted their ingenious signaling system to control opium prices. Jardine loaded clipper ships in India with opium and then sailed them to just outside Hong Kong's harbor, pausing there to wait. Meanwhile, on land, Jardine employees tracked the price of opium. As supplies dwindled and prices rose, a Jardine employee would climb to the top of one of Hong Kong's mountains, known as the Peak, to a spot known as "Jardine's lookout." There he would signal to the waiting clipper ships that it was time to sail into the harbor and sell their opium at high prices. Elias was too small an opium importer to set up his own signaling system, but he admired the strategy. The lesson of the value of tracking demand stuck with him. Two decades later he would use the new technology of telegraphs and steamships in a similar way to destroy Jardine's advantage and seize control of the opium market for the Sassoons.

From Hong Kong, Elias traveled to the other Chinese cities now open to trade. Hong Kong, he concluded, was too crowded with an influx of other small traders. Fierce competition on prices meant smaller profits on all products, including opium. He ultimately decided to move the Sassoons' headquarters to Shanghai. Besides being a bigger city than Hong Kong, he told his father, Shanghai was closer to colder northern Chinese cities eager to buy woolen yarn and textiles that the Sassoons could ship from India.

It was 1850, seven years since the first British arrivals had landed in Shanghai, and about a hundred more had joined them in the swampy settlement the daotai had allocated to them. Conditions were grim. A British doctor urged his fellow new arrivals to "seek elevated sites" to avoid yellow fever, plague, cholera, and typhus. Located at the same latitude as New Orleans and Cairo, Shanghai became a steam bath in summer. Newcomers battled prickly heat, ringworm, and other skin rashes. Mold discolored their boots and shoes. But the British showed no signs of leaving. They built warehouses and offices along the shore and added homes, a British club, even a racecourse. The swamp disappeared, replaced by a network of wide, European-style streets. Along the river ran a winding road that the British, many of whom like the Sassoons had come from India, dubbed with an Urdu word used to describe a causeway or river embankment: the Bund.

The daotai had hoped to isolate the foreigners and prevent any seepage of Western ideas into Shanghai. The only Chinese he allowed to live in the "International Settlement" initially were servants. But civil wars in the Chinese countryside drove many Chinese to seek refuge in the new International Settlement protected by British gunboats, which the Chinese saw as safer than the parts of Shanghai the emperor still controlled. Chinese and foreigners now lived side by side in a city where "hips touch hips. And shoulders rub shoulders," in the words of a Chinese scholar drawing up a new map of Shanghai.

"It is the destiny of Shanghai to become the permanent emporium of trade between [China] and all nations of the world," the editor of the city's new English-language newspaper wrote. Britain's ships and cannons "had opened the way" to colonize the Bund and the land around it, a European visitor observed, and "it is not very probable that they will ever be dislodged." The emperor dismissed the daotai and sent a series of Chinese officials to Shanghai to manage relations with the foreigners. None would be able to stop their ascension.

True to his father's vision, Elias's arrival in Shanghai at age thirty signaled that a new, more international era had begun for the Sassoons. Gone was the sailing ship that initially brought him and bedraggled sailors and merchants to Hong Kong a few years earlier. The Sassoons had purchased a steamship, cutting the voyage time between India and China dramatically and ensuring a much more

comfortable journey. Elias swept onshore in Shanghai proudly wearing his Baghdad cloak, with his account books, money bags, and a
gold snuffbox tucked into large pockets sewn into the fabric. He was
surrounded by a retinue of assistants educated in Bombay at the Sassoon schools in accounting, math, and the basics of commercial trading. Elias spoke several languages—though not Chinese. He immediately
began visiting the warehouses and docks along the river, talking in
his soft voice with the captains of the more than 400 ships that were
docking at Shanghai every year from Asian and European ports in
search of textiles, cotton, silk, and other products. Shanghai, a sea
captain declared, was a land flowing with "silk and money."

Applying the lessons of his father, Elias built his own warehouses
in Shanghai to avoid paying rent. He sold opium, Indian spices, and
Indian wool to the Chinese and bought silk, tea, and animal hides,
which he then sold to opium captains eager to fill their empty cargo
holds for the return trip to India. He acted as a broker for other traders looking to ship goods to India, using his connections with Chinese merchants to fill their cargo space. Ships sailing into Shanghai
began to vie for space at Elias's docks. Competition with other traders turned out to be fierce. Elias worried constantly about the dangers
of espionage. Because he didn't speak Chinese, he, like most foreigners, had to rely on English-speaking Chinese intermediaries, known
as compradors, to help negotiate deals and navigate the complex world
of Chinese business practices. Opportunities for corruption were rife.
Elias, like other foreigners, complained of having to pay bribes, known
as the "squeeze," to Chinese officials to get his goods to other parts
of China. Elias filed several lawsuits against compradors for stealing
and mismanaging the Sassoons' money.

Elias's impact on Shanghai was profound. He sought alliances and business opportunities with others, including the new class of Chinese entrepreneurs who were intrigued by the foreign arrivals and wanted to work with them. When local tensions in China's interior produced rebellions and uprisings that the emperor was hard-pressed to put down—most famously the Taiping Rebellion, a virtual civil war that began in 1850—tens of thousands of Chinese refugees poured into the British-run parts of Shanghai seeking safety, many of them well-off Chinese merchants. Elias purchased land and began building simple wooden houses that he rented to refugee families. They swelled Shanghai's population and added to the immigrant energy and ambition of the city.

David Sassoon was right that Elias was the best suited emotionally for the isolation of life in Shanghai. But the price Elias paid was evident in the disruption it caused in his family. Nine years elapsed between the births of his children—he was rarely able to sail home to Bombay to spend time with his wife. In Shanghai, Elias built a two-story house near the river, surrounding it with a protective wall and a courtyard in which he planted peonies and flowering cherries. He hired dozens of pigtailed Chinese servants. He occasionally stopped by the newly established Shanghai Club, filled with other foreign traders, for drinks and gossip. On Sundays he visited the new racetrack to watch dwarf Mongolian ponies run around the track. But he shunned most other expatriate social events.

His rivals considered Elias a smart and tough businessman—but also solitary and secretive. He would stroll across the courtyard of his house, dressed in aristocratic Chinese robes and spectacles. At other times he walked alone in a park along the Bund—seeking relief from the heat and cacophony of the city. When his older brother Abdullah came to visit, traders commented on how much more gregarious and charismatic he was than his younger brother. At one point, Elias was brutally assaulted by a "drunken freak" and had to seek help from the British consulate. He started carrying a gun. Though he remained disconnected from the city that had become his home, Elias had exceeded his father's commercial expectations for the company, building up the China business and establishing thriving outposts in Canton, Hong Kong, and Japan, all flowing through Shanghai. He now expected to be rewarded for the sacrifices he had made.

BACK IN BOMBAY, David had divided Elias's six younger brothers between India and China, dispatching some to work with Elias. Rarely ever living in the same cities, the eight Sassoon brothers wrote more than 7,000 letters to one another between 1860 and 1900. David wrote to each of his sons daily. They traded family gossip, compared prices of cotton and opium, worried about commercial spying, discussed improved welfare schemes to keep their workers loyal. "I hope next month to have good news on the price of cotton because there are financial profits resulting from the War in America," one brother wrote at the start of the American Civil War.

Seeking advantage over his rivals, David searched for ways to speed up the Sassoon business decisions. Waiting for approval for a business loan from bankers in Bombay or London took too long if Elias wanted to build warehouses in Shanghai or buy up land to construct houses or finance a shipment of goods. David sent one of Elias's brothers to Hong Kong to join with entrepreneurs at Jardine and other firms to form the Hongkong and Shanghai Bank, which could swiftly approve loans for businesses in China—especially loans to board members like the Sassoons. For its headquarters, Arthur Sassoon rented the bank a building that Elias had purchased decades earlier in Hong Kong. A few months later the bank opened a branch in Shanghai on the Bund, placing two majestic bronze lions out front. It soon became the richest and most powerful bank in Asia.

Large companies like Jardine might be making more money and becoming better known, but the upstart, multilingual Sassoons were rising rapidly. "Silver and gold, silks, gums and spices, opium and cotton, wool and wheat—whatever moves over sea or land feels the hand or bears the mark of Sassoon & Co.," a rival told an English-language newspaper in China. Jacob Saphir, a European researcher and writer who traveled throughout Asia, reported in 1859 that the Sassoons, with their combined interests in China and India, "have arrived at great wealth, approximately five million sterling"—almost $600 million in today's money.

Almost twenty years after dispatching Elias to Shanghai on a speculative mission with uncertain chances of success, David summoned him back to Bombay in 1862 to begin planning the family succession. David was seventy years old. It was time for Elias and his older brother Abdullah to work side by side and take over the business.

Abdullah, already favored as the eldest son, was pulling ahead in the family succession. Shanghai hadn't seemed an important posting when Elias the introspective loner had settled there. David gave Abdullah, the more gregarious and outgoing son, a much more plum international assignment. He was sent to Baghdad, which had reopened to the Sassoons' business after the overthrow of the local rulers. It was an easier and more lucrative post than Shanghai. Much of the Sassoons' business still passed through the Persian Gulf, and the

Sassoon name was well known. Everyone spoke Arabic, which was the Sassoons' native language. And Baghdad was much closer to Bombay than Shanghai, which meant Abdullah could come home more frequently to see his father and his family.

Both his father and his brother misjudged how much Elias had changed and grown in his years in Shanghai. He was more confident, more entrepreneurial. He had expanded the family business and traveled across China and to Japan establishing new offices. He had lived a single-minded life determined to increase the success and influence of the Sassoon family, and his father.

In contrast to the lonely, hard work that he had poured into their business in Shanghai, Elias found his elder brother in Bombay leading a life of luxury. Abdullah entertained lavishly in a new mansion high on the hills outside the city. He had returned from a successful stint in Baghdad and was spending more and more time at his father's side. David turned frequently to him for advice, and Abdullah assumed a more public role, overseeing the family's charitable donations. He laid out ambitious plans for further growth, including building factories to produce Indian textiles. He hobnobbed with British businessmen and colonial officials. Following a grand ball that featured 300 British guests and a performance of an Italian opera at his home, *The Bombay Gazette* congratulated Abdullah and his family "on their evident wish to ally themselves with English society in Bombay."

One November afternoon in 1864, David Sassoon took a walk in the gardens of his Sans Souci mansion and then retired to his bedroom to write his daily letters of instruction to his far-flung sons in Hong Kong, Shanghai, Bombay, and London. He died in his sleep, aged seventy-two. His sons, scattered across the globe, attended memorial services and lowered the Union Jack flying on Sassoon ships and in front of Sassoon warehouses to half-staff.

Under the terms of David's will, Abdullah became the new chairman, Elias his deputy. Elias's resentment grew as the future became clear. Abdullah assumed that Elias, the family introvert, would welcome working behind the scenes. He proposed that Elias and his son Jacob, twenty-three, oversee Shanghai, Hong Kong, and the Persian Gulf ports as roving managers, reprising many of Elias's own journeys twenty years earlier. When Abdullah was ready to give up the chairmanship, leadership of the Sassoons would of course pass to his own son. Elias tried to rally his brothers into a rebellion against their eldest sibling, but Abdullah won them over, dispatching them to London and promising them generous incomes. Shanghai may have revealed how Elias inherited his father's business acumen. But Abdullah had David's force of personality and command.

Less than three years after their father's death, in the autumn of 1867, Elias announced that he was resigning from the family company and starting a new company of his own. His share of his father's estate amounted to at least £250,000—more than $25 million in today's money. None of the other brothers joined him. They all decided to stay with Abdullah. Abdullah told the family he expected Elias to set up a small trading company in Shanghai—nothing that would trouble the powerful parent firm with its international reputation. Accompanied by his son, Jacob, Elias named his new company E. D. Sassoon & Co. and boarded a ship for the return trip to Shanghai. The Chinese, confused, dubbed Abdullah's company Old Sassoon and Elias's company New Sassoon.

As the "New Sassoons" expanded, social contact between Elias and his brothers ceased. They gathered for marriages and funerals and exchanged formal birthday greetings, but little more. But both would benefit from their biggest investment and the product that would cement their fortune and influence: opium.

EVEN BEFORE the First Opium War, and many years before Elias broke from his brothers to start his own company, the Sassoons had made money smuggling opium into China. But they were still small businessmen. They couldn't compete with the smuggling operations of a large British company like Jardine, Matheson, which deployed well-armed clipper ships and schooners to pick up chests of opium in India, where it was grown legally, then sailed it up the China coast to deliver the drug for sale in China, where it was banned. Smuggling opium into China meant eluding or fighting off pirates and Chinese patrols, bribing Chinese officials, and sneaking into Canton and other Chinese ports. Smuggling opium generated dizzying profits—more than trading in silk, cotton, or textiles. Even after deducting the cost of shipping the opium and distributing it to addicts in China, Jardine made 30 percent to 50 percent profit on every chest of opium. In one trip in 1832, a single Jardine captain sold $200,000 (in current dollars) worth of opium in four days.

Despite the British victory in the Opium War, opium was still technically illegal in China. Smaller firms like the Sassoons' had little choice but to rely on Jardine to carry their opium and smuggle it in for them. In 1851, British documents recorded forty-two opium clippers registered to British firms involved in the opium trade, many of them to Jardine. Eleven were registered to American companies. Just two were registered to David Sassoon Sons & Co. William Jardine gloated that the opium business kept out "men of small capital." Ledgers from 1842, their pages crumbling with age, record in careful script how Jardine bought opium from the Sassoons at a low price in India, made huge profits by selling it in China, and constantly squeezed and pressured the Sassoons. "We had given directions that your damaged opium should be replaced by fresh sound drug," a Jardine official in Shanghai wrote to Elias at one point. In another case, Jardine refused to pay for opium bought from the Sassoons—which was delivered in cakes and boiled to test for purity—"on account of ill appearance of cakes and boiling badly." Elias was building up a profitable business in every area he chose. But in the most lucrative trade in China, the Sassoons controlled at most only 20 percent of the opium market.

That all changed in 1857, seven years after Elias first landed in Shanghai. Determined to open all of China to trade, not just five cities, and to formally legalize the sale of opium, Britain invaded China again in what became known as the Second Opium War. A combined British and French force marched on Beijing and looted and burned the emperor's Summer Palace. China's Qing leadership surrendered to the Franco-British expeditionary force soon after, ending the Second Opium War and Chinese hopes of reversing the tide of foreign domination in its national affairs. European soldiers stripped the Summer Palace of its valuables; the British Museum was given two brass plates pried off a door during the looting. A Pekinese dog was taken from the palace and presented to Queen Victoria.

China was forced to surrender even more territory—the Kowloon Peninsula in southern China, which became part of Hong Kong. The sale of opium was made legal. Jardine, Matheson & Co. issued a press release hailing Britain's victory, declaring that "the use of opium is not a curse, but a comfort and benefit to hard working Chinese."

For the Sassoons, legalization changed everything. Selling opium switched from being a crime to being a business. David's sons, positioned in India, Hong Kong, Shanghai, and London, recognized that they no longer needed Jardine's armed schooners and network of smugglers to get their product to China. They could buy opium in India, ship it by commercial steamer or on their own boats, and hire Chinese at the other end to distribute the opium for them. They could create an end-to-end monopoly.

The monopoly chain began in India. Jardine didn't produce its own opium. It bought opium from Indian farmers through local Indian agents. The Sassoons decided to go around the agents by negotiating directly with Indian farmers, lending them money to cultivate the opium crop in exchange for the exclusive right to buy the harvest. They sought out farmers who cultivated Malwa opium, the most popular in China. By the time Jardine decided to match this strategy and buy opium directly from farmers, it was too late. The Sassoons had locked up contracts on much of the crop. They could buy the opium and hold on to it until they felt the time was right to sell.

Next came pricing. The opium was bought in India but sold in Shanghai. Remembering "Jardine's lookout" in Hong Kong and how Jardine would hold back opium deliveries until prices rose, Elias encouraged his brothers to use their well-established family intelligence network to share news of opium prices to determine the best time to flood the market. "The opium trade is showing losses as prices go down," a typical letter from the Sassoon office in Calcutta to Hong Kong read. "We have huge stocks in Calcutta. To sell it now would result in a huge loss." Instead, the Sassoons decided to hold on to the opium until prices rose. The Sassoons invested in the new technology of the telegraph, which was revolutionizing communications across countries and continents. Some of the first telegrams in Asia were coded messages from one Sassoon office to another discussing the price of opium—information shared before Jardine or any other competitor could obtain it. By the end of the nineteenth century, the Sassoons were considered among the leading experts on telegraph technology, invited to speak before the House of Commons.

Finally came distribution. Jardine relied on its long-established network of smugglers and corrupt Chinese officials. But with the opium trade now legalized, Elias saw a more efficient—and cheaper—way to reach customers. He negotiated with the Chaozhou, a Chinese minority group that had settled near the China coast but had contacts along trade routes throughout China. In return for a share of the profits, the Chaozhou sold the Sassoons' opium to other Chinese. To undercut Jardine and other dealers, the Sassoons sometimes sold their opium at discount or lent money to Chinese opium shops. The Chaozhou profited enormously from working with the Sassoons. A Western visitor remarked on the growing affluence of the "local opium men," who appeared "jolly, respectable . . . and . . . very civil." Critics of the opium trade expected it to be conducted by gangsters. Instead, it was creating a new class of Chinese business entrepreneurs: "The trade is conducted by men of the highest respectability, possessed of immense capital, who are known and esteemed as merchants of the first class." The Chaozhou used the money they made selling the Sassoons' opium to invest in banks and shops.

The impact of all this on Jardine was swift and devastating. With increasing alarm, Jardine executives watched the growing success of the Sassoons. "I cannot impress upon you too strongly the vast importance of carefully watching the proceedings of [the Sassoons] and speculators whose activities are seriously upsetting prices," a Jardine executive in India wrote to an employee. The Sassoons' tactics were allowing them to drive down opium prices and sell the drug more cheaply. "I am surprised that shippers are found at prices which cannot but lose money," the same executive wrote. The drop in prices was becoming "ruinous" for Jardine. The opium trade "altogether has gone to the dogs," another executive wrote. In one shipment of opium from India to Shanghai, 10 chests were from Jardine versus 42 from the Sassoons. In another shipment, 260 were from the Sassoons and just 42 from Jardine. By the 1870s, despite the rift between Elias and his brothers, the Sassoons controlled 70 percent of the opium flowing into China.

In 1872, thirty-three years after Jardine goaded Britain into invading China to protect its opium business, the company withdrew from the opium trade entirely. Jardine would go on to make huge profits in cotton, real estate, mines, and shipping. But opium and the profits that had powered Jardine's initial success now belonged to the Sassoons. So too did the power and access that came with it. The British colonial government in India relied on taxes on opium sales to support itself. The British viceroy now politely asked Abdullah Sassoon, David's eldest son and chosen successor, for "good information . . . [about] the prospects for the opium trade for the next 12 months," adding, "I know of no one better able to furnish it." A few years later the British asked Abdullah to join the Indian legislative assembly. Soon after that, they granted him a knighthood, and he became Sir Albert Sassoon.

The suffering of China's opium addicts rarely entered into the

Sassoons' letters, telegrams, or ledger books. The Sassoons knew the toll opium was taking on the health of Chinese workers. Opium sellers had "corrupted, degraded and annihilated the moral being" of the Chinese "while, every hour is bringing new victims," a British official in Hong Kong wrote as early as 1844. At one point, Elias's office in Shanghai wrote to the Sassoon office in Calcutta that it needed to fire its highest-ranking Chinese employee because he had become "useless" after excessive opium smoking. Protestant missionaries in China compiled data to demonstrate the harm of the drug and created the Anti-Opium League, which included leading doctors in Shanghai. In 1875, San Francisco, fearing the spread of opium among immigrant Chinese railway workers, passed the first American anti-drug law, making it a crime to frequent opium dens. Siegfried Sassoon, one of Britain's leading early twentieth-century poets, became estranged from the family and its "monstrous wealth." "They made it in the East by dirty trading, millions and millions of coins," he wrote. Under pressure from anti-opium groups, the British government set up a Royal Opium Commission in India in 1893. Testifying before the commission, representatives of the Sassoons insisted that, if used in moderation, opium was safe. It was "a mere entertainment activity for the upper classes," one Sassoon executive declared, while another added that "if taken moderately opium was very beneficial." Just as Europeans indulged in drinking alcohol, so the Chinese were instinctively drawn to opium. Indeed, "the Chinese who smoked or imbibed opium were better behaved, quieter, and far more sensible than those addicted to alcoholic drinks," the Sassoons declared.

The Sassoons fought vigorously against any effort to limit or ban the opium trade. Critical to their success was the growing influence of the family in British politics and at Buckingham Palace. In 1858,

S. D. Sassoon, who was working with his brother Elias in Shanghai, was sent by their father to London to open an office for the Sassoon family. S. D. leapt at the chance. He hated the humidity and heat of summers in Shanghai and, untraditionally, was told he could bring his wife and young son. The family left for England. S. D. opened an office on Fenchurch Street in London, the bustling financial equivalent of Wall Street, and bought an old royal castle at Ashley Park in Kent. In Baghdad, Sassoons had been groomed to be the Nasi, the adviser to kings and financial supporters of the government. The family understood the interplay of politicians, royalty, and business, the deals and alliances hatched at garden parties and dinners at wealthy estates. S. D. was soon joined by two of his younger brothers, so they could buy property and begin entertaining the British upper classes. The letters from brother to brother began focusing less on the prices of cotton and opium and more on wining and dining royalty. The London brothers sent newspaper clippings back to India boasting of their growing access and trading tips on social etiquette and social climbing. When British aristocrats visited India, the brothers urged one another to invite them to balls at the family mansion. "That will add to the fame of our family. Send a message to the press so they write about this in the newspaper."

The prime target was the most important man in Britain—the son of Queen Victoria and her heir apparent, Edward, Prince of Wales, popularly known as "Bertie." Before he became king in 1901 at age fifty-nine, Bertie was the heir apparent for longer than any of his predecessors. He was socially more broad-minded and cosmopolitan than many other royals and became friendly with several prominent and wealthy Jews, including the Rothschilds. He also needed money to support a profligate life. Bertie loved gambling, hunting, and yachting. He kept a string of mistresses, including actresses and singers, and wooed them with expensive gifts. Gossip swirled about his indebtedness.

The Sassoon brothers began romancing the heir to the British throne at house parties and horse races hosted by the Rothschilds. One brother, Reuben, began accompanying the corpulent prince on his monthlong "cures" to lose weight in the Czech Republic. The family stocked Bertie's favorite foods and stayed up as late as he wanted to play bridge, dance the Scottish reel, and smoke cigars. Most important, they helped cover his gambling debts, including giving him stock tips and an opportunity to take a "flyer" on opium—buying some stock in opium in India and then reaping a profit when it sold in Shanghai. The family made Bertie so much money that he joked that he should appoint Reuben Sassoon—his weight-loss companion—as his chancellor of the exchequer, Great Britain's treasury secretary.

When Bertie visited India, Albert hosted a party for the prince at the Sans Souci mansion he had inherited from his father. "It will cost us a lot of money, but it will add to the fame of the family," Albert wrote to his brothers in London. After Bertie left, Albert commissioned a colossal equestrian statue showing the prince astride a horse. Featured prominently in a carving at the base of the statue was a depiction of Albert's son Edward, named in honor of the future king.

The swift rise of the Sassoons also triggered a backlash. Many wealthy British families were land rich but cash poor. Just as British aristocrats suddenly developed a fondness for rich American women and their inheritances, so too did they learn to tolerate and even welcome outsiders like the Rothschilds and the Sassoons, who could afford to invest in new industries, host elaborate parties, entertain the king, and buy and renovate run-down country estates. "Say what you will, the Jews are the salt of smart Society, and the one intellectual stimulus," a London writer declared of the Sassoons. "Such humanizing influences as leaven fashionable London today come largely from the Jewish element."

But other members of the British aristocracy scorned the arrival of these newcomers and privately exchanged anti-Semitic slurs even as they joined the Sassoons for dinner. A British duke refused to rent his country house to Reuben Sassoon, notwithstanding Reuben's close ties to the royal family, "on account of religion." The duke told friends he would take "lower rent from a more desirable tenant." When the Prince of Wales visited the races north of London, in the company of several Sassoons, someone in the crowd shouted out: "Hail, King of the Jews."

"I am curious to know about the King," Winston Churchill wrote to his mother on the eve of Bertie's coronation in 1901. "Will it entirely revolutionize his way of life? Will he sell his horses and scatter his Jews, or will Reuben Sassoon be enshrined among the crown jewels and other regalia?"

When Albert Sassoon, the head of the family, decided to move from Bombay to London permanently to join his brothers, a British newspaper ran a limerick mocking him as a gold-loving "coon":

> Sir Albert Abdullah Sassoon
> That Indian auriferous coon
> has bought an estate called Queen's Gate
> And will enter upon it in June.

The Sassoons, collecting knighthoods and royal invitations and enjoying dinner and weight-loss cures with the heir to the British throne, saw themselves as British. The Chinese, seeing the Sassoon business interests advancing beneath the Union Jack, saw the Sassoons as British. But many British saw the Sassoons as Jews.

Nevertheless, the interest of the Sassoons and their allies in London came together to keep the opium trade thriving. In 1891, Britain's Parliament, under popular pressure, passed legislation ending the trade. Using their political and social connections, the Sassoons were able to delay implementation. In 1906, Parliament passed another law prohibiting the sale of opium in China. "We shall suffer enormous losses and whom shall we look to for compensation?" a Sassoon representative wrote. "Our losses are daily increasing. We as British merchants are entitled to have the support of our Government in the legitimate pursuit of our trade." The sale of opium continued. In 1909, an international conference to ban opium was convened in Shanghai. Three years later, dozens of countries, including the United States, signed an international agreement banning the opium trade. Representatives of the two Sassoon companies jointly wrote that the ban would lead to "enormous losses." Nevertheless, the ban went into effect. "The prohibition is now an accomplished fact," the Sassoons lamented. "The handling of opium" has become "a criminal offense."

Seen in the most favorable light, the Sassoons' view of the opium trade paralleled that later taken by entrepreneurs peddling tobacco and alcohol. They knew its harmful effects, yet their job was to make money, not to prohibit vice. Opium was legal. The British government in India taxed it. Chinese businessmen worked with the Sassoons to distribute it.

But the Sassoons' pursuit of the opium trade and decades-long battle to resist efforts to ban it reflected the racism at the heart of the colonial view of China. Reading the Sassoon letters about opium, it is hard to shake the belief that the Sassoons, like other British merchants and officials, viewed the Chinese with condescension and therefore distanced themselves from the devastating impact of opium addiction. The Sassoons avoided the drug themselves, and they, like many British in Shanghai, scolded and rebuked any Westerners they saw using it, especially when they developed the sallow yellow color of an addict.

Millions of Chinese suffered the effects of opium addiction, and the widespread use of opium—combined with myriad other factors—weakened the ability of the emperor to respond to the invasions of the West. A Chinese poet lamented the trail of opium from the blooming red poppy in the Indian desert to the green smoke that hovered over opium smokers:

> Hot Indian deserts exhale poisonous miasma,
> roast worms of sandy gold;
> Black crows tear flesh from the bones of corpses,
> peck at the fat, dripping blood;
> Blood red poppies spring up, for all this,
> they make a paste of yearning.
> Greenish smoke arises when paste is pounded to pieces,
> it drains gold and money out of the country.
> The vitality of a neighborhood disappears daily . . .

After opium was banned, the Sassoons invested their money in real estate and factories, building an even greater fortune. Upon taking power in 1949, the Communists seized the business records of the Sassoon companies in Shanghai. In the 1980s, the Chinese government allowed two Chinese economists to conduct a detailed investigation and accounting of the multiple Sassoon holdings over a century of business. The Chinese discovered that profits in opium had brought the Sassoons 140 million "liang" (a common name for the nineteenth-century Chinese currency)—the equivalent of $2.7 billion in 2018 dollars. They then invested that money in Shanghai property, stock, and companies to more than double their profit, to the equivalent of $5.6 billion. As the French writer Honoré de Balzac observed, reflecting on nineteenth-century robber barons around the world like the Sassoons: behind every great fortune lies a crime.

Laura and Elly Kadoorie

3

Laura and Elly

I n just one generation David Sassoon and his sons had vaulted from refugees fleeing Baghdad to the apex of British business and society. They sat in the colonial Indian legislative assembly and advised the British colonial government. They socialized with the king at their homes and visited him in Windsor Castle. They had pioneered many of the tools of modern capitalism and applied them ruthlessly, deploying steamships, the telegraph, and modern banks. Their London headquarters housed an entire floor of translators to translate bills of lading, contracts, insurance policies, and business inquiries that arrived written in Hebrew, Arabic, Persian, Chinese, and Hindustani. Forced to open Shanghai to foreign traders, the Chinese emperor had hoped to restrict their influence and eventually drive them away. Instead, the Sassoons kept expanding and began transforming China and the way the Chinese thought about business. "The name of Sassoon is less known in Europe than that of Rothschild," Shanghai's new English-language newspaper, *The North-*

China Herald, wrote in 1881, but among Chinese merchants, "it is a name to conjure with."

As word of the Sassoons' success and the success of other tycoons spread, other foreign businessmen from Great Britain, the United States, and Europe began to arrive to seize this new opportunity. David Sassoon's most striking innovation—the creation of the Sassoon schools to funnel new employees every year into the family firm—also held a danger. As word of the money to be made in China spread, so did the ambition of the poor Baghdadis flocking to work for the Sassoons. The Sassoons were minting money. They were also minting rivals.

Rima Kadoorie heard about the Sassoon schools as financial catastrophe overtook her family. She and her husband, Salih, were living well in Baghdad—not as rich as their distant cousins the Sassoons, but comfortable, nonetheless. Salih was a "merchant farmer"—the Baghdad equivalent of a merchant banker. In the countryside around Baghdad, flocks of sheep served as collateral for business deals. Nomads watched the sheep; Salih acted as a banker and middleman, providing credit, with the sheep serving as security. The Kadoories had seven children—six sons and a daughter. They sent their six boys to a private school run by a Paris-based Jewish organization, where the boys learned to read and write English, Hebrew, and French. In 1876, with his children still teenagers, Salih died, leaving Rima to support them alone. No one was old enough to take over the family business. Rima had heard that the Sassoons, with their new businesses in India and China, would provide training and apprenticeships and jobs. Though the boys were only teenagers, this was a great opportunity for them, since they could send money back to support their widowed mother. Surely the Sassoons would welcome them.

Their training in business and languages would make them valuable. Their faith would keep them close. Rima decided to send four of her sons to India to work for the Sassoons. Elly, the youngest, was fifteen. The Sassoons welcomed him: a family relative in Baghdad fallen on hard times; a teenager with a business mind; a position secured; gratitude and loyalty assured.

Elly's journey from Baghdad and the trajectory of his life could not have been more different from David Sassoon's. Several factors set them apart. David was thirty-seven when he fled Baghdad, a husband and a father, heir to a fortune and groomed to assume leadership of his family, the Jewish community, and a business that stretched across the Middle East. Elly was a boy of fifteen. He spoke English and French but lacked the network and contacts of the Sassoons and the respect and deference they commanded. Elly would grow up in China and make his most important business and family choices there. In contrast to the Sassoons, who carried the mantle of success and authority with them from Baghdad to Bombay to Shanghai, Elly was a striver, a self-made man with the dash of insecurity that many self-made men keep hidden. As much as David felt like an outsider, Elly's position was even more precarious. Being tossed into China forced Elly to build alliances and connections with other immigrants and with the Chinese. His determination and agility would impress many Chinese, who saw in his hunger and battles against the British establishment some of their own struggles and aspirations. He would tie the fate of his family to China and, operating in the shadow of the Sassoons, would rise until one day his family would surpass them.

After a brief stint in Bombay, where he apprenticed at the Sassoon school and learned the rudiments of trading in jute, coffee, and textiles, Elly was assigned a job as an apprentice clerk in Hong Kong working for E. D. Sassoon—the still-new venture set up by the renegade Elias, who had broken with the family to go out on his own. Elly first had to obtain a "laissez passer"—a travel document that allowed him to travel throughout the British Empire, India, and China. He arrived in Hong Kong on May 20, 1880, and reported to E. D. Sassoon's busy headquarters near the waterfront. By 1880—almost four decades after the First Opium War, with British rule firmly entrenched in Hong Kong and in the International Settlement of Shanghai—Hong Kong was teeming with ambition. The Sassoon headquarters overlooked the busy waterfront; the family already ranked among the city's dominant traders. Elly was given a salary of thirty-seven rupees a month, half of which he sent back to his mother in Baghdad.

Elly did well and soon was sent north to small port cities with Sassoon outposts along the China coast, ending at the small settlement of Weihaiwei, a three-day sail from Shanghai, where the Sassoons operated a warehouse. At eighteen, Elly moved into a large house with a garden, a view of the harbor, and the job title of "Number Three Clerk." A lucrative posting in Shanghai likely beckoned next.

Weihaiwei, like many Chinese cities, was beset with poor sanitation and repeated outbreaks of disease. An epidemic of bubonic plague broke out soon after Elly arrived. Elly's bosses were away on vacation and visiting other outposts. Temporarily in charge of the warehouse, Elly took a barrel of disinfectant out of storage and doused the building to repel the fleas and rats that were spreading the disease. When people started dying near the warehouse, Elly offered disinfectant to Chinese employees. For those who couldn't pay, he agreed to take payment later.

When the senior managers returned, they reprimanded Elly for using the disinfectant without permission. Plague or no plague, he had given away products that belonged to the Sassoons. He was summoned down to the Sassoon head office in Shanghai, where he argued vehemently. The Sassoon cousin in charge told him to stop being hotheaded. If Elly promised to "mend his ways," the incident would be forgotten.

"If that's the value you place on life, if you don't value humanity, I resign right now," Elly replied. The story entered the family's lore because it encapsulated how Elly saw himself: a principled, stubborn man railing against the foolishness and shortsightedness of others. It is equally likely that a young and ambitious Elly, captivated by the opportunities all around him in China, simply got tired of working for the overbearing Sassoons and decided it was time to strike out on his own. Looking back at the fortune the Kadoories subsequently amassed, Elly's son Lawrence would joke that the family should commemorate Elly's departure from the Sassoons by inscribing "a barrel of disinfectant" upon the Kadoorie family crest.

AFTER QUITTING THE SASSOON OFFICE in Shanghai, Elly traveled back down to Hong Kong to seek help from his elder brother Moses, who had also been sent out of Baghdad by his mother to find work with the Sassoons. Moses gave his brother 500 Hong Kong dollars and warned him, "Don't come back to me for more."

Elly took his $500 to the best hotel in town, the Hong Kong Hotel—four stories topped by an ornate cupola and observatory. Inside were a spacious courtyard, bar, and billiard room, and a grand staircase that led to guest rooms. Along three sides of the hotel ran a covered veranda to protect guests from the heat. Brokers and traders in Hong Kong met daily on the veranda to swap financial tips, tout stocks, and buy shares in companies—the forerunner of a formal stock exchange. David Sassoon had a name that opened doors and attracted traders. Not so Elly Kadoorie. Fearing that his name sounded too "foreign," Elly adopted an alias: E. S. Kelly. "E. S. Kelly," he reasoned, stood a better chance in business than "Eleazer Silas Kadoorie" of Baghdad with his thick Baghdadi accent and just $500 to his name. The veranda turned out to be an excellent avenue for a young outsider like Elly Kadoorie to make connections. With two other traders, Elly formed a stock brokerage company, Benjamin, Kelly & Potts. Now he could buy stakes in companies based on information gathered from other brokers and spot early investment opportunities. Working under an alias made him stealthy, allowing him not to tip his hand until he was ready to announce his investments publicly. In March 1891, at the age of twenty-five, he bought his first shares—in the company that owned the hotel he visited every morning.

Elly's more modest background and straitened circumstances prevented him from amassing the capital he needed to enter the opium trade. He was forced to become more diversified in his business and to develop a wider network of business associates than the British traders arriving from London to seek their fortunes, or even the Sassoons. He became a stockbroker, acquiring stakes in dozens of companies and working behind the scenes with partners and owners, accumulating influence and power as he went—a strategy American investor Warren Buffett would perfect a century later. Unfailingly polite and proper in public, Elly could be stubborn and ruthless in the boardroom, squeezing out partners and taking advantage of financial turmoil to seize control.

In pursuit of business, Elly began to cross social barriers, which was almost unheard of at the time. Hong Kong's population was overwhelmingly Chinese, but it was a British colony, and the Chinese were treated like second-class citizens. They could live only in certain neighborhoods and were barred from the scenic Victoria Peak that soared over the city center. Minor crimes were punished by public floggings. That didn't stop Elly from befriending the richest local businessman in Hong Kong—Robert Hotung. Hotung was a Eurasian tycoon whose father was Dutch and mother was Chinese. He learned English and worked as a comprador for Jardine, negotiating business deals with the Chinese and amassing investments of his own. He identified as Chinese, and by the time Elly returned to Hong Kong and was looking to buy shares in fledgling companies, Hotung was one of the richest Chinese men in town. The two began investing in new, innovative companies that, at the end of the nineteenth century, were transforming life and ushering in modernization. They acquired a stake in Hong Kong's nascent electric company, shares in the hotels that were attracting foreign businessmen and travelers, and part ownership of a mechanized tram that climbed the Peak, Hong Kong's tallest mountain, overlooking the harbor, displacing the coolies who had carried British families up in sedan chairs in the baking heat. The relationship between Elly and Hotung extended across the generations. Years later, Hotung would write affectionately to Elly's children that he had seen them grow up. It was an intimacy with the Chinese that no one in the Sassoon family could match.

AFTER ALMOST TWO DECADES of wheeling and dealing, Elly, at the age of thirty-two, began to think of marriage. The Sassoons, at the direction of their father, had all married women from well-to-do Baghdadi families, typically leaving them in Bombay to raise children while they moved from Shanghai to Hong Kong and on to London. Other British and foreign adventurers landing in China took up with Shanghai's "songbirds," the Chinese prostitutes who solicited men along the wharves. Elly's brother Ellis never married but appeared to have a series of liaisons with Chinese women. When he died, Ellis left a house and money in trust to support a Chinese woman and her daughters. Several other Chinese women came forward saying he had promised them property as well as jewels.

None of this was Elly's way. He sailed to England to see about forming business partnerships with wealthy Jews there and met Frederick Mocatta, the leader of the London Jewish community. Mocatta invited Elly to his home to meet his niece Laura.

Laura was everything Elly was not. She was an educated British aristocrat. Her family was part of the "cousinhood"—a group of wealthy Jewish families who had established themselves in England for hundreds of years. The Mocattas had been driven from Spain by the Inquisition in 1492, settling first in Holland, then moving to London following Oliver Cromwell's readmission of Jews to England. They had become wealthy running London's gold and silver exchange, and Frederick Mocatta turned to philanthropy, founding schools and libraries in the East End of London, where most poor Jews lived. Elly became infatuated with Laura. She was considered plain and was approaching forty, long past marrying age and several years older than Elly. She had traveled to India with a cousin, unusual for women in that time, and her mother had recently died. Laura was likely facing life as a wealthy unmarried woman involved in charity and helping London's poor.

But Elly was smitten. He delayed his return to China and, after a few months, proposed. In a time when arranged marriages were a sure route to business success, Elly could not have arranged a better one, marrying into a prominent wealthy family in London to complement his growing China investments. But if this is all Elly expected, he misjudged his wife. Whatever his motives, he ended up with a marriage that was far more a partnership than many others of its time. Laura gave Elly entrée into the world of London society. They raised their two boys as Britons, from their names—Lawrence and Horace— to their boarding schools to the mansion they would buy in London. But Laura was also determined not to settle for the life of the idle rich helping with the occasional charity lunch. Most China adventurers left their wives in England, China being too unpleasant. But Laura loved traveling and was eager for a change after her mother's death. When Elly announced he was returning to China to look for more business opportunities, Laura decided she was traveling with him.

It was "very hot" when she and her new husband arrived in Hong Kong, Laura confided to her diary. When the heat eased, they were immersed in a "terrible damp fog." She and Elly moved to a house halfway up the Peak, the mountain that loomed over central Hong Kong and was reserved for Europeans and other foreigners. There they could escape some of the heat and humidity. Soon after Laura arrived, a typhoon ripped off part of the Kadoories' veranda and flung it onto a greenhouse in a garden below. The house next door, perched above the ground on four-foot columns, was blown off its foundation. Across the harbor in Kowloon, Elly and Laura could spy workers picking up corpses. "At first, my mother found living in Hong

Kong somewhat difficult, being very different from the atmosphere to which she was accustomed in London," her son Lawrence observed drily many years later. Her uncle had donated considerable sums to help the poor Jewish immigrants crowding East London—analogous to New York's Lower East Side. Here in Hong Kong, the poverty and catastrophes were even worse. Many of the needs were the same. The beneficiaries wouldn't be Jews. They would be Chinese.

In London, Laura had been considered part of the British upper classes, her family's wealth and social connections smoothing her way. Not so in Hong Kong. The colony was a "snobbish" place, her son Lawrence recalled years later. Status literally ran in layers.

The governor's summer mansion sat atop the Peak. "As you went down, the social strata descended accordingly," Lawrence recalled. "The whole atmosphere from the point of view of anyone coming from England who had any situation at all was surprising. They couldn't at first understand what was going on."

As Laura tried to build a network of friends, she first had to adapt to the customs of Hong Kong high society. For example, no one would associate with Laura until she presented a visiting card—like a business card—at their home. She even had to bend down a corner of the card to show she had left the card herself and had not just sent it along with a servant or carriage driver. Until the longer-term resident dropped off one of her cards in response—thus recognizing her existence—protocol forbade Laura from visiting again.

Unlike Shanghai, which felt like the frontier, Hong Kong was a British colony with a royal governor, civil service, and an accompanying overlay of protocol, afternoon teas, and an acute awareness of class and accents. It was, visitors said, more British than Britain.

Ladies in Hong Kong "led lives of little responsibility as they circulated in carriages to distribute shoals of calling cards, arrange the next day's tiffin [lunch], gossip about the rising price of oysters and pheasants," a Protestant missionary wrote. "Some of the ladies were undoubtedly merry as well as irresponsible, but they usually looked washed out and slightly breathless during the hot days in their tight dresses." Heavy meals intensified their discomfort. The British made no concession to the heat of Hong Kong or to local cuisine. Dinner began at seven, just as it did in London, with sherry, followed by soup, fish, two meat courses, cheeses, and salads. Then came desserts, and fruits, all washed down with glasses of wine and port.

Laura had three children within four years. One baby, Victor, died at five months. In 1901, Elly dropped the pretense of "Kelly" and proudly renamed his company "Elly Kadoorie & Sons." Emulating the British, he adopted a coat of arms, and a motto taken from Laura's family, the wealthy Mocattas: "Adhere and Prosper."

LAURA WAS DETERMINED not to be suffocated by the prescribed colonial life of Hong Kong. Her family had been active in charity in London, and Elly's cousins the Sassoons had built and endowed synagogues and schools in India and across the Middle East. She now joined with Elly to start supporting a pioneering cause: schools for girls. The couple agreed to build a school for girls in Baghdad, named after Laura. Elly negotiated with his connections in Baghdad to buy the land and pay for the construction; Laura, writing in fluent French, negotiated with their wives to support scholarships for students and organize events.

Educating girls, Laura insisted, was crucial if Baghdad was to modernize, just as education and libraries had been crucial to improve the prospects of poor Jewish immigrants in the East End of London. Teachers at the new school fought against child marriage and succeeded in raising the age of brides who graduated from the school. The Kadoories supported a library at the school that women could use even after they left. More than 700 girls enrolled, most of them poor and Jewish, though a handful of Muslim parents, attracted by the progressive ideas, also sent their daughters. As the Baghdad school grew, Laura and Elly began supporting efforts by Elly's brother Ellis to open a network of schools for poor Chinese students typically shut out of education in Hong Kong and Canton. The schools taught arithmetic, Chinese language, and English, eventually enrolling 1,000 students.

Increasingly, Elly's hunt for new investments took him to Shanghai and across China. Laura, determined not to be left behind in stifling Hong Kong, decided she would travel with him, accompanied by her two young boys, a governess, and a dozen suitcases. Over the next two decades, Laura kept a diary of her experiences that at times recall Katharine Hepburn in *The African Queen*.

On an early voyage she noted how everyone, including Elly and the boys, had been up all night with seasickness. She had managed to overcome it. "I am quite a good sailor now," she wrote, though the unrelenting heat was still a problem. "It has been very hot since we left Hongkong [sic] but fortunately there was a pleasant breeze at Shanghai, though the temperature reached 105 degrees."

The smells and filth of China shocked her. The streets of Beijing were "horribly bad, thick mud all over. . . . Dirty wretched hovels, called bazaars, lined either side of the wide street." Alongside jostling crowds of people, camels "promenaded the streets carrying goods. They were wretched uncared-for looking animals. The rickshaw men rushed along as their rickshaws swerved from side to side over the terrible roads with ruts and holes at every turn." Careening through poverty in Beijing and Shanghai made London's tenement-filled East End look genteel. "We rushed in between the dirty shops and stalls placed in front of them, every minute expecting to be chucked for we had very few extra clothes with us, and we should have been thrown among those filthy, dirty and often quite naked children," she continued in her diary. A British couple traveling with Laura wanted to rush back to the hotel. "But I was struck by the comic part of the whole scene and would not have returned for the world," Laura declared.

The more she traveled, the bolder Laura became. "I noticed a sailing ship containing two men only cross our ship right across its bow," she wrote during one China voyage from Hong Kong to Shanghai. She was standing on deck showing seven-year-old Lawrence the scenery. "Before we knew what was happening, over went our boat on its side. Lower and lower it went." Laura grabbed her little boy. "We clung to the rail on the high side and then the awful feeling of what was to happen next—where was Elly, Baby [Horace] and Ah Ning [the baby's nanny]? What could I do to save Lawrence? Where should we all be in a minute more if this continued? rushed through my brain like a flash of lightning." As the boat tipped close to capsizing, it became stuck in the mud, with Laura and her son clinging to the high side. Elly and the nurse, holding Horace, rushed on deck to avoid being hurled into the river. Slowly the boat righted itself and

continued onward. "Of course, there were as usual some stupid people on board, who cried and shrieked and had to be given brandy,"
Laura noted. That evening many of the women slept with four life
belts tied around them. "I can't think how some people can be so
stupid," Laura wrote. She spent the rest of the trip calmly sketching
the sights, playing the piano, and leading passengers in singalongs.

As Laura traveled across China, she caught glimpses of the slow
deterioration of the country as other countries, now including Japan,
invaded and demanded territory and trading concessions. Like China,
Japan had been shocked by the arrival of Western ships and evidence
of the West's superior arms and technology. Unlike China, Japan had
responded by dispatching scholars and soldiers across the West to
learn from foreign countries, rearm, and prepare to expand on its
own. In 1894, Japan attacked China from the north and seized foreign concessions for itself.

During a sentimental 1905 trip to Chefoo, one of the cities where
Elly had worked as a clerk for the Sassoons "as a poor Baghdad boy,"
Laura noticed guns placed on all the ships, including the one she and
Elly boarded. The Chinese government insisted ships be armed to
fend off Japanese raiders. Laura climbed on deck, and the captain
showed her how to "manage" the guns if the Japanese attacked. "We
heard that a battle had just been fought in which the Japs had captured 5 of their [Russian] ships, some had been sunk. . . . All the
Baltic fleet which had been expected to do such wonders was captured or sunk by the Japs and the chief admirals taken." The Kadoories' trip ended without incident, but it was an ominous sign of
Japan's rise.

A few months later, aboard another ship with her family, Laura
confided to her diary that "there are certain places . . . which are

considered dangerous, and if we had arrived at these parts by night we must have to anchor on account of the floating mines." Still, she left the ship in good spirits, writing a humorous verse in the captain's logbook: "Thus we passed pleasantly over the wave / And encountered no mine to make us feel grave."

Laura relished the attention her adventuresome spirit attracted from other foreigners. Mingling among the first-class passengers on a boat crossing the Pacific to a vacation in Canada, she met the Russian and Japanese officials heading to the United States to discuss peace with President Theodore Roosevelt and talked with them about the "war question." She savored how the other passengers "seemed to think us marvels to have come from such a far-off land as China and they wanted to know every particular as to our life out there."

Driving in a horse and carriage down a street in Shanghai in 1905, Laura saw the terrible cost of the Russo-Japanese War, which had spilled into China's coastal waters: Wounded soldiers lay heaped on the shore, "rows of stretchers, 2 or 3 in a row, and continuing for about a mile, and on them were poor wounded Russians, covered by a sheet but with their agonized faces turned up to the boiling sun: it was indeed a painful scene."

A DOZEN YEARS after marrying Laura and establishing a life in China, Elly was rich enough to settle down and cease his endless traveling. Shanghai was a good place to make money, but no place to raise a family. Elly moved Laura and their two boys to London. They bought a house near Laura's family and enrolled the boys in an elite English prep school. Elly began looking for a country house.

Their London sojourn didn't last long. Elly and Laura had barely settled into their new home in London when Elly received a letter that a manager in his Hong Kong business had been speculating with company money and stealing company funds. His firm was facing "severe losses." Elly headed back to Hong Kong to recoup what he could.

It turned out that the problem was worse than a single dishonest employee. Elly had expanded his investments to a new industry with huge potential—rubber—and he had begun buying up stock in rubber companies in Malaysia and elsewhere in Southeast Asia. The industry was booming thanks to the rapidly growing auto industry in Europe and the United States, which required rubber to manufacture tires. When Henry Ford began mass-producing his Model T cars in 1908, interest in rubber stocks soared, rising 20 percent to 30 percent a week.

Unfortunately, the surge in the price of rubber company stocks was a classic "bubble" in which the stock prices far outstrip the reality of the business. When American demand for rubber slowed, the market crashed. Elly had been borrowing money from one of Hong Kong's biggest banks, Chartered Bank, to buy shares of Malaysian rubber companies, using the shares as collateral. With stock prices falling, the bank was demanding immediate repayment of its loans, known as "overdrafts." Back in Hong Kong to deal with the problem, Elly met with his bankers to negotiate, but the bankers held firm. They wanted their money back now.

Elly stepped outside to a small park in front of the bank in downtown Hong Kong and slumped on a bench, head down.

A mustachioed British man came by, dressed in a waistcoat and tie, and patted him on the back. Elly was already well known around town. "Now, young Kadoorie, why are you looking so miserable?" It was Thomas Jackson, head of the Hongkong and Shanghai Bank, backed by the Sassoons, already the premier bank in Asia.

"Well, you know, if all your interests were in rubber, and rubber has crashed, and your banker has asked for your overdraft to be drawn, you'd also look miserable," Kadoorie responded.

"Haven't you heard there's another bank?" Jackson asked. He invited Elly to meet with him in his office.

Within a few days Elly had new loans from the Hongkong and Shanghai Bank and was solvent again. Jackson had another offer for him as well. More than 300 rubber companies in Malaysia had borrowed money from the bank and were now teetering on the edge of bankruptcy as the price of rubber fell. With the backing and pressure of the bank, would Kadoorie consider working to consolidate them into a handful of larger companies, cutting expenses and personnel? Indeed, he would.

The rubber investment turned out to be not only a financial turning point for Elly but a personal one as well. Up to this point, Elly's investments had been focused on China's future and its modernization. Now he also learned that he could capitalize on a crisis, risking some of his own money in return for a much greater profit. That took a certain kind of business mettle and patience—investing when everyone else was bailing out. Elly learned something about himself: that when he believed in a plan and trusted his instincts, he could take a big risk and make it pay off.

In a matter of months Elly Kadoorie was transformed from a stockbroker to a financier, liquidating companies with the backing of the Hongkong and Shanghai Bank, creating new ones, and investing in the most promising. Operating from Shanghai and Hong Kong, he guaranteed loans and provided mortgages to save many rubber companies from bankruptcy. Some of them were run by wealthy British businessmen, who suddenly found themselves taking orders from this immigrant from Baghdad. As the price of rubber recovered by 1912, stock prices soared. Elly was a millionaire again. Returning to London, Elly told Laura that the future of his business increasingly lay in Shanghai. A year after she thought she had left China for good, Laura moved back, leaving the two boys—Lawrence and Horace—enrolled in British boarding school.

THE RUBBER CRISIS that made Elly a millionaire turned out to be one of the sparks that ignited the 1911 Chinese revolution and toppled the emperor. Ever since the British had invaded China in the First Opium War, the imperial court in Beijing struggled to respond. The effective British annexation of part of Shanghai and the opening of other treaty ports led to other countries invading China and lopping off territory. Fourteen years later, Britain invaded again and forced China to cede Kowloon, the southern peninsula across the bay from Hong Kong, giving Britain control of one of the world's great natural harbors. The United States, envying the concessions the British were wringing out of the Chinese empire, demanded similar favorable trading rights to help merchants sailing from New England to Shanghai and the China coast. The French, Germans, and Japanese followed with their own gunboats, soldiers, and demands. Aroused by the success of foreign invaders and sensing the weakness of the emperor, Chinese rebels mounted their own challenges. In 1850, the Taiping Rebellion convulsed China. Efforts to reform China's government and catch up with the West were repeatedly thwarted by the conservative emperors and their court.

Chinese reformers began to think that the problem lay not just in the invasions of the imperialists but in the inability of the emperor and China's imperial rule to respond effectively.

"As soon as the European race discovered our internal condition they mobilized their national imperialism as swarms of ants attach themselves to what is rank and foul and as a myriad of arrows concentrate on a target," Liang Qichao-chai, one of China's most influential thinkers, wrote, advocating vast reforms to allow China to modernize and expel the foreigners. Sun Yat-sen went even further. Trained as a doctor and educated in part overseas, Sun became increasingly frustrated by the refusal of the emperor and his advisers to adopt knowledge from the technologically advanced West. He called for the overthrow of the emperor, installation of a democratic, republican government, and the expulsion of the imperialist Europeans and Japanese.

Sun attracted the support of many wealthy Chinese, including Elly's business colleague Robert Hotung. Hotung profited enormously from working with foreigners. He had gotten his start in business working at Jardine and had a working—and profitable—relationship with Elly. But he also identified as Chinese, typically wore a traditional Chinese silk gown in public, and believed that the treaties imposed by the British after the Opium Wars were unfair. He was rich and comfortable and a nationalist and anti-imperialist.

Many Chinese banks and small Chinese investors were caught up in the rubber bubble. As rubber prices plunged, wave after wave of Chinese banks filed for bankruptcy, infuriating small depositors desperate to save their money. Half the Chinese banks in Shanghai went under. When it was discovered that local Chinese officials had used government funds to speculate on rubber stocks—and lost millions—

the emperor seized control of China's growing railway network and announced plans to sell it to foreigners to raise cash. The move angered not only Chinese patriots but local governments and Chinese businessmen who had been managing the growing and profitable rail system. Riots broke out, which led the emperor to call out the army to suppress the protests. On October 10, 1911, revolutionary groups organized an uprising in Wuchang in the province of Hubei, which ignited a series of revolts and led to the collapse of the Qing dynasty and the establishment of the Republic of China. After many failed attempts, the revolutionaries had succeeded. Sun, who was overseas fund-raising and organizing when the revolution broke out, returned and was named the first president of the Republic of China.

Many British businessmen in Shanghai mocked the revolution from their seats at the Long Bar at the Shanghai Club on the Bund. They welcomed the fall of the emperor and China's weakened state, and over the next few years formed alliances with whichever local Chinese warlord or military chief could benefit their business as central rule in China crumbled. Elly was more sympathetic. He was both part of the British establishment and apart from it. Several of his business associates, like Hotung, were Chinese and supported the revolution. Elly's travel with Laura around China had exposed him to the scope of China's problems and unhappiness with the imperial government. No one could deny that China was in a desperate condition. In 1912, when a triumphant Sun Yat-sen visited Shanghai and was given a reception at the mansion of a senior executive of the Sassoon companies, Elly kept an open mind. This new leader of China intrigued him.

Part of Elly's sympathy for the Chinese and their anger at foreign occupation stemmed from his own situation. Unlike David Sassoon, who had become a British citizen in 1853, and the Sassoon sons, who were collecting knighthoods in London and dining with the Prince of Wales, Elly on the eve of World War I was essentially a man without a country. Under various treaties, citizens of Baghdad living in China were considered French nationals and looked after by the French. Elly kept applying for British citizenship, citing his British wife, his children's education in British boarding schools, his success in business, and his mastery of English. Every time he was rebuffed. "The application should be refused as, if it is granted in this case, countless others will follow," the British vice consul in Hong Kong wrote to the foreign office.

World War I heightened Elly's sense of vulnerability. Joining Germany in alliance against Britain, France, and the United States was the Ottoman Turkish Empire, the rulers of Baghdad. On the eve of the war, Laura and Elly set sail across the Pacific for Canada, where they rendezvoused with their teenage sons, who had sailed across the Atlantic from London for a summer holiday. They planned to all return to England after vacation. When war broke out in August 1914, the Kadoories were unable to continue as planned to England— whether because of the dangers of war or questions about citizenship isn't clear. The Kadoories had to scramble to borrow money from friends and book passage back to Shanghai, where they enrolled the boys in a local English-language school. "I have never in my life been so much worried over passports," Laura wrote in her diary. "Many of my friends found it unbearable and returned without completing their proposed trips. Officials meet one on boarding the train and again on arrival at station and hotel, asking many totally unnecessary questions and taking the greatest delight in prolonging the agony."

Laura described one young man and his family confronted by British officials when they discovered that he, like Elly, was born in Baghdad. "After the usual questions as to his age, etc., they inquired, 'What is your nationality?'

"'French,' he replied.

"'Where were you born?'

"'In Baghdad.'

"'Where do you live?'

"'In France.'

"'Oh, I see you live in Baghdad which is somewhere in France.'"

The British colonial government in Hong Kong issued a regulation that prevented non-British residents from joining the boards of directors of major British companies in China and Hong Kong. Elly had been using the money he reaped in rubber to buy up shares in companies that were betting on Shanghai's future: the gas company, a land development company. These companies were attractive because their owners had deep ties to the British establishment and the Shanghai Municipal Council, which ran the day-to-day affairs of the International Settlement. The new regulations ensured that Hong Kong and Shanghai businesses would remain a British gentleman's club. Though his investments were growing, Elly was blocked from joining the boards of directors where decisions were made.

ELLY HAD MARRIED a spirited and confident woman. Laura was inspired by the new suffragette and emancipation movements that were starting to lap up on the shores of Shanghai. Local newspapers dubbed her the most "emancipated" foreign woman in the city.

When motorcars became available in China, Laura became one of the first women in China to drive one, steering it along Bubbling Well Road. She won the "Ladies Pistol Shooting Championship." Spurred in part by Elly's quest for British citizenship, but also by the desire to help ease the poverty and suffering she saw across China, Laura expanded her charity work. She visited Chinese orphanages and schools and raised money for the Shanghai Red Cross, spurring other British women to do the same. She organized charity events and bazaars, the first Shanghai had seen. "She took delight from morn till night in devoting her energies, her abilities and her means to the cause of the poor and the needy," a local Shanghai newspaper wrote. One of the Kadoories' Jewish friends began giving away money to Chinese victims of floods who lined up in front of his mansion. To Western eyes, especially a hundred years later, such behavior might smack of the worst kind of noblesse oblige. But for China such notions of philanthropy were new. Chinese merchants gave money to support their clans or villages when times were hard. They didn't give money to people they didn't know. Wealthy Chinese began to take note of the Kadoories' efforts and soon began similar efforts, often partnering with Westerners.

Laura also began pushing for more opportunities for women. She lobbied the British all-male clubs to open their doors to women, at least at certain times. She looked askance at how women were treated across Asia, recalling in her diary how on a trip to Korea she saw a large bell that "used to be rung at 9 o'clock pm to inform the men it was time to go home and let the women go out, which they could do only after dark." In too many societies, "women were never supposed to be seen by any man but their husbands, and even the latter looked down upon them." Educating girls, Laura believed, could end this and ensure that women in China and elsewhere would no longer be "kept secluded and like prisoners."

Horace and Lawrence were preparing for their university-level education in England. Elly was strict, but Laura oversaw family matters. Lawrence wanted to attend Lincoln's Inn and become a barrister in England. Horace contemplated entering agriculture and becoming a gentleman farmer, perhaps in Canada, where the family enjoyed vacationing. "You would be surprised if you could see our boys now," Laura wrote in her diary. "It is wonderful how quickly boys outgrow their fathers." In the fall of 1918, the family spent six weeks in Japan, hiking and fishing. Laura spent "many happy hours sketching." She wrote with optimism about trips to come, aided by new innovations like plane travel, "when everyone goes about in aero planes, and the distances which now seem so great can be passed in a few days."

In shuttling from London to Hong Kong to Shanghai and back again, Laura often complained to Elly of missing "a fixed home." Elly bought a mansion on Shanghai's most fashionable street, Bubbling Well Road—so called, Laura noted with her typical dry humor, "As it contains a well with horribly dirty water with a few bubbles on it."

Six weeks after the family returned to Shanghai from their Japanese vacation, fire broke out in the mansion on Bubbling Well Road as everyone slept. It spread quickly, choking the main staircase with smoke. Elly stumbled out of his first-floor bedroom and across the hall to Laura's bedroom and woke his wife. He then went to wake the boys. They had already been awoken by the servants and escaped. As the smoke thickened, Elly rushed out and the family gathered on a veranda away from the flames. Laura realized the family governess was missing and rushed back into the house to search for her. When the fire brigade arrived, they found Laura collapsed by a linen closet, suffocated by the smoke. The governess had already escaped.

Hundreds attended Laura's funeral the next day and a citywide memorial service a week later. "Her virtues are all the rarer and more priceless in that they have been manifested in an age of crude materialism, where the pursuit of wealth has engrossed the majority of men and women, to the extent of almost bringing about the death of their souls," an admirer wrote. Elly packed up the children and headed to England. They left Laura's body buried in a Shanghai cemetery.

They wouldn't stay away long.

PART TWO

Kings of Shanghai

Elly Kadoorie and his sons,
Lawrence (left) and Horace

4

Shanghai Rising

As China fell, Shanghai rose.

A few months after he was declared president of the new Republic of China, Sun Yat-sen was ousted and replaced by a powerful general, Yuan Shikai. The general declared himself emperor in late 1915 and then abdicated after a few months, leaving a power vacuum that ushered in a new warlord period in China. Generals in different parts of the country ruled their fiefdoms with terror and military force. The British, French, Americans, Germans, and Japanese all continued to run their spheres of influence, extending their control over almost every major city in China except Beijing. Imagine that, despite early America's nominal independence, the British still occupied New York, Boston, and Atlanta while a besieged American government in Washington, D.C., kept losing battles against rebellious Native Americans in the West and secessionists in the South.

Shanghai, by contrast, enjoyed what most of China lacked: a

stable government that could protect its citizens. The International Settlement had been established in 1863, when the American Concession—land fronting the Huangpu River adjacent to the British-controlled land—joined the British Settlement. Presiding over this increasingly pleasant colonial enclave was a seven-member panel of prominent British financiers and industrialists elected by the Shanghai British business community—the Shanghai Municipal Council. (The French Concession remained independent and was ruled by a similar group of foreign businessmen.) The Shanghai Municipal Council oversaw the construction of roads, collection of garbage, and payment of taxes. It regulated gas suppliers, trams, rickshaws, and prostitution. It oversaw the police. All the policies of the International Settlement were designed by its business leaders to create the stability, prosperity, and lack of government interference yearned for by foreign capitalists. Representatives of the Sassoons, of course, were permanent members. Shanghai had become, in the words of one historian, a "Republic of Merchants." Foreign investors flocked to the city, lured by modern conveniences, low taxes, and a business-friendly lack of regulation. For ambitious foreign businessmen and financiers, Shanghai no longer smelled of sewage, cooking food, and burning incense. It smelled of money.

Daily life was far more pleasant than the city Laura had complained about in her diary. Gone, at least where the foreigners lived, were the stink of illness and filth, the brawling men, the sense of being on the frontier of empire. Colonnades now adorned banks, trading houses, and official buildings along the Bund. The lack of a sewage system that had so appalled early foreign settlers, the sight of Chinese hauling people around in wheelbarrows as if they were loads of bricks, the lack of proper lights and running water—all these were replaced by new technology. The streets where foreigners lived now had trams, gas lighting, and running water. Villas built by wealthy foreigners on Bubbling Well Road now extended well beyond the popular racecourse. The hardships of China yielded to the cosseting of colonialism. The number of Western women in Shanghai—most accompanying their husbands—rose from just seven in 1850 to more than three thousand by 1895, an indicator of just how much better living conditions were becoming. A popular phrase book offered newly arriving foreign women language tips for dealing with Chinese servants: "*Nung hiau tuh Ying koh kuh sau feh va?*" (Can you cook according to the English method?) "*Hiniung tan long kuh bung zung tan t'seh chepah.*" (Take the carpet out and beat the dust out.) "*Pau seau non t'seh chepeh seang seang.*" (Take the child out for a walk.)

"One had but to shout . . . and everything would arrive," a young British businessman recalled. "First the water-carrier to fill the tub for the daily bath, then the 'number-two boy' with the glass of 'breakfast claret,' the steak and eggs (both so cheap one couldn't afford not to eat them), and then the same shout would summon the . . . coolie who pulled one to the office for the business of the day."

"I remember that until I was twelve years old I never took a bath by myself," recalled a Bubbling Well Road neighbor of the Kadoories. She was always attended by a maid. "I didn't know how to rinse a cup. I had a nursemaid who was closer to me than my own mother."

The growth and modernization weren't limited to the foreign neighborhoods and the European families that lived there; they rippled outward. Ever since the Opium Wars, China's best minds had struggled with how to respond to the technologically more advanced and better-armed West. For many Chinese entrepreneurs and businessmen, Shanghai now offered an answer: learn from foreign businessmen, and take advantage of the city's open borders and foreign competition. For some Chinese, Shanghai was a daily reminder of China's military defeats and humiliation. For others, it illuminated the future.

By the 1920s, about 40,000 foreigners lived in Shanghai's International Settlement administered by the British. So did 1 million Chinese, plus another 2 million Chinese who lived in Chinese-controlled parts of the city. The British imposed social restrictions on the entire Chinese population. They could not enter British clubs or walk in certain parks. But they could walk or ride through the International Settlement without interference, shop in stores, work in offices and factories. Aspiring Chinese began to pour into Shanghai determined to work for the foreign businesses lining the Bund. The new arrivals acted like immigrants in their own country—hardworking, entrepreneurial, packed into slums, seeking work with the rich foreigners or with new Chinese companies infected by the city's innovative energy. They launched companies in cotton, rubber, tobacco, iron, flour, cigarettes, and food processing. Between the end of the nineteenth century and the 1920s, more than half of China's new factories were started—by Chinese businessmen—in Shanghai. The local film industry boomed. Billboards on building walls across the city featured Chinese women in Western dress smoking Western cigarettes surrounded by Western luxuries.

The British also allowed more dissent and a freer Chinese press in the International Settlement than did the Chinese authorities in the rest of China. As a result, the International Settlement became a haven for political radicals, including Communists who wished to topple the capitalists and drive the foreigners out of China. Both Mao Zedong and Zhou Enlai, two leaders of the Communist Chinese revolution that would triumph in 1949, lived in the International Settlement or the nearby French Concession in the 1920s and spread propaganda and held meetings designed to foment revolution. More than 1,000 Chinese-language dailies, weeklies, and monthlies circulated in China at that time, many published in Shanghai. Factory workers were passionate about politics. "Almost everybody in the factory reads newspapers," recalled a worker at a cotton mill. One illiterate woman bought a newspaper every day and asked her son to read it, so she could "understand society and the present political situation." Even rickshaw pullers kept up with news, one out of two reading newspapers.

The first time he visited Shanghai in the 1920s, the American soldier Joseph Stilwell, who would play a pivotal role in America's views on and relations with China during World War II, was stunned by the modernity of the city. Instead of an Oriental skyline of wooden pagodas and temples with gently sloping roofs, Stilwell saw modern hotels and banks, broad streets and the parks of a Western-style city. From his hotel window, Stilwell thought Shanghai looked like Philadelphia.

Then he stepped into the streets. Leaving his hotel, he plunged into the narrow alleyways filled with "bustle, crowds, smells and the incessant din of voices calling, businessmen selling and bargaining, hurling imprecations and warnings and crying their wares with shouts, chants, tinkling bells or the clacking of sticks on blocks of wood." He marveled in his diary at the energy of the Chinese: "With the right direction, 400 million people with their working and manufacturing ability will dominate and we'd better be with them," he wrote.

"There never was and never will be another city like Shanghai between the two wars," Elly's son Lawrence Kadoorie would recall years later. "A city of extreme contrasts, combining the attributes of East and West. The Paris of the Orient . . . a paradise for adventurers. Here my brother and I continued our education—the international outlook of Shanghai broadening ours and giving us an understanding of what it was to become a citizen of the world."

For the rich twenty-five-year-old scion of a rising dynasty, the city was paradise. "The winters were cold, which made one feel brisk and energetic," Lawrence recalled. "Shanghai was a place where one could dance all night, go riding at 6 o'clock in the morning, work all day and yet not feel tired."

REELING FROM LAURA's DEATH, a despondent Elly Kadoorie, back in London, pondered what to do. Moving back to Shanghai started to seem like a good option. He had already enrolled Lawrence, then twenty, at Lincoln's Inn, the prominent London law school. Horace, a few years younger, talked about studying architecture or perhaps agriculture and becoming a gentleman farmer. Elly was a wealthy man and had the backing of his wife's family, the rich and socially well-connected Mocattas. But Elly's horizons in Britain felt limited. He didn't have British citizenship. Elly's British rivals looked down on him and mocked the death of his wife. Describing the fire that had killed Laura, Jardine executive J. K. Patterson wrote to his bosses: "In the general scramble the mother of the family was forgotten, when it was all over she was found as smoked and as dead as a kipper in a cupboard into which she had bolted." The executive went on that Elly "unfortunately . . . found the door!" William Keswick, the head of the Jardine office in Shanghai and one of the city's most powerful men, privately mocked the Kadoories' "Semitic" appearance. The Kadoories, he complained in a letter, were "never-ending in their nosing and queries" on business deals. "One can truthfully say that the Kadoories have good noses for nosing."

By contrast, the Chinese whom Elly dealt with in Shanghai and Hong Kong didn't make any distinction between British businessmen and Jews. They treated him with deference. There was no history of anti-Semitism in China that Elly could see. At fifty-five, Elly lacked the polish to play the relaxed country squire. Elly was "a bouncing ball of energy," as one employee described him. "A man who didn't like red tape, a law unto himself. . . . He expected all the jobs he asked for to be done immediately. . . . He was a rough task master, fond of a good-looking finished job," and, with Laura gone, of "a good-looking woman too." The British newspapers reported daily the comings and goings of various Sassoons at court as they entertained and mingled with the king and his circle. Elly sensed that in London, despite his success, he would forever remain an outsider, and in the shadow of the richer, more successful Sassoons.

A second family tragedy sealed his decision. A year after Laura's death, Elly's brother Ellis died of a heart attack in Hong Kong, leaving him a large stake in a network of hotels in Hong Kong, Shanghai, and Beijing. Elly now sat astride an empire spread across China and Asia: his late brother's luxury hotels; an electric company in Hong Kong and southern China; rubber companies in Malaysia; growing stock holdings in Shanghai. His sprawling investments required constant attention. The last time he had moved to England—in 1910—he had left his business in the hands of local managers; embezzlement and a business crisis had pulled him back. The Sassoons also provided a cautionary tale. During World War I, the Sassoon companies in Shanghai had been accused of trading with the enemy Germans, the details filling the newspapers. The companies were acquitted, but it showed how lack of strong oversight could tarnish the family name.

Elly decided to move back to Shanghai and take his sons with him. He had relied on Laura; now he relied on Lawrence and Horace. In 1924, he ordered Lawrence to end his legal studies at Lincoln's Inn and Horace to abandon his dreams of architecture and farming. (In a small act of rebellion, Lawrence never formally withdrew from Lincoln's Inn but kept his connection active until well into his eighties.) The Kadoories announced the family's return to Shanghai by building the city's largest mansion. Modeled on the royal palace at Versailles outside Paris, where the Allies had just held the peace conference that ended World War I, Marble Hall was twice the size of any existing home in Shanghai and sat just down the street from the more modest home of Jardine's William Keswick, whose executives often mocked Elly and his family. The veranda along the front of Marble Hall stretched 220 feet, longer than a city block. A series of garages held several Rolls Royces. Inside, the ballroom was eighty feet long, fifty feet wide, and sixty-five feet high, with 3,600 electric lightbulbs glittering from the ceiling. A visitor counted more than four dozen sofas in the ballroom, living rooms, and parlors. The dining room could seat fifty. There were twelve bedrooms, though just three people lived in the house—Elly, Lawrence, and Horace, attended by forty-two servants. They ate their meals at a small table set up in the corner of the vast dining room. In later years Elly's sons blamed the extravagance on an alcoholic architect who they said had built Marble Hall while they were in London and without their knowledge—a claim that seems far-fetched. It didn't stop the Kadoories from filling Marble

Hall with Chinese antiques, Persian carpets, even a whole ceiling imported from an Indian temple.

Marble Hall became the most famous address in Shanghai. Unlike the parties at the stuffy Shanghai British Club and other British residences that were staid and predictable, those at Marble Hall burst with the energy of the Jazz Age that was sweeping the United States and Europe. The home linked Shanghai to London, but also to Paris and New York. The Kadoories hosted Charles Lindbergh at a party when he was flying around the world, then welcomed Katherine Stinson as the first woman to fly to Shanghai from England. A group of American pilots flying around the world landed one day at four in the afternoon. A film was made of the landing and shown in the ballroom of Marble Hall at nine the same night. Marble Hall parties featured a "bevy of pretty girls" who greeted guests at the door and ushered them into the ballroom and gardens to see "solos, dancers, musical numbers, clever variety turns, some smart dresses and a few stunts not seen before in Shanghai," Shanghai's English-language newspaper reported. After an American-themed ball in 1924, a newspaper wrote that "the ball struck an unusual note of informality—almost Bohemianism— that threw into even stronger relief the grandeur and spaciousness of Mr. Kadoorie's hall."

About a mile away from Marble Hall, across the street from Elly's former mansion where Laura had died in the fire, sat a large house and estate that belonged to Scottish friends of the Kadoories. When the friends decided to move, Elly's company bought the property and decided to build the "best, fanciest hotel in Asia." It would be called the Majestic. A few years later he followed it with another hotel in Hong Kong, the Peninsula.

It is difficult today in a world of cookie-cutter hotel chains and frequent business travel to appreciate the importance hotels played in establishing the identity of a city and its social meeting points. For the British, hotels were an extension of colonialism and a symbol of British civility and culture in chaotic surroundings. The hotel chain Elly inherited from his brother ran a series of colonial—and quintessentially British—hotels across China. For those sipping tea in leather club chairs, seated in heavily carpeted and draped rooms, with the muffled chaos of China safely outside, it would be easy to believe the hotel was owned by a British lord, not some immigrant from Baghdad. Indeed, one visitor wrote that "only the waiters in their long blue gowns and pigtails gave any impression that Europe was some distance away."

For the Majestic in Shanghai, Elly hired a team that envisioned something different, a hotel where he and his sons would feel comfortable and welcome, one that reflected their experiences and the city's emergence as a globalized, cosmopolitan city in an interconnected world. The British Shanghai Club didn't allow Chinese to join. The British-run racecourse was segregated, forcing Chinese into their own section. The new Majestic Hotel, by contrast, was advertised as an "international" hotel open to Westerners and (affluent) Chinese alike, a place where the different parts of Shanghai could come together and where wealthy Chinese could get a glimpse and taste of the wider world. The motive for opening the hotel was economic; Elly saw a market of globe-trotting tourists, local businessmen, wealthy expatriates, and striving Chinese businessmen. It was cracking open the establishment and making room for ambitious and talented outsiders to elbow into the clubby world of colonial Shanghai.

Elly hired a Spanish/French architect to build his dream hotel and staffed it with French chefs, Swiss managers, and American entertainers. Guests dined on French food and danced to a jazz orchestra led by American Whitey Smith, who encouraged Chinese women to wear the cheongsam, a body-hugging dress with a slit running up one leg that became the rage among movie stars and ordinary young women alike, allowing them to more easily dance the latest "rags," including the Charleston. Hollywood celebrities began to visit Shanghai and stay at the Majestic. At the height of their popularity, Hollywood movie stars Douglas Fairbanks and his wife, Mary Pickford, stayed for a week. More than 2,000 people attended a dance in their honor. "There are only five prominent cities in the world and Shanghai in my opinion occupies the limelight as the most colorful and interesting and progressive," Fairbanks told reporters.

Elly stepped up his charitable giving, coordinating it with Britain's foreign policy, pushing British efforts to improve its image in the Middle East and in China. He gave money to hospitals in England, France, Constantinople, and the Middle East. In Laura's memory he supported the school for girls in Baghdad she had helped found. He endowed another school for girls in Shanghai. On a visit to London, he assisted the government by hosting and entertaining visiting royalty, among them King Faisal of Iraq and Emperor Haile Selassie of Ethiopia.

In 1926, Elly achieved his long-sought acceptance from Great Britain: King George V gave Elly citizenship and a knighthood. Now Elly was free to begin to expand his stock holdings and take his place on British corporate boards. Together with his longtime friend and business partner Robert Hotung, he began buying stock in the Shanghai Land Co., the largest real estate company in Shanghai. The company was controlled by a handful of Shanghai's British elite—all its founders were members of the Shanghai Municipal Council, which controlled land and zoning in the International Settlement. As a result, the company owned most of the best parcels for development. Elly and Hotung bought enough shares on the open market to take control of the company. They invited the Sassoons to join them—fellow outsiders triumphing over the old elite. Next came the Shanghai Gas Co., which had become one of the most important and profitable utilities as the city grew. It was originally founded by British merchants, but Elly took control, buying up shares as the company expanded, until he controlled it with about 40 percent of the stock. He installed his other son, Horace, on the board, and eventually made him chairman.

THE SASSOONS AND THE KADOORIES had both emerged from the rich religious and cultural soil of Baghdad's Jewish community. As the memory of Baghdad faded, replaced by their new lives in the British Empire as British citizens, their views of their position in the world—and by extension, in China—diverged. Zionism—the dream of returning to Palestine and Jerusalem—galvanized Jews around the world in the early twentieth century as they confronted rising anti-Semitism in Europe and anti-Jewish pogroms in Russia. The Sassoons kept their distance from Zionism. They embraced the British, trusting that their money and growing influence with the royalty and aristocracy in London ensured their safety and ascent.

Zionism was more compelling to Elly. He had less money than the Sassoons, and fewer connections. He had battled for more than a decade to get British citizenship. He had needed to adopt a Christian surname—Kelly—to get his start in Hong Kong. The idea of a Jewish

homeland appealed to a man whose place in the world seemed uncertain.

Elly had become the leader of the small Zionist movement in China
in 1909, and he and his brother donated money to acquire land for the
Hebrew University in Jerusalem. In 1917, under international pressure, England issued the Balfour Declaration, which supported the
creation of a Jewish homeland in Palestine and was the first step to
what would become the creation of the state of Israel in 1948. Around
the world, Jews mobilized to rally public opinion and persuade governments to endorse the idea of a new Jewish state. The same year the
Balfour Declaration was issued, Elly decided to approach the putative
leader of China, Sun Yat-sen, and ask him for support.

Like most Chinese, Sun Yat-sen knew very little about Jews. But
they were not completely absent in Chinese history. A small group of
Jews from the Middle East had settled in Kaifeng centuries earlier
and had adopted a Chinese-inspired Judaism. On a stone monument
in 1489 they had written diffidently: "Our religion and Confucianism
differ only in minor details." Both religions "venerate ancestors, are
loyal to sovereigns and ministers, and filial to parents." By the twentieth century, the Kaifeng Jews had nearly all disappeared through
intermarriage. Most Chinese followed Buddhism, Taoism, or Confucianism and had little experience with or animus toward Jews, treat-
ing them as another curiosity imported from the West, just like
Christians. "The native Chinese make no difference between a Jew
and a Christian," a friend of Elly's remarked in the 1920s. "Both are
foreigners in their eyes."

Sun Yat-sen had met some Jews as he traveled the world seeking
support for his efforts to overthrow China's emperor. Visiting

Moscow, where the Communists had just toppled the czar, Sun met several top Communists who were Jewish, his eventual successor Chiang Kai-shek later recalled, and "were comparatively speaking sincerer in their friendliness." In the United States, Sun met Morris Cohen, a Jewish former boxer who became his head of security. In Shanghai, he visited the estate of Silas Hardoon, who ran the Sassoon operations there. Sun sympathized with the plight of the Jews, which, he wrote, reminded him of some of China's own struggles. "Chinese nationalism disappeared when China was conquered by foreigners," he wrote. "But China was not the only country that had been conquered. The Jewish people also lost their country."

After Elly's face-to-face meeting with Sun to discuss Zionism, Palestine, and the Jews, Sun endorsed the Balfour Declaration in a personal letter to Elly, writing that "all lovers of democracy cannot help but support the movement to restore your wonderful and historic nation, which has contributed so much to the civilization of the world and which rightfully deserves an honorable place in the family of nations." In return, Elly offered his expertise to the government and likely indicated that he was prepared to buy bonds to support Sun's new republican government.

The relationship lasted even after Sun died of cancer in 1925, the connection sustained by Sun's increasingly influential and politically powerful widow, Madame Sun Yat-sen, also known as Soong Qing-ling.

Madame Sun came from one of China's most influential Western-educated families. Her father, Charles Soong, sent his three daughters to be educated in the United States and arranged their marriages into China's political elite. Soong Qing-ling became Madame Sun Yat-sen, marrying China's first president. Years later, her two sisters married into the Nationalist power structure as well. Soong Mei-ling married China's new leader, General Chiang Kai-shek, and became known throughout the West as Madame Chiang Kai-shek. A third sister, Ai-ling, married H. H. Kung, a descendant of Confucius and a wealthy banker. The Chinese waspishly joked that one Soong sister (Ai-ling) loved money, and one (Mei-ling) loved power, but Madame Sun (Qing-ling) loved China.

HORACE AND LAWRENCE KADOORIE gradually acquiesced to the roles Elly was carving out for them. Upon returning to Shanghai in 1924, Elly put Horace in charge of the Kadoories' social calendar—overseeing management of Marble Hall, arranging the lavish parties, and supervising the charity work that had been started by his mother. Horace gave up his dream of studying agriculture and becoming a gentleman farmer in the West. He had an eye for fine things and good food, and his shy temperament made him unlikely to challenge his father.

Lawrence was more conflicted. He resented the way his father sometimes turned him into an errand boy and secretary. "I didn't have much of a boyhood," Lawrence recalled later. "I lost perhaps some of the fun of being young because I was plunged immediately into quite heavy responsibilities."

Elly took Lawrence with him on overseas trips, employing him as his private secretary, having him draft letters and arrange meetings. Even before Laura's death, when Lawrence was still a teenager, Elly brought him down to Hong Kong to visit China Light and Power and carry his briefcase. The chairman of China Light, Elly's British partner, also represented Harley-Davidson motorcycles. Lawrence admired the motorcycles longingly.

"I will give you one of those!" Elly's partner announced.

"He will not accept it," Elly barked.

That was the end of that. At home as at work, Elly's word was law.

Like David Sassoon, Elly was turning his sons into extensions of himself and his business. He trained them to be loyal and follow his lead. Elly believed—correctly—that Lawrence was the better businessman of his two sons and was grooming him to take over the family's Hong Kong businesses. Lawrence craved the power and independence that would come with the role—though it would mean spending less time in Shanghai. It was an opportunity to make his own mark. His brother, Horace, would remain in Shanghai to tend to their father's needs.

Opponents stood little chance before Elly's efforts to empower his sons. Soon after winning Sun Yat-sen's endorsement of the Balfour Declaration, Elly proposed a massive donation to Zionists in Palestine to build a "garden city" near Jerusalem that would include schools, hospitals, and farms. The only condition was that Lawrence and Horace would oversee the project. After two years, Elly visited Palestine to see the progress only to find that the money had been used for other causes and there were no signs of construction. Bitterly disappointed and saying he had been misled, Elly quit as head of the Shanghai Zionists, severing an important tie with the Jewish community. "I'm much richer than the Rothschilds yet they do whatever they please," he complained. "Only on me are these strictures."

In April 1928, one of the directors of China Light and Power died. Elly bought the shares and named Lawrence, not yet thirty, as his representative on the board of directors. Some executives at China Light and Power in Hong Kong grumbled about Elly's determination to bring his sons "with pink cheeks, down from Shanghai" into the boardroom. A few years later, he ousted his longtime partner Robert Shewan as chairman and elevated Lawrence to the chairman's job. He began putting Lawrence on boards of his other Hong Kong companies as well.

"I met today Lawrence Kadoorie who told me with that charming smile of his that he was joining the Wharf Board in Hong Kong," Elly's bête noire, William Keswick of Jardine, wrote to a colleague. "Last year I resisted their advances. But I know how persistent they are, and money talks."

A FEW MILES from Marble Hall, another Shanghai was overwhelmed by poverty and overcrowding. Shanghai's slums were some of the most crowded and desperate on earth—twice as crowded as New York's Lower East Side. Factory owners reaped huge profits by paying the world's lowest industrial wages. Officials of the Shanghai Municipal Council visited the slums and found as many as fifteen families sharing a single home. Municipal workers pushed wagons along the streets, picking up bodies as if they were trash. Visiting British writers Christopher Isherwood and W. H. Auden described how in some Shanghai factories "half the children have already the blue line in their gums which is a symptom of lead-poisoning. Few of them will survive longer than a year or eighteen months."

In the opening pages of his widely read Chinese novel *Midnight*, the writer Mao Dun described how Shanghai was changing again,

from its architecture along the Bund to the new technology flowing through the city. Arriving from the countryside, a Chinese visitor stared anxiously at the new buildings: "To the west, one saw with
a shock of wonder on the roof of a foreign style building a huge
neon sign in flaming red and phosphorescent green: LIGHT, HEAT,
POWER!"

Elly had been more charitable than most foreigners, building several schools in Shanghai to educate poor Chinese children, especially
girls. But foreigners like the Kadoories and the Sassoons lived in a
"hermetically sealed and isolated glass case," British journalist Arthur
Ransome wrote after visiting Shanghai. "Europe is far away from them
and China, at their very doors, seems almost as far." They "look round
on their magnificent buildings and are surprised that China is not
grateful to them for these gifts, forgetting that the money to build
them came out of China."

"My family lived in a bubble," Elly's grandson Michael observed
decades later.

The bubble was about to be punctured.

IN 1920, a round-faced librarian and political activist arrived in
Shanghai and rented a room in the International Settlement in a
building owned by Silas Hardoon, a real estate tycoon and the former
manager of the Sassoon family's Shanghai operations.

Mao Zedong was not yet a Communist—the first Chinese trans-
lation of *The Communist Manifesto* didn't appear until later that year—
but he had supported several radical movements and denounced the
foreign occupation of Shanghai. Living in the more tolerant International Settlement and renting from a foreign landlord benefited

Mao. Communist literature circulated widely, and protests were frequent. In Shanghai, Mao met a professor named Chen Duxiu who was organizing the nascent Communist Party. Chen invited Mao to the party's first congress, held in Shanghai in July 1921. Fifteen delegates, posing as university professors on a summer excursion, met in a two-story house in the French Concession. Even with the International Settlement's relative freedom, the organizers were on edge. When a stranger unexpectedly wandered into the meeting, Mao and the other delegates, fearing a police raid, fled south, where they concluded the meeting. Mao returned to Shanghai dozens of times in the 1920s, almost always staying in the International Settlement or the adjacent French Concession and building alliances with like-minded radicals such as Zhou Enlai, who lived nearby. As the British celebrated the stability and prosperity they brought to Shanghai, a Chinese professor who had founded the Communist Party with Mao mourned that before the foreigners arrived "every stone and every blade of grass" in Shanghai belonged to Chinese. But now there were parks they couldn't enter. Though China was now a democratic republic, Chinese living in the foreign-run settlements couldn't vote. The Chinese who worked with and benefited from the Westerners, he proclaimed, were "the dog of the foreigners." Sun Yat-sen, who liked living in Shanghai, enjoyed playing croquet, and worked with Elly to endorse the Balfour Declaration, complained that he couldn't meet foreign supporters for dinner in foreign-owned clubs or walk in British parks on the Bund. He moved closer toward an alliance with the Communists.

The purpose of "foreign imperialists," Mao wrote, is to transform China into a colony. In the face of such "enemies" the Chinese need to be "ruthless."

Communism terrified the Kadoories. Capitalists above all, they viewed the growing strength of the Chinese Communists with alarm. In March 1927, Zhou Enlai launched an armed Communist uprising in Shanghai. Workers seized control of the city except for the International Settlement. With the tacit backing of the British and Shanghai's moneyed elite, General Chiang Kai-shek, who had succeeded Sun Yat-sen as leader of the Nationalists, ordered his troops to march on Shanghai and retake the city.

The Kadoories and the British community sent an emergency appeal to London demanding that British troops be sent to protect them from the fighting that was about to erupt. As the British soldiers arrived, Elly opened Marble Hall to them and ordered Horace to make sure they were entertained. The British set up barricades around the International Settlement to protect it from what looked to be the start of a civil war between the Communists and Nationalists.

It ended up being a massacre instead. Chiang and the Nationalist troops surrounded the Communists in Shanghai, declared martial law, and began executing Communist supporters—as many as 12,000 in three weeks. Chiang issued a secret order to all provinces under the control of his forces to purge Communists. More than 10,000 Communists across the country were also arrested and killed. Over the next year, anti-Communist suppression campaigns killed 300,000 people.

Mao escaped. He fled Shanghai and led a small peasant army in retreat—the start of what would become the People's Liberation Army. The International Settlement was untouched. The British soldiers watched the massacres from a distance and wrote home praising the luxury of their rooms in Marble Hall and the "excellent" and exotic Baghdad-influenced cuisine.

The crisis, for now, had passed. Chiang Kai-shek and the Nationalists now controlled Shanghai and the rest of the country. The International Settlement remained an enclave governed by British criminal and commercial law and protected by British troops. But that didn't make it completely immune to the changes sweeping China. Chiang and his government summoned Elly and other Chinese and foreign businessmen in Shanghai and demanded they buy government bonds to "help balance the budget." It was a reasonable price to pay for stability.

Three months after the Shanghai massacre, Chiang Kai-shek arrived at the Kadoories' Majestic Hotel for the "wedding of the decade"—his marriage to the younger sister of Madame Sun Yat-sen. Both the Communists and the Nationalists were trying to claim Sun, the father of the nation, as their inspiration. After her husband's death, Madame Sun herself had chosen the Communist side and was living in Shanghai, safe for now but powerless. By marrying Madame Sun's sister, Chiang Kai-shek was establishing a direct link to Sun's legacy and popularity. More than 1,000 people packed the Kadoories' hotel ballroom. The walls were decorated with bunting and white flowers. An American tenor serenaded the couple as they walked in to thunderous applause. *The New York Times* covered the wedding at the top of its front page the next day. Chiang was well on his way to establishing a dynasty. So was Elly.

THE SASSOONS, MEANWHILE, had fallen into disarray, with feuds dividing the dynasty that David had tried to establish with his eight sons. In the wake of David's death in 1864, most of his sons had moved to London. Elias Sassoon, the most business-minded brother, was still living in Shanghai, but was estranged from the family and running his own successful company, E. D. Sassoon. As Elias had predicted, his brothers were being seduced by London and showing less and less interest in business in China and India, even as their demands for money to fund their real estate and entertaining increased.

Upon the death of Solomon Sassoon, the last of David's eight sons remaining in India, followed swiftly by the death of the nephew who was supposed to succeed him, the Sassoons faced a crisis. While the London brothers debated who should run the company and whether—for the first time—they should turn management over to someone outside the family, Solomon's wife, Flora, announced from Bombay that she would take over the firm as a kind of regent until her son was old enough to step in. She was thirty-five—almost twenty years younger than her husband—but her lineage was unimpeachable. She was the great-granddaughter of David Sassoon. Her marriage to one of his sons had raised eyebrows; she essentially had married her uncle. But no one could argue with her intelligence and education. Her parents were both well educated and scholarly and had ensured that Flora received an excellent education denied most women of the time. They had brought eminent rabbis from Baghdad to teach her and had enrolled her in an elite Bombay school. By the time Flora was seventeen, she knew Hebrew, Aramaic, and Hindustani, as well as English, French, and German. She could quote Shakespeare. Many Hindu and Muslim women operated under "purdah," the physical separation of men and women and the demand that women cover their faces and bodies in public. Flora refused to go along, and sometimes accompanied her husband to the office, to the shocked looks of colleagues who had never seen a woman at a business before.

With her husband dead, Flora knew better than to challenge her brothers-in-law directly. Like the Empress Dowager Cixi in China, she would be the regent ruler of David Sassoon and Co. only until her son was old enough to take over, thus ensuring the male line of Sassoon control. The London brothers agreed. They established separate lines of communication with other Sassoon company executives in Bombay to ensure that Flora would be an easy-to-control figurehead.

By any measure, Flora produced spectacular results. She was a good listener, attentive to detail, with a gift for unobtrusively extracting useful information from employees and rivals. Women were not supposed to be seen in public and rarely left their homes. Deferring to local custom, Flora initially restricted her appearances as well, spending mornings at home, seated in a high-backed chair at a card table, answering letters from China, Japan, and the Persian Gulf. But in the late afternoons she started visiting the Sassoon cotton mills on her way to the office. Employees found her charming and approachable. The Royal Bombay Yacht Club, a male bastion, invited her to become a member. With opium exports declining, Flora shifted to trading merchandise such as copper, tea, silver, and spices. Telegrams from London praised the accomplishments of "our dearest sister."

In the spring of 1897, an epidemic of bubonic plague broke out in Bombay, spreading through the slums where most of the population—and many of Flora's workers—lived. Almost 20,000 people died. Trade in Bombay came to a standstill as goods piled up and were left to rot in the quarantined port. An outbreak of cholera followed, intensifying the crisis.

Determined to calm the growing panic, Flora joined the "Plague Committee" of doctors, civil servants, and businessmen. She supported the efforts of a young bacteriologist who had developed an anti-cholera vaccine. When some Muslim and Hindu leaders denounced the vaccination as unclean and against their religion, Flora had herself inoculated—and photographed—and went out with other women, dubbed the "Purdah Club," to persuade others to join them.

The plague outbreak damaged the Sassoon businesses. Flora was forced to close several factories and operate others at half capacity. Her dark hair became thickly streaked with white.

As profits slumped, Flora's brothers-in-law in London became impatient. The younger generation of Sassoon men—sons of the eight brothers—questioned why a woman should be in charge, especially one raising three children, one of whom was disabled. Flora felt more and more isolated.

The London brothers waited for the right moment to strike. The day before Christmas 1901, they staged a business coup, changing the financial structure of the company to effectively squeeze out Flora. David Sassoon and Co. announced it was changing management of the firm from a private partnership of the Sassoon brothers and their sister-in-law Flora to a joint stock company—with all the stock in the new company held by the Sassoon brothers. One brother would become chairman; three others would become directors. The new head of the Bombay office would be a longtime male family aide who had been advising Flora in recent years. Flora was cut out completely.

Rumors flew around Bombay that Flora would form her own company now that she'd been forced out of the family business. A clerk loyal to Flora wrote to deplore her "catastrophic" departure; another lamented "one pleasure less in this sordid world of ours." Flora wrote a note to a female friend, taking a parting shot at her brothers-in-law in London: "I am retiring from the firm tomorrow, as I do not think I can any longer drudge all day while the others take a superficial interest only, doing more harm than good when they suddenly awake." With the business taken away from her in Bombay, Flora decided to move to London, where she could obtain better medical care for her disabled daughter. Boarding a ship at the pier, she and her children were seen off by a crowd of officials, tearful servants, and well-wishers. Her stateroom was choked with bouquets and gifts. Just before the ship set sail, a young Indian girl ran forward and placed a garland around Flora's neck, inscribed to "Her Majesty, the Queen of Bombay and Empress of Malabar Hill"—the site of the Sassoon mansion. Flora sailed away. She would become a well-known philanthropist in London and a respected amateur scholar. She never set foot in the Sassoon businesses again.

At the same time Flora was fighting—and losing—the battle over succession in Bombay, in London another Sassoon woman was battling the British establishment and her own family to push ahead.

Rachel Sassoon was a child when David Sassoon sent her father, S. D., to London to represent the Sassoons' business interests and master London society. He succeeded beyond all expectations, acquiring a lavish mansion, servants, and a garden estate. He sent all three of his sons to Oxford. Rachel, as was the custom at the time, was kept at home. She entertained visitors and played the piano. Women at the time were denied the vote. They were denied equal access to education. A good marriage was to be Rachel's career; her mother, who had been born and raised in Baghdad, had married at sixteen.

Rachel rebelled. She was, she wrote later, a "clever daughter." She mocked the daughters of other British aristocrats who were "driven yearly to the market, and who go cackling to meet their fate" as wives. Those with "good heads" like hers "are set apart to lead celibate lives."

Rachel's father died when she was just nine years old. He left firm instructions in his will that even though the family now lived in London, she should marry someone from the Baghdadi Jewish community. He left the family's mansion and lush gardens to her brother and set aside a trust fund for Rachel. Bright and strong willed, Rachel rebelled against expectations that she should marry a young Baghdadi man, or even get married at all. "Few among women can be lover, mother, gourmet, saint, brilliant conversationalist, a good housekeeper, mistress, companion, and nurse all at the same time," she declared. "Men expect too much." At twenty-six—already past marriageable age—Rachel moved from the family house in the British countryside to London and trained as a nurse. Though she had many suitors, the family became resigned to the fact that she would grow old as an "unmarried spinster." Then, nearing thirty, Rachel fell in love with Frederick Beer, a German tycoon who had inherited a fortune and admired Rachel's independent spirit. Among his many business interests, Beer had decided to focus his energies on a London newspaper his family had bought: *The Observer*, a Sunday weekly that covered art and social justice.

Beer, who was born Jewish, had converted to Christianity. The day before her wedding in 1887, Rachel converted as well. Her mother and the Sassoon family were outraged. As a family, the Sassoons were so concerned about their children marrying Christians that they inserted explicit codicils in their wills disinheriting their children if they married non-Jews, or even non-Baghdadis. But the pull of assimilation was strong. As the Sassoons rose higher and higher in British society, more began to leave the Jewish faith, enraging family traditionalists. The Sassoons cut off contact with Rachel; her own mother declared a public period of mourning—as if Rachel had died—to show her displeasure.

Undeterred, Rachel abandoned nursing and found her calling in journalism. She became a reporter and columnist for her husband's newspaper. Running into opposition from the male staff, many of whom opposed growing calls for women's emancipation, Rachel declared she wanted a newspaper of her own. Her doting husband, Frederick, bought *The Sunday Times* and named Rachel editor in chief. Soon, the editor of *The Observer* quit, and Rachel was named editor of that paper as well—the first woman in Britain to edit two national newspapers. It would be eighty years before another woman was to have so senior a position on Fleet Street.

Rachel emerged as a feminist and a liberal. She proposed raising taxes on the rich and supported laws for better pay and improved working conditions. Recalling being marooned at home while her brothers went to Oxford, she called for equality in education, demanding that "colleges be opened to both sexes under the same terms." Invited to speak at the Women's International Congress, Rachel surveyed the gains she and other women had made and declared, "The nineteenth century is the women's century."

Rachel's greatest scoop came when she plunged into the controversy over the Dreyfus affair. Near the end of 1894, Captain Alfred Dreyfus, the only Jewish member of the French General Staff, was accused of being a spy and passing secret military documents to German officials. He was sentenced to life imprisonment on Devil's Island and stripped of his rank and uniform in a public ceremony before 20,000 Parisians who shouted, "Death to the Jews!"

Although Rachel herself had converted to Protestantism, she

worried that the charges of dual loyalty against Dreyfus could imperil the gains she and other Jews had made. Nothing is more remarkable, she wrote, "than the attachment and loyalty shown by the Hebrew race to any country which treats it well."

A reporter at *The Observer* uncovered evidence that Dreyfus's accusers had used forged documents to smear him. She confronted the forger, cross-examined him in a hotel room, and decided to publish the story. Dreyfus's conviction was subsequently overturned, and he was restored to his full rank.

None of this reopened the doors of the Sassoon family to her. Rachel defended the Sassoons' opium trade in the pages of *The Observer*, but she was never invited to join the family firm or attend the parties and balls they threw to entertain the Prince of Wales. In 1896, Rachel's husband, Frederick, fell ill. Doctors said it was tuberculosis, but it may well have been syphilis, a result of his philandering. Rachel, trained as a nurse, began caring for him in addition to running her two newspapers. After he died in 1901, she fell into a depression, unable to finish her columns and editorials. The Sassoon family mobilized. Rachel was a rebellious, nontraditional career woman doing a man's job. Her family had always considered her eccentric and unpredictable. She was now a childless wealthy widow. One Sassoon relative declared that Rachel appeared listless at one moment and then started "raving wildly." She refused to file her husband's will with the court, which raised suspicions about who would inherit his fortune. Her brother, who hadn't seen her for fifteen years, filed a petition that she was a person of "unsound mind." Three doctors and the Sassoon family lawyer agreed. Rachel was brought before a court-appointed "master in lunacy," who declared Rachel insane. Lacking family support and unable to resist, the woman who oversaw *The Sunday Times* and *The Observer* failed to mount a defense or call doctors to testify on her behalf. The newspapers were sold. Rachel spent the rest of her life alone in a large mansion, looked after by nurses. She died in 1927.

Like her cousin Flora, and like ill-fated Laura Kadoorie, Rachel Sassoon had her ambitions cut short. Her career epitomized the paradoxes buffeting the Sassoons: a social liberal and feminist who also supported the British Empire and defended the opium trade that made her family so rich and influential; a barrier-breaking Jewish woman who strove for social acceptance by converting to Christianity but found herself caught between the traditions of her Jewish family and the virulent anti-Semitism of Europe; a woman of talent and ambition thwarted. For the Sassoons, there was little sign that the nineteenth century—or the twentieth—was going to go down as a century for women.

As life in Shanghai returned to normal after Chiang Kai-shek's suppression of the Communist insurrection, the British businessmen in the International Settlement and at the Shanghai Club began to gossip about a rich bachelor from England who walked with a cane but exuded charisma and sexuality. After the family turmoil with Flora and her departure for London, the Sassoons had scrambled to find someone to run their businesses in Asia, the financial lifeblood of the dynasty. This new scion, based in Bombay, was visiting Shanghai more and more frequently, inquiring about business deals and squiring beautiful women to the racecourse, a carnation boutonniere in his buttonhole and a silver cigarette holder poking jauntily out of his mouth. His name was Victor Sassoon, heir to the Sassoon fortune. The Sassoons were about to make a comeback.

Victor Sassoon and friends

5

The Impresario

"How are you, darling?"

Victor Sassoon leaned in, his dark eyes dancing with curiosity and a hint of mischief. His pencil-thin mustache and the monocle he wore over his right eye gave every joke and observation he made an insouciant tone. More than six feet tall, with broad shoulders, he had been a strong college swimmer at Cambridge, as well as a boxer and a better-than-average tennis player. One could see why men and women were drawn to him—the confidence, the quick wit, the mockery. Plus, Victor was single, and one of the richest men in the world. He had the politician's gift of making whomever he was talking to feel like the center of his attention, as if he—or often she—were the only one in the room. Victor was "unusually quick and witty, especially for a businessman," wrote *The New Yorker* writer Emily Hahn, who would have an affair with Victor in Shanghai, in a letter to her mother. "He liked intelligence."

Victor Sassoon, the grandson of David Sassoon, the family patriarch, loved everything new in the 1920s: fast cars, airplanes, motion pictures, movie stars. He kept his own handheld movie camera close at hand, so he could rush outside and shoot friends or departing yachts or, later, bombing attacks by the Japanese. He outfitted a private photography studio to take portraits of his female friends, in all stages of undress. He built racing stables and bred horses to compete around the globe.

His piercing eyes and quick wit drew attention away from the two crutches that kept him upright and propelled him across the floor of his office, his hotel, and his dance club. Below the waist he was a crippled man. He had injured his hip in a plane crash while serving during World War I when he was thirty-five. His private diaries reflected his struggles—sleepless nights, quests for cures, the pursuit of doctors who could make him walk normally again. Like Franklin Roosevelt, he projected a confidence and virility that defied his handicap. A relentless host of extravagant parties, he would leave suddenly for an upstairs private room when a stab of pain shot through his body. The circle of friends left behind would occasionally hear a thump in the ceiling above them when he fell. They pretended not to notice.

Victor's affectations and frivolous pursuits hid a shrewd business mind. He spoke fluent French, loved to give speeches, and kept a careful record of everyone he met so he could charm them later. Business rivals often underestimated him—and so, too, would the Japanese.

IN SHANGHAI, the Sassoon business DNA was running thin. David Sassoon's company was being run by a grandson, Reginald, whom a family biographer described as "a war hero, crack golfer and horse-man but no commercial genius." Reginald spent most of his time at Shanghai clubs and the racetrack. A clumsy man, he tried to ride his own horses and fell off five times in five weeks, breaking bones each time. After being carried off on a stretcher at one race, he insisted on returning to the saddle a few hours later for the last race, to the applause of the crowd.

The rise of Victor the playboy initially appeared to be a poor solution to the Sassoons' leadership problems. Born in Naples while his parents were traveling, he attended Harrow, the English boarding school, and Cambridge, where he majored in history. He became close to "Nunkie," a Sassoon uncle who dated chorus girls and spent lavishly. Worldlier and wealthier than most of his friends, Victor formed a university club for bachelors fueled by fine wine and became an accomplished ballroom dancer. He swore he would never have children. After studying his Sassoon pedigree, he said: "I am convinced that I would either produce a genius or an idiot. It's a risk I'm not prepared to take."

Most "posh" students like Victor from the upper classes received "third-class honors" at Cambridge—the equivalent of a "gentleman's C" in the United States. But Victor showed a keen intelligence. In between the parties, dancing, and spending on clothes and wine, he wrote a thesis that received a respectable second-class honor in history, better than many of his cousins or Siegfried Sassoon, the famed British poet who a few years later would leave Cambridge without a degree at all.

Upon graduation, Victor was told by his father that, as a Sassoon, he was expected to begin working in the family firm's London head-quarters and find a bride among the wealthy Jewish families of

England. He bridled. Instead he took up an invitation from his uncle Jacob—the son of the rogue Elias Sassoon—to visit the family's operations in India and Shanghai.

ACCOMPANIED BY JACOB, who organized his trip, Victor first traveled to Bombay, where he visited the Sassoon textile mills. He tinkered with the spindles and took an interest in the latest technology from both Manchester and the United States, asking intelligent questions of the maintenance workers.

Jacob next sent Victor to Shanghai, which the young man found even more exciting. He bought jade and ivories for sale on Bubbling Well Road and attended parties thrown in his honor by Cambridge alumni, drinking and joining in sing-alongs. With no children of his own, Jacob developed a fondness for his nephew, who seemed to move easily from the upper reaches of society to the bungalows of soldiers he could join for hunting or a game of polo. By the time Victor left Shanghai, Jacob had named him a junior partner of the company, in the hope that one day he would return.

VICTOR'S TRIP TO ASIA sparked some family hope that he would turn serious, but he soon returned to his familiar ways in London, avoiding the office to drive his new motorcar and watch balloon races in the countryside in a top hat, morning coat, and carnation, with his monocle squeezed into a supercilious eye and the "inevitable chorus belle on his arm," in the words of a family biographer.

Victor was thirty-three when World War I broke out. He enlisted in the newly formed Royal Naval Air Service. His fellow soldiers called him "Daddy" because he was a decade older than most of them. One early morning in February 1915, Victor was seated in the observation seat of his plane studying his maps as his young pilot took off. Suddenly, the engine faltered, spluttered, and died. The plane went into a tailspin, spiraling downward. Victor stayed "methodical and precise, cool as a cucumber," the pilot later reported. The crash crippled Victor. It broke both of his legs and damaged his hip. He was given a shot of morphine and taken off by stretcher to a hospital. "The machine was a write-off and would be reduced to scrap," recalled the pilot.

Victor stayed in a plaster cast for eight months. He refused to use a wheelchair. He told friends he was convinced no one would marry him now except for his money and position. "If I had healthy and attractive children," he told a relative, "I could not help becoming horribly jealous of them."

Victor was assigned to work with the American Air Force and apply his business knowledge to speed up production of bombers being made in Italy—the start of what would become a lifelong affection for America. Even though Victor was a British officer in charge of an American detachment, the American soldiers showed "great faith" in his judgment, he recalled later. They welcomed the way he cut through bureaucracy, at one point going over a U.S. general's head to get approval to visit factories by threatening to approach a friend who worked in the administration in Washington. On board a train in Italy escorting senior American officers on an inspection visit, the Italian officer in charge of logistics turned out to have been headwaiter at one of Victor's favorite London restaurants. The Italian assigned Victor to a luxurious sleeping car while the higher-ranking Americans slept all night sitting up in coaches. "I realize now how it pays to be a cripple," an American officer told Victor the next morning.

Both the original David Sassoon and Co. and E. D. Sassoon & Co. had boomed during the war, supplying cotton to the British army for uniforms and trading actively with China, India, and England. The end of the war meant slowing demand for Indian cotton in England. That was compounded by growing unrest among Indian workers, who were rallying around Mahatma Gandhi and his calls for self-rule. His symbol was Indian homespun cloth, which undercut the textile industry in which the Sassoons made much of their money now that the opium trade was illegal. Workers in India were demanding higher wages. Gandhi began launching boycotts against British goods. In China, Japan was starting to build factories of its own and flooding the Chinese market.

To regain their edge, the Sassoons needed to raise capital to modernize their factories. But as business challenges rose, the London-based Sassoons continued to show only perfunctory interest in running the company. Victor's cousin Philip, rising rapidly in the British government, ignored the company completely, spending his time furnishing three separate estates with Aubusson carpets and tapestries and masterworks including those of Velázquez, John Singer Sargent, and Gainsborough.

Other potential leaders weren't faring much better. Victor's father, Edward, who reluctantly took over E. D. Sassoon as his more business-minded relatives died, suffered a series of strokes in his fifties that left him weak and suffering from dementia. Frustrated by the aimless drift at the top of the firm, Silas Hardoon, one of the original "Baghdad Boys" David Sassoon had hired to work in Shanghai, quit the company in 1920 and set up his own firm, buying up real estate all across the city. Soon after, yet another potential heir dropped dead of a heart attack.

Victor himself lusted after a political career. But in his first run for office as a Conservative for the London city council, he lost by a hundred votes. Forty years old, handsome and rich but stymied by the war injury that seemed destined to push him to the margins of wealthy society, Victor decided to move to Bombay and take over the Sassoon businesses.

Surprising everyone, including his managers, who assumed that he would be a dilettante figurehead, Victor seized control of the company. Pulling himself along the factory floor with his two crutches, he continued his research that had started when he'd first visited Bombay, photographing spindles and intricate pieces of machinery at the Sassoon textile mills and sending cables to England with ideas for redesigns. He cross-examined the managers of the different Sassoon offices across Asia about industrial plants, insurance, and real estate. He showed a special talent for finance. With factories, assets, and investments in India, China, and Britain, Victor recognized that moving money could be as profitable as exporting cotton or importing spices. He expanded the network of Sassoon-controlled banks, giving him access to different currencies in different countries to take advantage of fluctuating exchange rates. If Parliament was raising taxes in Britain, he could funnel profits through subsidiaries and trusts in Hong Kong to avoid them. If political uncertainty in India and China was making their currency less stable, he could shift his money into pounds sterling. The currency transactions protected his assets and increased his profits and sent a rich stream of dividends to his London relatives to fund their shooting parties and art collections.

Dismissed in London as a playboy, Victor in India became a man
of influence. He was appointed to the colonial National Legislative
Assembly as a representative of the textile industry. He immersed
himself in debates over currency reform and factory conditions. He
believed in colonial rule and was convinced that his own family's paternalism had benefited India's workers. Labor conditions and wages
in the Sassoon factories were the best in India. He supported a law
that limited the workweek to sixty hours and raised the minimum
age of child workers to twelve, over the objections of many of his fellow millionaires. "I don't pretend to know anything about debating,
as until I went to Delhi the only debate I had even listened to [was at
university] and I have never set foot in the House of Commons," he
wrote to a friend. But with a few exceptions, he felt there was no one
in the British colonial government he couldn't outargue.

Victor saw multiple threats looming on India's political horizon:
Mahatma Gandhi, socialism, Indian independence. In 1922 the handsome Prince of Wales—later to become King Edward VIII—visited
New Delhi. Victor greeted him as he disembarked, along with other
leaders. Gandhi's supporters quickly organized riots and strikes to
wreck the royal goodwill tour. Winston Churchill, a rising politician
in London, dismissed Gandhi and his spreading campaign of civil
disobedience as the "alarming and nauseating" efforts of a "seditious
fakir . . . striding half-naked up the steps of the vice regal palace." But
Victor, who knew Churchill socially, warned a friend in a letter that
Gandhi's name "is one to conjure with in India." The British couldn't
continue to suppress Gandhi by putting him in jail, Victor believed.
To his friend, he described meeting with a wealthy Indian businessman in Bombay and being taken aback by the businessman's
suspicion of British rule and sympathy for Gandhi's calls for inde-

pendence. "If a man like him is still suspicious, what must the half-educated man think?"

The British, Sassoon proposed, should woo Gandhi to their side, creating a coalition to oppose Communist members of his movement that Gandhi was having increasing trouble controlling. "The moment you remove the British regime you remove the only thing on which India is united," Victor predicted in a letter to a friend. "Gandhi's difficulties . . . look like increasing instead of diminishing as [his] success comes nearer."

Victor himself was being challenged by anti-British anger and the demands of Indian workers. In 1925, he proposed building a private racecourse in Bombay at the cost of $500,000 (in 1925 U.S. dollars). Victor and the Bombay mill owners were proposing at the same time to reduce wages because of a falloff in demand for textiles. A local Bombay newspaper raged: "How can one reconcile the cries of the mill owners that they are down with Sir Victor's ambitious project?" *The Times* of India called Victor's proposal "preposterous" and insulting to workers. "There is enough in the world for rich men to spend money on without indulging in idle vanities and luxurious and extravagant tastes," the newspaper declared. And yet he couldn't avoid the condescension of the British aristocrats and civil servants who ruled Indian politics. Victor was one of the largest employers in India; his staff boasted that, in public, the British governor-general often walked behind Victor Sassoon. But despite Victor's wealth, British officials still spurned Victor and his wealthy family as upstarts, "boxwallahs," merchants who had made money but lacked the polish and the acumen to rule.

Victor began visiting Shanghai for two or three months a year to inspect E. D. Sassoon's China operations. In contrast to India,

Shanghai was stable and booming, with little political agitation. Chiang Kai-shek had put an end to the Communist threats. British gunships sat in the harbor protecting British business. The seven-member Shanghai Municipal Council, which included a representative from the Sassoons, oversaw everything from police to public works. Taxes were low. Sassoon noticed how Silas Hardoon, once a night watchman for the Sassoons and later the manager of their Shanghai office, had gone off on his own and become wealthy by buying up thousands of Shanghai apartments and renting them to the Chinese. Hardoon's wealth now rivaled Victor's. Sitting in a suite in one of the Kadoories' hotels overlooking the Bund, Victor watched Cadillacs drive along the street jockeying with rickshaws. He attended lavish parties and escorted fashionably dressed women to the races.

"Things never really get bad in China if we are firm with troops in the end," he wrote to a friend in 1927 after one of his visits. "The foreign devils . . . developed the present settlements. As these are free from Chinese interference and taxation, they prospered." Gandhi's growing power was threatening colonial presence in India, but in China, the new Nationalist government was weak—and, Sassoon believed, ineffectual. Foreign businessmen could do as they pleased, which proved irresistible to Victor.

Victor decided to liquidate his family's near-century's worth of holdings in India and move his money to Shanghai. He told an Indian newspaper he was leaving because of "the cut-throat competition with Indian firms" and because of "anti-foreign prejudice." The news that one of Britain's richest men was abandoning India for Shanghai made newspapers worldwide. Victor planned to transfer the equivalent of sixty "lakhs" of silver—$400 million in today's dollars. Jardine, the old Sassoon rival, noted the news with a typical dose of anti-Semitism. The directors of the new Sassoon Company in Shanghai "contain a large number who must be of the best 'Scottish' descent," a Jardine executive wrote, referring sarcastically to the well-known Jewish background of many of Victor's executives. Still, the executive warned, "they will probably be our most serious competitors in the future, and difficult nuts to crack."

Victor bought the most prominent site on the Bund, a full city block, at the intersection of Nanjing Road and the waterfront, and began construction of a new family headquarters, to be known as Sassoon House. It would be nine stories tall with a copper tower on top—fifty feet taller than the current tallest building, the Hongkong and Shanghai Bank, a few blocks down the Bund and far grander than the Kadoories' recently completed Majestic Hotel a mile away. He notified the architects that he wanted to incorporate a new hotel into the building as well. It would carry the name Marco Polo used for China: Cathay.

Victor routinely stayed in the world's most luxurious hotels: the Taj Mahal in Bombay, the George V in Paris, Claridge's in London. The Cathay, he vowed, would rival them all.

In the words of one architectural critic, the resulting hotel soared over the Bund "like an Art Deco rocket ship rising from the Huangpu River." Before the Cathay, tourists, foreigners, and Chinese had had to pick their way through Shanghai's chaotic streets and markets to buy even luxury goods. Under mosaic ceilings, the Cathay lobby arcade housed twenty shops that sold the latest hats, lingerie, linens from Paris, and objects for tourists, such as silver swizzle sticks with jade handles. The hallways were lined with Lalique crystal lamp sconces and mirrors. The lobby corridors from each of the hotel's entrances intersected beneath a dramatic dome. In addition to the guest rooms, the Cathay featured a floor of "national suites," each decorated in a different foreign style: tatami mats in the Japan Suite, Indian rugs and cushions in the India Suite, Chinese furniture and ceramics in the China Suite. Behind the luxury pulsed modern conveniences never widely available before in Shanghai or China. Guests could summon a waiter, room boy, maid, dry cleaner, valet, or laundryman by telephone. The deep bathtubs had silver taps supplying purified water from Bubbling Springs Well outside the city.

Previous generations of Sassoons settling in Shanghai had relied on a tight-knit group of fellow Baghdadis—like Silas Hardoon—to run their businesses. Victor jettisoned that approach, creating instead a global management team. He recruited the manager of the Cathay from the Taj Mahal Hotel in Bombay, the general manager of the hotel company from Claridge's in London, and the manager of the Cathay's nightclub from Berlin, adding a dash of Weimar Germany spice and decadence.

Victor moved into a ninth-floor suite. His windows jutted over the Bund like the prow of a ship, giving him an unobstructed view down onto the harbor and along art deco buildings below. He called the view his "muse." In the bathroom he installed two bathtubs. "I like sharing my bed but not my bath," he told a friend.

The Cathay made the Kadoories' hotels, even the famed Majestic Hotel, look dowdy by comparison. Guests abandoned the Kadoories' Astor House Hotel, just down the Bund from the Cathay, which still required room boys to pick up chamber pots, while the Cathay had indoor plumbing. Overnight, Victor's Cathay turned the Kadoorie hotel into "a second-rate establishment," an English-language newspaper in Shanghai wrote. An American visitor described the Astor House as "a faded green, cavern-like wooden structure, with tall rooms smelling of must and mildew." By contrast, slender Chinese women in elegant cheongsams spurned the Majestic and flocked to the Cathay, blending with foreign hotel guests looking for the trendiest tea dances—a British tradition combining afternoon tea with dancing—and the latest jazz. The world's leading cabaret artists performed in the Cathay's ballroom, which was outfitted with a sprung floor to encourage dancing. Guests ordered Victor's custom cocktails—among them the "Cobra's Kiss," which mixed equal parts brandy, curaçao, and cream and added three dashes of absinthe. They enjoyed "tiffin"—the multicourse India-inspired lunch that, on Thursdays, included a Bombay-style vegetable curry accompanied by a bottle of ice-cold Bass ale. Room service delivered "Capon Sourdough" cooked with Madeira, foie gras, and truffles, and "Crêpes Georgette" sprinkled with finely chopped pineapples marinated in kirsch. (Victor himself, trim but always worried about his weight, ate more carefully: "Keeping trim on vegetables," he recorded in his diary. "Nine day diet. Everyday breakfast: half a grapefruit, black coffee. Salad made with lemon.") Victor's extensive land holdings allowed him to guarantee his guests that safe fertilizers, rather than human waste, were used to raise the vegetables served in his kitchens.

Wealthy Chinese flocked to the hotel to celebrate birthdays, anniversaries, and other special occasions. In the lobby of the hotel, Victor installed a recording booth that looked like a phone booth where guests could record toasts and greetings and be handed a pressed vinyl record as a souvenir. "The Chinese have been going out much more than they used to, and one meets them at a lot of parties," Victor wrote to a friend. "It really is amazing how Europeanized they are getting, and the ladies are quite ready to rag which was unheard of even a few years ago."

By the mid-1930s, 40,000 tourists a year were stopping in Shanghai, disembarking from the new ocean liners circling the globe. Every day, tourists poured off liners from Trieste, Hamburg, London, Oslo, Seattle, and Vancouver. No world cruise was complete without a stop in Shanghai. Celebrities who had once made the Majestic their home in Shanghai switched to the more modern and glamorous Cathay. Noël Coward checked in, came down with the flu, and wrote a draft of *Private Lives* propped up on pillows in his suite. Shanghai was a city of easy money and easy morals. Wallis Simpson, who would scandalize Great Britain with her marriage to King Edward VIII, had reportedly once posed for photographs in the city clad only in a life preserver. Now Victor was literally putting Shanghai on the world map.

Vicki Baum, author of the novel *Grand Hotel*, which was later made into a movie starring Greta Garbo, came to Shanghai and wrote a sequel based on cosmopolitan lives that intersected at the Cathay: "Optimists, pessimists, Westerners, Easterners, men, women. Europeans, Americans, orients. Courage and cowardice. Idealism and greed. Enmity and love. People of every sort and color and tendency. Voices, noise, laughter, tea, whiskey. The full orchestra of every description of humanity: that was teatime on the roof garden." Charlie Chaplin and Paulette Goddard, his wife-to-be, holidayed in Shanghai in 1936 and stayed at the Cathay (the previous time they visited, they stayed at the Kadoories' Astor House Hotel farther down the Bund). In the Tower Night Club, Chaplin told Victor he was keen to make a film set in China about a White Russian countess reduced to making a living as a taxi dancer—the movie that later became *A Countess from Hong Kong.*

Bookings at the Kadoories' Majestic Hotel tumbled. Within a year of the opening of the Cathay, Victor put together a group of investors, bought the Majestic, and soon closed it down and auctioned off its contents.

The Cathay's success ignited a building boom that transformed Shanghai. Victor built a second hotel, the Metropole, aimed at business travelers. He followed that with several apartment and office blocks—Grosvenor House, Embankment House, Cathay Mansions, and Hamilton House—all with regal British names. Together they offered tenants 1,000 air-conditioned bedrooms and suites—some spread over three levels. When Silas Hardoon died, and his children began fighting over his inheritance, Victor swooped in and bought up dozens of his properties. One evening, Victor visited a popular nightclub and ballroom and was escorted, along with his party, to a table distant from the dance floor. When he complained, the waiter apologized and said that because Victor was using two canes, he assumed he was unable to dance. Victor left, bought a site nearby, and built Ciro's, which became the city's most popular dance club.

The building boom made property on the Bund more expensive than many building sites in fashionable parts of London or New York. By 1935, Victor had recouped his entire investment in Shanghai through property alone, worth 87 million yuan, or $460 million in today's dollars. To his property empire, Victor now added textile mills, timber trading, shipyards, the Shanghai bus company, auto dealers, storage services, and a brewery. When a vacant lot became available next to the Cathay, word reached Victor that the Nationalist government planned to build the Bank of China on the site and send it thirty-three stories in the air, dwarfing the Cathay. But his vast property holdings gave him control of the Shanghai Municipal Council, the foreigner-dominated body that controlled building permits along the Bund. The council rejected the bank's proposal on "technical grounds," ensuring that the Cathay would remain the tallest and most prominent building on the strip.

. . .

UNLIKE THE KADOORIES, the Sassoons had never dealt much on a personal level with the Chinese. They never saw them as equals and devoted much more energy to cultivating the British aristocracy. Descendants recall that they had real affection for India and for Baghdad, where they had come from. They served Indian curries and sweet Middle Eastern desserts and talked affectionately about Bombay. Their letters reveal few mentions of substantial relations with the Chinese. China was business.

Victor was different. He had once thought of entering politics in Britain and had the politician's interest in building alliances. In India, he was already a more cosmopolitan figure, conscious of the interplay of business and social gatherings—something the Sassoons mastered in London, where their cultivation of the king and the aristocracy had led to the opium trade being maintained in the face of popular disapproval. Victor's social diaries included a careful color-coded system: he underlined the names of people he knew in blue, the ones he was meeting for the first time in red. He kept the seating plans for his luncheons and dinners, paying special attention to Indian royalty and prominent businessmen.

Chiang Kai-shek and the new Nationalist government saw early on how useful Victor could be economically and politically. Shanghai, by the late 1920s, was the economic center of China, home to almost half the major banks and factories. The Nationalists had an ambitious agenda to modernize the country. They needed taxes to fund the army that was battling the Communist "bandits" led by Mao in the northern mountains and in parts of the countryside. Chiang initially raised the money he needed by allying with Shanghai's gangsters and extorting and kidnapping Chinese businessmen made wealthy by Shanghai's boom. "The plight of the Chinese merchant in and about Shanghai is pitiable," *The New York Times* reported. "At the mercy of General Chiang Kai-shek's dictatorship, the merchants do not know what the next day will bring, confiscations, compulsory loans, exile, or possible execution." The son of a dye merchant was arrested by Chiang Kai-shek's Nationalists as a "counterrevolutionary," but was released when his father "donated" $200,000 to Chiang. Another merchant paid half a million dollars when his three-year-old heir vanished. China ordered the arrest of Rong Zongjing, the cotton king, when Rong declined to buy government bonds.

Such strong-arm tactics wouldn't work on Victor or on other foreigners like the Kadoories. Winning their backing was crucial not just for business investment, but for maintaining the support of the United States and Britain. It would signal to other foreign companies and to Chinese investors that the Nationalist government was politically reliable. The road to Chinese modernization, and Nationalist political success, ran along the Bund.

From the moment Victor announced his intention to move his fortune to Shanghai, Chiang Kai-shek dispatched his top financial officials, Western educated and fluent in English, to a series of lunches, offering lucrative business deals and high returns on investment.

Chiang Kai-shek and the officials around him spent enormous amounts of time wooing American officials and power brokers, including Henry Luce, the powerful publisher of Time Inc. They created what became known as the China Lobby in the United States, mobilized to win American popular backing for China's Nationalist regime. T. V. Soong, China's finance minister, touted the Ivy League–educated elite that were running China. "Do you realize that more than half the present Cabinet of our government are graduates of your colleges?" T. V. Soong told an American audience in a radio address. "I have the honor of being an alumnus of Harvard. In my immediate family, one of my sisters, Mrs. Chiang Kai-shek, went to Wellesley. Two sisters, Mrs. Sun Yat-sen and Mrs. H. H. Kung . . . attended Wesleyan College in Macon, Georgia."

Victor saw himself as the consummate political insider. He had represented the Bombay mill owners in India's legislative assembly. He understood currency flows and had helped write India's currency regulations. He had, he believed, correctly diagnosed India's future and the problem Gandhi's rise would cause Britain and capitalists like himself. He was convinced that moving his fortune to China and investing in Shanghai had been a shrewd move despite the upheavals that regularly rocked the Chinese Nationalist government. "Time does fly here faster than anywhere I know," Victor wrote from Shanghai to a friend. "I suppose it is because there is always so much doing. We have wars, revolutions, panics, alarums and excursions of all kinds daily." Nevertheless, Victor believed "nothing really happens."

The Nationalists believed in Victor, too. A week after moving to Shanghai he was guest of honor sitting at the head of a table for a dinner of leading Chinese and foreign businessmen, with Finance Minister Soong at his right. They offered Victor the chance to buy government bonds that yielded 12 percent to 15 percent a year—a better rate than any other investment. The Nationalists also appealed to Victor's fear of communism. At one lunch, the Nationalists brought along a top military official with good sources among the "bolshies" to brief him on the military situation. At another, he met a group of wealthy Chinese businessmen backing the Nationalists. "No doubt they all believe in Nationalists in government," he recorded. And they all seemed "pretty informed" about "Bolshie elements."

Victor's alliance with the Nationalists profited both sides. With the Depression enveloping the rest of the world, Victor continued to make money in Shanghai. He used it to buy up assets in countries wracked by the Depression. He bought stock in American companies, bonds in Australia, the controlling interest in a small French bank. The Nationalists used the money from bonds that Victor bought to fund their army and their modernization of the economy. Plus, they had the prestige and endorsement of one of the world's richest men consulting with them over lunches and visits to the racecourse. In June 1935, senior Nationalist officials came to the Cathay and personally presented Victor with a "First Class Gold Medal," China's highest honor.

Victor's reputation benefited as well from the support of the formidable China Lobby in the United States, led by Henry Luce. Luce was the son of a missionary and had come to believe that the Nationalists were the key to China's future. He put the resources of his Time Inc. empire behind the Nationalists, extolling Chiang Kai-shek and Madame Chiang in *Time* magazine, the most influential newsmagazine of the day, and in *Fortune*, the leading business publication. In 1935, *Fortune* did a lavish feature on the "Shanghai boom," declaring that "a new vitality has come to the Chinese. Nationalism and westernization have released new forces that were not present in 1860 or even in 1927." If at any time in the 1920s "you had taken your money out of American stocks and transferred it to Shanghai in the form of real estate investments, you would have trebled it in seven years."

"One man in the world actually did this," the magazine declared—and there in the pages of *Fortune*, hands folded on an ivory-tipped cane and smiling knowingly at the reader, was Victor Sassoon.

"A bachelor will probably live in one of Sir Victor Sassoon's smart new apartments," the magazine declared. The Cathay Hotel was "one of the most luxurious hostelries in the world, rivalling the best in Manhattan." And Victor Sassoon himself? "He has left his imprint on Shanghai in the towering bulk of his buildings, he has found a sanctuary for his wealth, and he is great."

WHILE VICTOR INCREASED his bet on Shanghai, Elly Kadoorie began to move some of his investments out of the city and down to Hong Kong, which, unlike Shanghai, was a British colony. It was a fixed part of the British Empire, run by a British administrator and protected by British troops. In 1920, he decided to build his own luxurious hotel, the Repulse Bay, on Hong Kong Island and followed it later in the decade with an even more luxurious hotel, the Peninsula, on the Kowloon side of Hong Kong harbor. He continued to operate a tramway—a vertical railroad—that chugged up the Peak and was one of the engineering marvels of Asia. When Elly finally won his British citizenship, he emerged from the shadows and joined the board of directors of China Light and Power. He had been knighted in 1926 and was "almost one of us," in the words of one Englishman in Shanghai.

Elly still found his best business opportunities working with other outsiders. In 1926, José Pedro Braga, whose Portuguese father had settled in Macau and who had gotten a job working at China Light and Power, took a drive with Elly in the rural part of Kowloon to see a large parcel of land covered with rice paddy fields. It was about to go up for auction. Its commercial possibilities, Braga told Elly, were "limitless." Elly formed a partnership with Braga, the Portuguese immigrant, and Robert Hotung, who in addition to his other investments had become one of Hong Kong's largest property owners.

Elly quietly began selling some of his stock in Shanghai to raise funds for the land in Kowloon. In a furious bidding war, he outbid a group of Chinese investors. Elly and his partners named the site Kadoorie Hill and plotted out Kadoorie Avenue. Elly began building dozens of luxury colonial-style homes, with tennis courts and garages for motorcars—the biggest development Hong Kong had ever seen, and one appealing to outsiders such as Elly, Braga, and Hotung as an alternative to Hong Kong's other, snobbish luxury encampment across the harbor on Hong Kong Island atop the British-dominated Peak. On a promontory overlooking the sea, even farther north than Kowloon in the New Territories, Elly started building a weekend retreat known as Boulder Lodge. Victor Sassoon had judged Shanghai a safer bet than India. To the Kadoories, Hong Kong was starting to look like a safer bet than Shanghai—or at least a good hedge.

VICTOR, DESPITE PERSISTENT PAIN from his war injuries, maintained a business and social calendar that would have exhausted most men, spending mornings at his Cathay office, lunches with business associates, afternoons at the races or visiting his investments, and formal dinners in the evenings, often followed by a cruise aboard his yacht or after-dinner drinks at one of his clubs. He turned the Cathay into a stage for parties that scandalized the city even as people scrambled for invitations. One school-themed costume ball required guests to arrive dressed like schoolchildren. Victor greeted them dressed as a schoolmaster, with mortarboard and a birch switch to hit recalcitrant students. For another party, Shanghai's high society was invited to a Cathay Hotel ballroom transformed for the night into a big top. The city's leading businessmen arrived dressed as high-wire artists; one wife came dressed as a seal. Victor dressed as the ringmaster, complete with top hat, mustache, and whip.

Some bridled at what they saw as his relentless social climbing. One evening at the Cathay, Victor elbowed into a conversation between a visiting British aristocrat and a young woman. The aristocrat shouted: "Back to Baghdad! Back to Baghdad!"

"He was Jewish, but one couldn't very well snub a man who played golf with the Prince of Wales," a wealthy British woman observed. "It was a perplexing topic at the Club, I can tell you."

When Victor wasn't negotiating business deals, photographing women, or planning parties—and often while he was doing these things—he attended the races and his growing racing stables. Racing appealed to the gambler in Victor but also, as he confessed, fed his social ambition. Others in his family "are more famous than I," he confessed: The poet Siegfried Sassoon was known throughout England for his poetry coming out of World War I. Another cousin, Philip Sassoon, was an aide to Prime Minister David Lloyd George and then served in the British cabinet.

"My fame is due to the fact that I own the best English racing horses of the century," Victor said. Victor's horses were indeed famous. They regularly won the major English races, and he often watched them from the royal box, chatting with aristocrats and businessmen. In Shanghai, his private box at the local racetrack was always filled with business contacts and Chinese and Western women.

Though he went by the name Victor, his full name was Ellice Victor Sassoon, and he used a play on his first two initials to name many of his horses: Dewey Eve, Happy Eve, Holiday Eve, Courting Eve, Wedding Eve, Honeymoon Eve, Opera Eve. Others he named to curry favor with the famous—for example, naming one horse "Pinza" after the famous Italian opera singer Ezio Pinza. Pinza won the premier English horse race, known as the Derby. As befitted a financier who enjoyed financial manipulation and mastered currency fluctuations, Victor enjoyed studying bloodlines and breeding stocks, connecting breeds to produce champions.

Victor Sassoon was pioneering the idea of the businessman as celebrity. Staying at the Cathay, renting an apartment in one of his buildings, sitting with him in his box at the races, attending one of his parties—all brought visitors into Victor's charmed circle. Victor Sassoon became the face of Shanghai. When the American humorist and performer Will Rogers visited the city, he dubbed Victor "the J. P. Morgan of China and India."

VICTOR'S SEX LIFE WAS a popular topic of speculation. It was said he met with Serge Voronoff, a Russian-born surgeon who advocated transplanting thin slices of baboon testicles into human scrotums to rejuvenate sexual performance. In his diary, amid notes of lunches with Chinese politicians and businessmen, he carefully pasted nude pictures he had taken of European and Chinese women. Some reclined seductively on a sofa. Others struck athletic poses or stood bare-breasted in front of a Buddha, the jewels from an elaborate headdress hanging over their nipples. He hired chorus girls to work for him as "secretaries." Once, a business partner was meeting with

Victor in his Cathay office when a young woman came in to announce she was leaving Shanghai. Victor pulled out a drawer in his
desk filled with diamond bracelets and told her to pick out one as a
gift. When she said she couldn't decide, Victor snapped, "Take the
drawer!" and resumed the meeting.

Gossip circulated that Victor was bisexual. At one party, the daughter of a wealthy Chinese financier objected when Victor put his hand
on her knee. She pushed it away. Victor promptly put his hand on the
knee of her brother. He didn't marry until he was sixty-five, when,
in exile in the Bahamas after the Communists had seized power, he
married his American nurse.

Of all the women linked to Victor, the most intriguing was an
American writer named Emily Hahn, who began writing essays and
articles for *The New Yorker* in her early twenties. At twenty-five, she
moved to the Belgian Congo, where she spent two years working for
the Red Cross. She smoked large cigars and drank with gusto. She
arrived in Shanghai in April 1935 on a round-the-world trip with her
sister, intending to stay just a few weeks to see the sights before continuing to Africa. She was thirty-two, wore her brown hair in a fashionable bob, and had a "voluptuous" figure. "Emily Hahn is here too,"
gushed *Time* magazine correspondent Theodore White in a letter
to his mother. He described her as "a superb mad woman, brilliant,
beautiful . . . extraordinarily clever, smokes cigars, talks Chinese, has
every man in love with her."

Her first night in Shanghai, Hahn attended a lecture on D. H. Lawrence arranged by a friend of Victor's in one of the buildings he owned
a few blocks from the Cathay. After the lecture and dinner, Victor
drove Hahn and her sister in his Rolls Royce to his country house.
Four days later he invited them back and asked Hahn to pose for him

in his photography studio. He showed the sisters a big album in which he kept the nude photos he had taken of many of Shanghai's most beautiful women. Hahn readily agreed, flattered that he had asked her and not her sister, Helen: "Sir Victor didn't ask to photograph Helen, and she kept saying, 'I wish I had a good figure,'" Hahn recalled. "Sir Victor just smiled. 'But you have such a nice nature,' he said."

Hahn decided to stay on in Shanghai. Victor installed her in a suite in a luxury apartment building he owned.

"Now we're back at the Cathay Mansions, in a suite instead of a room, because Sir Victor made them give it to us at a terrific reduction. He owns almost all the important property in Shanghai," she wrote to her mother. "When we moved in yesterday we found a great basket of liqueurs—one of almost anything you can think of, including vodka, and on top a carton of delicious cream cheese."

Hahn took a job at the *North-China Daily News* and was named China Coast correspondent of *The New Yorker*. She dined and gossiped with Victor regularly. She was like a "cat," she wrote to her sister, who "saved up all my scratching to do with him, once a week." She attended Victor's parties and accompanied him to the races. On weekends, they raced a yacht he'd had built in Norway, and took friends duck shooting.

Hahn—like Victor—had a wandering eye. She met Zau Sinmay, a handsome married Chinese writer who had lived in Paris and published a literary magazine. She described him in a story published in *The New Yorker*: "When he was not laughing or talking his ivory-colored face was perfectly oval, but one did not think of perfection, one looked at his eyes. In their oblique and startling beauty, they were full of light and life. . . . His soft carved mouth [he] had decorated with mustaches like those of his ancestors, marking sharply the corners of his lips. His tiny beard, no more than a brush of whiskers at the end of his chin, was a sly joke at his youth. In repose his face was impossibly pure, but it was rarely in repose."

Her first night meeting Victor Sassoon, Hahn had talked to him late into the night and returned to pose for nude pictures. Her first night meeting Zau, she went off with him, smoked opium, and started an affair.

At the same time she was sleeping with Zau, Hahn became friendly with his wife, children, family, and social circle and began writing about them in thinly fictionalized stories for *The New Yorker*. "Little by little, because of all the Chinese people I met, and all their histories which I heard, I was able to see through new windows," Hahn wrote. She wrote a series of popular stories for *The New Yorker* that transformed Zau into "Mr. Pan" and mocked the way Western visitors— including those who stayed at the Cathay—embraced caricatures of China. "Pale and wraith-like, bearded with a few wisps of real Chinese hair, gowned in sober brown, his long, narrow eyes blank and faraway, he is calculated to make the most hardened tourist gape and gasp," Hahn wrote of her Mr. Pan. "In the beginning he would quote Confucius, with one eye on me for my approval, and he talked real Chinese with the waiters. . . . He never failed to say after some dull evening at a restaurant, 'You are the first foreigner who has ever been there, do you know?'" Mr. Pan, Hahn wrote, "does not care what foreigners say of him."

Hahn wrote often to her mother and sister about her "emotional complications" shuttling between Zau and Victor. "Once in a while Sir Victor, who is the nicest man in the world, finds some way to make me a present, and I take it without blushing, everybody does, because he is also the richest man in the world and unlike Mr.

Rockefeller he seems to like to waste his money like that," she wrote. "So long as I never let myself slip into the habit of expecting him to help me, I think it's safe, don't you?"

When Victor left on a trip to India, Hahn wrote to her sister, Helen, "Really Helen I do love him; everything we know about him and all."

For his part, Victor treated Hahn differently from the other women who flitted through his diary. What began as a brief affair evolved into a friendship; Hahn was one of several women that Victor would become close to and confide in. When Hahn signed a contract to write a book about the Soong family, she showed Victor a draft of the first chapters. "He did me an enormous favor," she recalled. "Up until then I had used my old friends from the Monday Night Club as victims, trying the book out on them chapter by chapter. They listened, appreciated, made a few gentle suggestions, asked a few questions, but kept telling me that it was too soon to judge." Victor wasn't so polite. "He sent me my precious chapters with a blunt note: 'This is dull,' he said flatly. 'It bored me to death. If I hadn't been in bed already, I would have fallen asleep in my chair, reading it.'"

Hahn started rewriting. When Victor read the second version, he told her it kept him awake until one o'clock in the morning. The book went on to be a bestseller.

But their expert advice did not go both ways. Victor didn't pay as much attention to his lover's warnings that support for the Communists was growing in Shanghai. As a reporter, Emily saw the inequality between foreign wealth and Chinese poverty that was fueling it. Emily hobnobbed with millionaires like Victor, but her Chinese lover Zau Sinmay also introduced her to Chinese intellectuals and leftist thinkers, including Zhou Enlai. "Even the aristocrats here, the ones I know, admit that Communism is the only way out," she wrote. Hahn became friends with Chinese politicians, one of whom warned her, "The British are in for a rude awakening."

Victor dismissed her fears, his judgment clouded by his own business dealings with Nationalists who assured him that communism wasn't a threat, and by jealousy over Hahn's ongoing affair with Zau, which was an open secret in Victor's social circle. He flared when she used Chinese pronunciation of foreign names. Once when Emily showed up for a ride on his yacht in her bathing suit, Victor noticed that her skin was tinged yellow—a sign of possible jaundice from her opium smoking with Zau. "You're getting too damn Chinese," he shouted.

Hahn felt conflicted by the poverty she saw. Being in China, she believed, meant being complicit in exploitation. "Why balk at a ricksha," she wrote in her memoirs, "when you are doing just as much harm in every other way, merely by living like a foreigner in the overcrowded country of China? The shoes I walk in have been made by sweated labor; the shoemaker, beaten down by my bargaining, takes it out of his workers, and so they are being exploited (by me) just as much as the ricksha coolie is. . . .

"Cheap labor in a vast city like Shanghai means cheap production: furniture and housework and clothing and green stuff. In placid ignorance I sat on top of a heap of underfed coolies."

IN 1935, the year *Fortune* lauded Victor and the "Shanghai boom," the Shanghai Municipal Council collected 5,950 Chinese corpses from the streets of the International Settlement—Chinese residents who had died of starvation or disease and whose families were too poor to bury them. Jimmy's Kitchen, a popular restaurant started by an ex–American Navy cook that Victor visited frequently, served hamburgers and corned beef hash in portions so large that every customer left with a doggie bag—not for the family dog, but to be given to the beggars who waited outside. American journalist Edgar Snow, who would soon journey to Yenan and document sympathetically the rise of Mao and the Communists, stayed in Room 303 of the Kadoories' Astor House Hotel, down the Bund from the Cathay, and wrote succinctly of the stark divide between rich and poor, foreigners and Chinese in Shanghai. A foreigner in Shanghai "lives in a world unto himself," Snow wrote. "To him, some 3,000,000 Chinese workers in Greater Shanghai are so much background—necessary for trade and industry, but isn't it—ah—unfortunate that they couldn't all be like us?"

As unrest spread in Shanghai, radicalism infiltrated the staff of the Cathay. Yang Mengliang, the poor son of a Shanghai family, was hired to greet people at the door of the Cathay Hotel's restaurant. He was twelve years old. "You'd better work hard for me. You know, it's easier for me to hire 100 waiters rather than to look for 100 dogs," the restaurant's foreign manager told him.

To move up and become a waiter, Yang studied English at night school and began buying English books and magazines, including books on communism and the humiliation of China by the British— books that were available in the International Settlement in stores near the Cathay. "Everyone is responsible for the rise and fall of his country," he concluded. He joined the underground Communist Party, and as he worked as a waiter in the Cathay's popular restaurant and at private parties in the hotel, he became a useful spy on the comings and goings of Nationalist Chinese leaders and, later, Japanese businessmen and officials. When the Communists conquered Shanghai in 1949, he became a top-ranking official of the People's Liberation Army occupying the city.

Victor occasionally seemed to understand the fragility of Shanghai, and how widespread poverty among its Chinese residents limited even his economic success. "The west will never be able to keep furnishing the orient with industrial manufactures if it does not also provide some means to increase the buying power of the people the machine-made goods are intended for," he wrote in 1932. He prided himself on paying his Chinese workers higher wages than almost every other Western businessman in Shanghai.

But the Cathay was off-limits to all but the wealthiest Chinese. In 1933, a Chinese customer wrote to a local newspaper complaining that Victor's office floors in the Cathay contained segregated bathrooms, one marked "Gentlemen" and the other "Chinese."

"We may suggest that the hotel management build a chute from its cashiers counter" to the river outside the hotel "so that the money of the undesirable Chinese may be dumped into that river. It just can't be clean enough to mix with the coins turned in by White hands," he wrote.

A few years later, the Chinese leftist writer Lu Xun visited the Cathay to see a British friend. When he entered the lobby elevator, the Chinese elevator operator ignored him. After waiting a few minutes, Lu Xun walked up seven floors. No wonder, Lu Xun wrote later, that confronting such humiliations drove many Chinese to "living in a small room and literally feeding their bodies to bedbugs."

LOOMING OVER THE POLITICS, economics, and divisions of Shanghai was the growing specter of Japan. Like China, Japan resisted trade with Western powers before the arrival of Western warships toward the middle of the nineteenth century. Unlike China, Japan had responded effectively and forcefully, reforming its political system, sending students and experts overseas to learn from the West, and rearming to become the dominant power in Asia. In 1895, Japan defeated China in a war that again exposed China's weakness. Ten years later Japan defeated Russia, becoming the first Asian power to defeat a European adversary. Determined to turn northern China into a virtual colony, and jealous of the trade concessions Western countries had extracted since the Opium Wars, Japan began in 1931 to manufacture a series of incidents to allow its troops to conquer more and more Chinese territory. Japanese trade with China was already increasing. The Japanese operated thirty textile mills around Shanghai, drawn, as were other foreigners, by the vast pool of cheap Chinese labor. By then, more than 30,000 Japanese lived in Shanghai—three times the number of British. That same year, the Japanese army staged an explosion near a railway line owned by the Japanese, blamed it on Chinese dissidents, and invaded Manchuria, creating the puppet state of Manchukuo. Chinese students and workers took to the street to protest the Japanese occupation of Manchuria and demand a boycott of Japanese products. Victor dismissed the protests as hopeless. Those in Chinese government "see they cannot go to war with Japan," which was much more powerful, he wrote to a friend, and the "student demand to fight all foreigners is not practical."

Saying it had to protect Japanese citizens, the Japanese bombed Shanghai in 1932, and thousands of Japanese troops invaded the city, focusing on the Japanese settlement known as Hongkew north of the International Settlement. Chinese troops counterattacked, and the battles spread throughout Chinese-controlled Shanghai, carefully steering clear of the International Settlement to avoid involving the British or other Western powers.

Victor was lunching in the Cathay when the Chinese exploded a bomb near the Japanese flagship in the harbor. The hotel swayed. Victor grabbed his camera and limped out to take photographs. A bullet fired by a Chinese soldier passed over his head and shattered a window in one of the banks on the Bund. Rather than hole up in the safety of the settlement, where, Victor wrote, "we have always been in less danger than an American city on the Fourth of July," he grabbed his new movie camera and toured the destroyed areas with an American officer. "The actual scene of fighting looks like the ruins of Ypres," he wrote in his diary. "Frightened stiff of booby traps I may say."

He pasted a photograph in his diary of a nearby railway station in flames. Beneath it he wrote, "It really is a war."

Within a few months, the fighting had eased. The Japanese apologized to Victor for shooting at him. Under a cease-fire agreement, the Chinese were forced to withdraw most of their troops from Shanghai. The Japanese now controlled Manchuria, and thousands of Japanese poured into the city to take up residence in the Hongkew neighborhood north of the Bund, which was under effective Japanese control. Life at the Cathay started to pick up. Victor recorded in his diary that the Cathay was "packed for dinner and small parties," though there were "very few young people."

The Japanese, he wrote a friend, "treat Shanghai as theirs and everybody as their enemy," while the Chinese "are just playing for time and refusing to settle anything, as there is no Government who can really govern at the moment."

Victor resumed his favorite activities, attending the races and throwing memorable parties at the Cathay, but the stress was taking its toll. When Victor, now in his fifties, visited London, a friend was shocked to see his sleek black hair streaked with gray and his face lined with wrinkles. "I have not been entertaining very much," he confided to his diary. "My Chinese friends are still here but they seemed to have changed a good deal. Some have gone off to Canton and some to Nanking, although I have given a couple of parties for them."

His profitable relations with Chiang Kai-shek's Nationalist government began to sour. Victor learned, as America would learn later, that the Nationalists had their own agenda. The Shanghai boom lauded by *Fortune* in 1935 was in many ways a state-created chimera. The high yield of government bonds was sucking money that would have otherwise been invested in Chinese banking and industry and putting it instead in the hands of investors such as Victor, Chiang Kai-shek's government, and the army. Shanghai boomed while China's farmers and countryside fell deep into economic depression and the Communist political messages became more appealing.

China had benefited from globalization as investors like Victor looked for high returns during the Depression. Now it suffered from the same forces. Suspicious of paper money, Victor held most of his money in silver, which he could convert into paper money or trade as he wished. In 1933, the United States abandoned the gold standard. To appease the political demands of Western mining states, it started buying silver at artificially high prices and storing that silver in the U.S. treasury. To financiers in Shanghai—and to Victor Sassoon—this meant that instead of buying Nationalist bonds, they could now sell their silver holdings to the United States for a quick, clear profit of 10 percent. The consequence for the Chinese economy was catastrophic. More than $170 million worth of silver poured out of China in the first eight months of 1934—the equivalent of $3 billion today. Bond sales plummeted. Without bond sales, Chiang's military buildup slowed; Mao's Red Army was able to break through the weakened Nationalist blockade and begin the Long March to a safe new base in Yenan. The Nationalist government was on the verge of financial collapse.

The Nationalists took a series of steps that effectively nationalized China banks and put them under the control of Chiang Kai-shek. They required all silver held by banks or individuals to be turned over to the government in exchange for paper money. The Nationalists now controlled the money supply and the value of silver. Victor and others dubbed it the "Shanghai Banking Coup." It came out of nowhere, and likely cost Victor millions of dollars and froze his silver, forcing him to exchange it for Chinese currency controlled by the Nationalists.

Furious, Victor confronted Li Ming, his financial liaison to the Nationalists. How could Chiang and the Nationalist leadership—the same people who lunched and dined with Victor—make such a decision without warning him? Li Ming blithely informed Victor that the Nationalists had "consulted no one outside" the Chinese government.

The Nationalist Chinese also began demanding changes in the notion of extraterritoriality—the doctrine that placed foreigners and foreign business transactions outside the scope of Chinese law and the power of the Chinese government. Not only did foreigners essentially operate as an independent state in Shanghai, the lives of 1 million Chinese living in the International Settlement also were controlled by the foreigners, not by China. The Nationalists found this unacceptable. In 1930, Britain bowed to Nationalist demands and returned control of Weihaiwei, where Elly Kadoorie had gotten his start, to China. Under pressure, the Shanghai Municipal Council added five Chinese members to its ranks, though foreigners still held a majority. The future of foreign investment in Shanghai was "precarious," a study commissioned by the British business community warned in 1931. "It depends on the continuance of the protection of the troops and ships" of Great Britain, the United States, and France "and on a certain degree of tolerance on the part of the Chinese government."

Victor was trapped. Shanghai had made him one of the richest men in the world. His real estate holdings alone were worth more than a half billion dollars. But he was a prisoner in a golden cage. The success of real estate depended on Shanghai's continued growth, and he was no longer free to send his profits out of the country. If the Nationalists controlled silver, they controlled the banks, the loans given to investors, the ability of foreigners like Victor to move money in and out of the country. The Shanghai Banking Coup ended Victor's infatuation with the Nationalists and Chiang Kai-shek. When the Chinese approached him in future years for help against the rising Japanese and threats of invasion, Victor refused. "A plague on both your houses is my motto in this business, but one has to be careful what one says, for telling the brutal truth will get us nowhere," he wrote to a friend in London.

Like the British and the Americans, Victor refused to believe that the Japanese, despite growing nationalism and bellicose statements, would go to war. Japan's army was "modern" and "well-trained" but fell below "modern European standards," he wrote to a friend. Japanese aviation was in "very bad shape" and their pilots in China "third rate." In the summer of 1937, Victor left on a trip to India. On July 8, he checked the news ticker tape and read that Japanese and Chinese troops had clashed on the Marco Polo Bridge outside Beijing. It was another "incident" staged by Japan. Within twenty-four hours, a flotilla of Japanese cruisers and destroyers was steaming for Shanghai while low-flying bombers strafed the countryside. Preparing for another outbreak of fighting between the Chinese and the Japanese, British troops and American marines ringed the International Settlement with barbed wire and sandbags. On Saturday morning, August 14, 1937, Chinese aircraft attacked a Japanese ship moored alongside the Bund. Two Chinese planes fleeing Japanese fire jettisoned their bombs. One fell just opposite the Cathay Hotel, on a street packed with civilians, sending up a wall of flame and debris. On the street, cars burned fiercely, the passenger seats filled with blackened corpses. Hundreds of bodies lay strewn about—many of them dismembered beyond recognition. Pieces of human flesh spattered the Cathay's walls up to the fifth and sixth floors.

When Victor returned to Shanghai a month later, fighting was continuing. He wrote in his diary that he went into a "number of houses" and saw "dead bodies, one of a gardener and family." Another Chinese gardener told Victor his daughter had been raped by Japanese soldiers. In December, Japanese troops moved farther south and invaded and conquered Nanjing. Reports reached Shanghai of Japanese soldiers engaging in the mass rape and murder of Chinese civilians. Victor worried that Japan might indeed one day go to war with Britain and the United States. Most ominously for him, he saw that he was coming under Japanese suspicion. He cut out an article that quoted a Japanese newspaper attacking Britain for trying to thwart Japan's rise. "British policy has been designed to place economic obstacles in the path of Japan, while hoping for Japan's economic and financial collapse," read the article that Victor pasted in his diary. It named two British citizens as Japan's enemies in China: the British ambassador to China and Victor Sassoon.

Shortly after New Year's Day 1938, Victor sat down at his desk at the Cathay and wrote to the head of his European operations in London. "The situation here appears to me more serious and dangerous than it ever has been, both from a political and a financial point of view," he wrote. The Japanese "have got to the stage where they do not seem to be afraid of anyone." He complained that Japanese soldiers in Shanghai had recently beaten a British police officer patrolling the streets "merely because, they say, he did not pull his car out of the way quickly enough to allow a Japanese Naval Landing Party motorcycle to pass, and I think that in this respect things will get worse instead of better." He complained about the ongoing impact of the Banking Coup, which meant the Nationalists wouldn't allow him to get his money out of China. If the Japanese took over, it would get even worse.

Four days later, he wrote again: "Things are looking really serious now, and I cannot see what is to be done." The Japanese, he believed, were preparing to take over China economically. If the British tried to blockade Japan or impose trade restrictions, "they will declare war on us, anticipating that they will be able to live on China by wholesale expropriation." The British, Victor concluded, should "start withdrawing every Britisher from China including civilians from Hong Kong . . . and then stop all trade with Japan."

Victor ended the letter by telling his London manager that he wasn't sharing his views with his executives and workers in Shanghai. "I do not want them to know how depressed I am."

In photographs taken by Victor Sassoon and kept in his personal scrapbook, Koreshige Inuzuka (far left), the anti-Semitic Japanese navy captain in charge of Shanghai's "Jewish problem," visits the Cathay Hotel and socializes and jokes with Japanese military colleagues and women.

6

"Me Voila Therefore Walking a Tightrope"

O n a cold, rainy day in November 1938, eleven months after Victor wrote his worried letters to London, the luxury Italian passenger vessel *Conte Biancamano* docked in Shanghai carrying more than a hundred Jewish refugees from Germany and Austria. For many years, the *Conte Biancamano* had brought celebrities and the wealthy to Shanghai to stay at the Cathay Hotel. Now it was shuttling Jewish passengers paying double or triple the price on the black market for passage to the only place left in the world that would take in Jews fleeing the Nazis. As country after country refused sanctuary to Jews fleeing rising Nazism, Shanghai—with power divided among the Chinese, the Japanese, the British, and the French—was an open city. No one needed a visa to enter. No one could be turned away.

One of the passengers was twelve-year-old Erich Reisman from Vienna. The previous nine months had been a blur of fear and desperation for Erich and his family. His father ran a wholesale fruit business; his mother was a homemaker who had opened a successful delicatessen in downtown Vienna. Anti-Semitic comments and taunts were a part of life, but when German troops marched into Vienna in March 1938 to annex the country in the Anschluss, the atmosphere darkened. The Friday after cheering crowds welcomed Hitler into Vienna, Erich came home to his apartment from a Boy Scout meeting and asked where his mother was. "Look here out the window," his brother said. There, on the street that ran alongside the apartment building, Erich saw his mother scrubbing the street while a crowd looked down and jeered. Erich ran down the stairs to help her. The crowd pushed him to the ground and made him start scrubbing, too. "Jew, help your mother like a good Jew!" they shouted. The next week Erich's brother, Paul, walked to his high school and saw a crowd gathered near the entrance. Inside, on the fourth floor, a gang of students with Nazi armbands grabbed a Jewish student and hurled him over the balustrade to the lobby below. Erich's brother panicked and ran home, refusing to go to school again. Their father came home despondent. His business had been seized by his Christian partners.

The Reismans began looking for ways to escape Vienna. They wrote to family members who lived overseas. Erich, his brother, and his father took turns standing in line with other Jews in front of foreign consulates, seeking visas that would allow them to leave Austria. They would stand in line starting the evening before until nine in the morning, when the consulates opened. Sometimes the first fifteen would be let in, sometimes only the first ten. But all that got them was a visa application or a chance to meet an ambassador or a consul to plead their case.

Embassy after embassy turned down his father's plea for a visa, until one day they stumbled on the Chinese consulate. The Chinese consul, a man named Ho who spoke German and seemed unusually sympathetic, told them about Shanghai.

The diplomat was Ho Feng-Shan, one of a generation of Chinese who had left the Chinese countryside for Shanghai to get rich and see the world. Ho was born in rural China in 1901. After his father died when Ho was seven, his mother enrolled him in a free Norwegian Lutheran Mission and then a school recently established nearby by Yale University. Like most Chinese, his beliefs were firmly rooted in Confucian principles; he would name his two children after tenets of Confucianism, "Virtue" and "Decorum." But he was also attracted by Western religion, including Judaism and Christianity, and became fluent in English and German. In 1926 he made his way to Shanghai. The cosmopolitanism of the city intoxicated him. He was spotted by the Nationalists, who were eager to train a new generation of Chinese students in Western languages and knowledge, and they sent him to study physics in Germany. When Ho returned to China, he was assigned to the foreign ministry. In 1932, he was dispatched to Germany again, to earn a doctorate in political economics at the University of Munich. He arrived just as Adolf Hitler was coming to power. Fascinated by European culture, he asked to go to Vienna and was posted there as a consul in 1937. Ho was frequently asked to lecture on Chinese history and culture and befriended members of the Jewish intelligentsia, including three wealthy Jewish sisters. When Nationalist Chinese politicians came to visit Europe, Ho warned them that the Nazi threat was real and that the Nazis' anti-Semitism was deadly. "The situation now is like a fire in a paper bag and it is going to burn through," Ho told a visiting Chinese delegation. "The consequences will be very dire especially for the Jews."

When Hitler marched into Vienna in March 1938, the enthusiastic reception he received appalled Ho. It was like fans greeting a movie star. Ho went to the home of the Jewish sisters he had met, the Doron family, and said he would protect them. "He claimed that, thanks to his diplomatic status, the [Nazis] would not dare harm us," one of the sisters recalled. Ho was in a Vienna coffee shop where Nazi hoodlums came in looking for Jews. He urged the Chinese foreign ministry to do something to help Vienna's Jews escape, but the Nationalists were buying arms from Germany and did not want to upset the German government.

So, Ho decided to act on his own. He gave the Doron sisters an exit visa, so they could escape to Palestine. In a café down the street from the Chinese consulate, he began inviting Jews standing in line hoping for a visa to meet with him. He explained that they did not need a visa to enter Shanghai. But they did need to show a Shanghai visa to obtain an exit permit to escape Austria. So, Ho began issuing visas. By June 1938, three months after Hitler had annexed Austria, he had issued 300. Four months later, he had issued 1,900. The holders of Ho's visas didn't all travel to Shanghai, but they were able to use the papers to get transit visas and escape elsewhere—the United States, Palestine, and the Philippines. "I thought it only natural to feel compassion and to want to help," Ho wrote later in a family memoir. "From the standpoint of humanity, that is the way it should be." In a poem he gave to his wife he wrote:

> The gifts Heaven bestows are not by chance
> The convictions of heroes not lightly formed.

Armed with Ho's Shanghai visa, Erich's father obtained an exit permit for his family. He sold the family's Oriental rugs and bought tickets on a train through Switzerland to Italy, where they boarded the *Conte Biancamano* in Naples, steamed through the Suez Canal and the Red Sea, past Bombay, Singapore, and Hong Kong before arriving a month later in the muddy waters of the Shanghai harbor bordering the Bund. Erich was wearing his winter clothes and a pith helmet he bought when the ship stopped in Egypt to transit across the Suez Canal. He was accompanied by his brother—who was still traumatized after having seen the Nazi thugs hurl his Jewish classmate to his death—and his parents. From the deck of the ocean liner, Erich and his brother gaped at the art deco buildings lining the waterfront and at the throngs of Chinese below, jostling along the docks and in the street, shouting, screaming, and yelling in their unfamiliar language.

Scanning the crowd, they spotted a sign in German held up by someone in the crowd: WELCOME TO SHANGHAI, it read. YOU ARE NO LONGER JEWS BUT CITIZENS OF THE WORLD. ALL SHANGHAI WELCOMES YOU.

"The people look like ants," his fifteen-year-old brother said.

The Reismans stepped off the boat and, along with a dozen other refugees, were bundled onto a truck with their luggage, taken to a dormitory where they were given a room, and fed. Though they didn't know it, their benefactor was Victor Sassoon.

JAPAN'S FASCINATION WITH JEWS started in 1905 when the Japanese finance minister went to Europe to raise money to fight the Russians. To finance their attack, Takahashi Korekiyo, deputy governor of the Bank of Japan, traveled to London to see if he could persuade European and American banks to lend Japan money. It was an audacious plea—an Asian upstart planning to attack a major European power. At a dinner party in April 1905, Takahashi met Jacob H. Schiff, the German-born Jewish president of the Wall Street firm Kuhn, Loeb & Co. Schiff, like many American Jews, loathed Russia and the czar for their anti-Semitic attacks on Jews that terrorized Jewish towns and neighborhoods. Two years earlier, gangs of Russians armed with knives and hatchets had stormed the streets of Kishinev, killing forty-nine Jews and raping scores of women. In the wake of the Kishinev pogrom, tens of thousands of Russian Jews fled to the United States and to Palestine. Influential American Jews, including Schiff, pleaded with President Theodore Roosevelt to intervene, to no avail.

In Japan's quest to build a navy and attack Russia, Schiff saw an opportunity to weaken the hated czar. He arranged more than $200 million in loans for Japan's military (more than $33 billion in current dollars) and encouraged other American bankers to lend money as well. The loans ended up financing construction of half the Japanese navy, which then decisively defeated Russia's Baltic fleet and helped Japan triumph over Russia in 1905. Takahashi became finance minister, and then premier. He sent his daughter to live with Schiff when she studied in the United States. Schiff became the first foreigner to be awarded the Order of the Rising Sun by Japan's emperor.

One consequence of Japan's victory over Russia was that soldiers returned from the war with copies of the infamous *Protocols of the Elders of Zion*, a forged Russian booklet first published in 1903 that claimed to be the minutes of a meeting of Jewish leaders preparing to dominate the world. Drawing on centuries of anti-Semitism and anti-Jewish myths and fables, *Protocols* was translated and reproduced around the world; Henry Ford sponsored the printing of 500,000 copies in the United States in 1920. The Nazis used *Protocols* in their anti-Semitic propaganda and ordered that *Protocols* be taught in many schools. *Protocols* struck a chord with many Japanese militarists as well. They were trying to understand why the West and, after World War I, the League of Nations opposed Japan's rise and expansion into China. *Protocols* gave an easy answer: the Jews and their diabolical hold on power stood between Japan and its rightful place in the world.

Helping to spread these views was a fast-rising Japanese navy captain, Koreshige Inuzuka. Writing under a pseudonym, Inuzuka translated *Protocols* and anti-Jewish propaganda into Japanese and published them in Japanese military periodicals. Inuzuka labeled the Jews "the source of evil thoughts" who were "masterminding international intrigues against Japan behind the scene in Britain, the United States, China and Russia." Jews were to blame for the "immorality of the Japanese youth by showing of their films." They controlled "the American press and thereby public opinion, turning it against Japan." Hitler's attacks on Jews were "imperative," Inuzuka wrote.

But *Protocols* did not become viral in Japan as it had in Germany, where it drew on centuries of Christian hatred and anti-Semitism, leading to the confinement of Jews in ghettos and their expulsion. In Shanghai, the only Jew most Japanese had dealt with or even heard of was Jacob Schiff himself. The upshot was that as they continued to study and try to understand the West, senior officers of the Japanese army and navy concocted an unusual anti-Semitic stew. They concluded that Jews indeed controlled the levers of world power. But unlike the Nazis or other anti-Semites who believed the Jews needed to be destroyed, the Japanese militarists concluded that they could cultivate useful allies among the Jews, like Jacob Schiff, if approached the right way. Inuzuka didn't want to annihilate the Jews. He wanted to woo them and harness their wealth and power to finance Japan's "Greater East Asia Co-Prosperity Sphere," especially the industrial development of its puppet state Manchukuo in northeast China. The Jews, Inuzuka concluded, could indeed be powerful enemies. But they could also be powerful allies.

In China, Inuzuka believed, the linchpin of Jewish power was Victor Sassoon, the richest man in Shanghai, financial backer of the Nationalist government, and a close friend of Chiang Kai-shek's top aides H. H. Kung and T. V. Soong. The Jews are the "true rulers of China, both its economy and its leaders," Inuzuka wrote. "Chiang is considered a mere puppet of his masters, the Jewish plutocrats, especially Sir Victor Sassoon."

The goal: to turn Victor Sassoon into Jacob Schiff. "It will be important to study in detail and find to what extent we can make use of the Jewish people," Inuzuka wrote. "It is emphatically advised, therefore, that our intelligence agencies should be strengthened and investigations on the spot intensified." In the fall of 1938, Inuzuka arrived in Shanghai to begin his work.

RELIGION MEANT LITTLE to Victor. He didn't observe Jewish dietary rules and was more likely to give a donation to a synagogue to honor his family than attend religious services. Despite hearing the occasional anti-Semitic slurs, he personified the triumph of Jewish assimilation and social acceptance. In public he shrugged off his Jewish background, embracing instead his renown as a businessman and bon vivant. "The only race greater than the Jews," he reportedly declared, "is the Derby"—the elite British horse race that Victor attended and in which he entered his thoroughbred horses.

By contrast, Elly Kadoorie, despite occasional clashes with other Jews in Shanghai, was the biggest Jewish benefactor in Shanghai's Jewish community and its de facto leader. He had persuaded Sun Yat-sen to endorse the Balfour Declaration and had long been involved in Zionism. His investments in Hong Kong were growing, but he still had millions invested in Shanghai and had lived there for almost three decades. When small groups of Jewish refugees began arriving in Shanghai starting in the mid-1930s, Elly and other Jewish leaders began organizing and donating money to help them. They provided refugee families coming off the boat—most of whom were middle-class professionals—with rooms in private boarding houses, at the Salvation Army, and at the Chinese YMCA. They gave the refugees meals and helped them look for jobs. They urged Chinese intellectuals and politicians to pressure the German government to ease its policies against the Jews. Recalling the alliance between her late husband and Elly Kadoorie, Madame Sun Yat-sen led a delegation to Shanghai's German consulate to protest anti-Jewish policies.

By the end of 1937, however, with more than a hundred refugees arriving every month and the Nazis encouraging Jews to flee Germany, Elly and the other Jewish leaders began to seek help to deal with the developing crisis. They cabled Jewish organizations in New York and London seeking donations and sent an emissary to both cities to seek donations in person from large Jewish agencies that were trying to deal with the exodus of Jews from Germany. Everyone turned them down. "Very sorry, we have no budget for this," an American Jewish group responded. American and British Jews knew how wealthy the Jewish businessmen in Shanghai were. Why don't they ask the millionaire playboy, Victor Sassoon?

Elly decided to go see Victor in his office at the Cathay Hotel. It was a humbling visit. In the years since he had moved from India to Shanghai, Victor had restored the primacy of the Sassoons in Shanghai. The Cathay Hotel dwarfed Elly's smaller Palace Hotel across Nanjing Road. He had bought out and closed Elly's once-preeminent Majestic Hotel. Marble Hall was still the scene of elegant parties, but they couldn't compete with the glamour and excitement of Victor's costume balls. The Kadoories rarely made the invitation list for Victor's parties—they weren't much fun. But Elly recognized that the growing influx of refugees to Shanghai required a united front. Victor had influence in London and among the Japanese. Whatever Victor's own feelings about Judaism, Elly and the refugees needed his wealth and connections. The news from Germany and the desperation of the refugees pouring into Shanghai showed that the Nazis and their anti-Semitic allies weren't going to spare wealthy Jews. Elly took the elevator up to Victor's suite and appealed to his ego and his heritage.

"Victor, there is a war going on," Elly said. "Stop being a playboy. You are a Sassoon. You are the leader. We will be behind you. But you are the leader."

Victor agreed to join the effort to help the refugees. Zionism didn't interest him; he was British born and bred. But privately, Victor now recognized the threat the Nazis posed and was worried. His family had settled in England, and Hitler's growing power frightened many in England, especially the Jews. In Asia, the growing power of the Japanese threatened the stability of China and Shanghai where Victor had built the family fortune. Many of his closest advisers were Jewish, some from the same Baghdadi roots as his family. The rise of Hitler, he recognized, posed an existential threat even to someone as rich as Victor Sassoon.

In typical style, Victor contacted Charlie Chaplin and enlisted him in efforts to raise money for the Shanghai Jewish refugees in the United States and Europe. He tried to persuade Hollywood stars to follow Chaplin's example, contributing income from their movies as Chaplin had contributed some of his income from *The Great Dictator*. Victor himself established a "rehabilitation fund" to help 700 families. Doctors were able to open successful clinics, and others established workshops and industries. Victor approached the refugee crisis with the same confidence and verve he applied to building his hotels or planning his parties.

THE FIRST MEETING BETWEEN VICTOR and the anti-Semitic Japanese captain Inuzuka took place in 1938. Inuzuka began by urging Victor to modify his open dislike of the Japanese and criticism of their invasion of China. He invoked the financial assistance rendered to Japan three decades earlier by Jacob Schiff. The Japanese and the Jews once again had a common enemy. Back then, the danger to Jews had come from Russian czarist pogroms. Now it was communism in the Soviet Union and the threat of communism in China and India that was spreading attacks on capitalism and imperiled the Sassoon business empire. Inuzuka suggested investing in Japanese factories at a high rate of return, greater than what Victor received from his vast holdings in Chinese bonds. He could begin by investing $700,000 in a Japanese factory in Manchuria. "In making use of the Jewish people," Inuzuka wrote to his superiors, "it is necessary first to find out their desires in detail and then clarify demands on our part." Inuzuka's secretary, who later became his wife, put the goal more simply: "We were trying to persuade him to support us," she recalled.

No one could charm people like Victor Sassoon. Inuzuka left the initial meetings with Victor buoyant. Victor told Inuzuka that Japanese officers were welcomed at the Cathay bars and dining rooms, where they would be treated with scrupulous politeness. Sassoon was a "leading figure" and "willing to cooperate," Inuzuka reported to Tokyo. "The leading class of the Jews in Shanghai has become very pro-Japanese." In a proposal adopted by the Japanese government, Inuzuka directed that Jews arriving in or living in Shanghai "are to be treated fairly and in the same manner as other foreign nationals. No special effort to expel them is to be made."

In fact, Victor distrusted the Japanese. Starting in 1937, Victor had set up a network of spies and informants and was cooperating with intelligence agents of Great Britain and the United States, two countries whose alliance he believed to be crucial. Following the Japanese-Chinese battle that led to a bomb falling outside the Cathay Hotel, Victor reported in his diary that he had given $500 to a Chinese man for "intelligence work." Years later, when they were living in the Bahamas, Victor's wife at the time recalled his telling her that the United States had assigned Victor a bodyguard in Shanghai as a "precautionary measure."

"I think it was a very hush-hush affair," she recalled.

Victor now began gathering information on his new Japanese acquaintances. "Japanese ambassador Ito on verge of being offensive—rather tight [drunk]," he recorded in his diary. "Last night understand he was clamoring . . . for a woman."

The normally voluble and quick-witted Victor began to play it cagey in public, to preserve the illusion that he was considering the offers of the Japanese. On a visit to the United States in 1938, he privately told friends on Wall Street and officials in the State Department that an economic embargo could soon drive the Japanese out of

China. But when he arrived in San Francisco and was interviewed by reporters, he surprised them with a curt "no comment" when asked about Shanghai. When he opened his newspaper in the St. Francis Hotel the next morning, he was furious to read a headline: SIR VICTOR SASSOON KNOWS NOTHING.

"Can you imagine me knowing nothing!" he fumed.

Even Victor's colleagues on the committees helping the Jewish refugees remained in the dark about what Victor was doing behind the scenes. "We heard lots of facts and some conjectures at our committee meetings," Jacob Alkow, a Jewish leader, recalled. Sassoon "refused to divulge" all his conversations with the Japanese and "avoided answering my questions. However, I can remember no plea to the Japanese that was unanswered."

Victor knew scores of bankers, industrialists, and members of Parliament in Japan. He believed that the country and the military were divided, and that this, in the end, would keep Japan out of war. The hard-line army "wants Japan to be a continental power and damn all foreigners and the world." The navy, represented by Inuzuka, "say[s] this is impossible, and that Japan must remain an Island power dependent on trade and so she must be careful of Great Britain who can cut her right off from everywhere." He cautioned Elly Kadoorie not to panic. "Sir Victor believes that it will not be long before the Japanese and the British become good friends," Lawrence wrote to his brother. "In fact, he was very optimistic as to conditions in this part of the world."

Victor wrote to a friend about the ballet taking place between himself and Inuzuka. "They hint at [several million sterling] and sympathy and then we can be left alone in settlements," he wrote. "I smile and say it is always wrong to give in to blackmail and any loans must follow complete settlement of all questions including China.

They say they are not anti-British. Army still suspicious of me but the rest say that I am their best bet as a liaison" with Great Britain.

He concluded: "Me voila therefore walking a tightrope."

ON OCTOBER 19, 1938, Elly invited the wealthy Jewish businessmen in Shanghai to a meeting at his office to coordinate their efforts. More than 1,000 refugees had arrived, and ships were bringing several hundred more every week. At the end of the meeting, Jacob Alcok, who was overseeing the distribution of money, housing, and food, said money was running out and the refugees would soon be cut off from any help. Elly pulled out his checkbook and wrote out a check for $50,000. Handing the check to Alcok, Elly barked: "Now go to Victor!"

Alcok went to the Cathay Hotel and Victor's office. Sassoon smiled. "Whatever Elly gave, I'll give," he said, and wrote a matching check.

Victor was confident that he could handle the Japanese and that Shanghai could handle the refugees. He assumed the crisis was temporary. "I think that we should be able to gradually work up to taking care of 3 to 4 thousand people, as long as we have the funds made available, and as long as we know that these people will be eventually taken off our hands," Victor wrote to a friend.

Despite his bravado, Victor was increasingly worried—and started planning for an uncertain future. In 1938, he flew to Brazil and purchased 10,000 square miles of land. Ostensibly he made the purchase as an investment. With Germany and Japan rising and threatening Asia and Europe, he believed that the future lay in the United States and Great Britain linking up and harnessing the natural resources of

South America. But his real purpose was to try to find a refuge for the Jews. Victor was not a Zionist. He didn't believe that the answer to the refugee crisis was sending Jews to Palestine; South America was more practical. He met with Brazil's president, Getúlio Vargas, and proposed the creation of a colony "where the Jews do everything from being sweepers to president." Like every other government in the world, the Brazilian government wasn't interested in helping Jewish refugees.

Vargas "told me he wanted the right sort of people to come . . . a race like Danes and Scandinavians with no imagination, no brains, but with great capacity for tilling the ground," Victor reported later. "He didn't want anybody who desired to live in their towns. He wanted them out in the country to till the soil and stay there."

Returning to Shanghai, Victor found the powerful non-Jewish members of the Shanghai Municipal Council, in effect the government of the International Settlement, becoming impatient. "It is quite impossible to absorb any large numbers of foreign refugees," the council told Victor. The city "may be compelled to take steps to prevent further refugees landing."

IN JULY 1938, thirty-two countries including Canada, Australia, and New Zealand met in Évian, France, to decide what to do about the tens of thousands of desperate Jews trying to flee Germany, Austria, and the rest of Europe. All but one—the Dominican Republic—announced they were refusing entry. In Vienna, Ho Feng-Shan began issuing even more documents to enable Jews to leave Austria and head for Shanghai. In November 1938, Elly and Horace traveled to Hong Kong to attend Lawrence's wedding to Muriel Gubbay, the daughter of a prominent Jewish family that also traced its roots to Baghdad, whose mother had been great friends with Lawrence's mother, Laura. Lawrence, too, had been trying to help Jewish refugees landing in Hong Kong, giving them jobs at China Light and Power. Even amid the rise of the Nazis and growing talk of war, the head of Jardine in Hong Kong, J. J. Paterson, couldn't resist another anti-Semitic swipe at the Kadoories, writing to his boss William Keswick in Shanghai that Lawrence's wedding took place at Ohel Leah Synagogue in Hong Kong—Hebrew for "House of Leah," after the biblical Jewish matriarch—with a reception at the Jewish community center.

Punning on "hell," Paterson chortled: "'Ohel!' is right." He added that he hoped the Kadoories had enjoyed themselves at the "Jew boy's club."

Lawrence's wedding took place on November 9, 1938. The next morning the Kadoories woke up and learned that half a world away, Kristallnacht—the "Night of Broken Glass"—had erupted in Austria and Germany. Mobs had burned and looted synagogues and Jewish-owned stores while police looked on or encouraged the attacks. The alarm among German and Austrian Jews turned into full-scale panic. The stream of refugees landing in Shanghai became a flood. "Five hundred and sixty-two additional refugees are arriving by Saturday's steamer and I understand another 700 will be arriving" in two weeks, Horace Kadoorie wrote to a friend in London. "Shanghai cannot cope with them."

Victor made available the first floor of one of his luxury skyscrapers, the Embankment Building, as a reception center for refugees, where each was given blankets, bedsheets, a tin dish, a cup, and a spoon. He installed a kitchen in the basement to provide 1,800 meals a day. He turned one of his factories into a dormitory for the refugees. Under the pseudonym Val Seymour, Victor paid the entry fee that allowed many refugees to get through customs. He established a fund to supply free milk daily to every refugee in Shanghai. He donated the money for an expensive iron lung to one of the three hospitals set up to serve the refugees and turned one of his buildings on Nanjing Road into the Immigrants' Thrift Shop, where refugees could raise funds by selling their belongings. He established a training camp to give vocational training to 200 men as mechanics, joiners, and carpenters. He started hiring refugees in his own enterprises. One of the refugees, a botanist by profession, was put in charge of his country estate in the Shanghai suburbs. Another set up a sewing machine in a kitchen he shared with three other families and sewed new shirts from fabric donated by Victor from his textile mills.

Sylvia Chancellor, a British resident of Shanghai who had criticized Victor for being a playboy and ignoring the poverty and inequality of the city, changed her mind. "God will forgive him all his sins because of the charity he gives" to the refugees, she declared. The refugees caught glimpses of their benefactor but didn't fully understand who he was. "The people who helped us—they were Moroccan," Erich Reisman recalled.

For the Reismans, who landed in November 1938, Shanghai was a shock after the sophistication of Vienna. On the street, Erich stared at Chinese families living in cardboard boxes. Once, walking along, he saw a package lying on the ground wrapped in either a straw mat or a piece of newspaper, a small leg sticking out. He realized with a start that it was a dead child laid out by the parents on the sidewalk. The child had died overnight of starvation.

None of the new arrivals spoke Chinese; only a few spoke English. Though they had lived middle-class lives in Germany and Austria, the Nazis had confiscated their money and belongings as they left. They were disoriented and scared. Erich's family was lucky; the one-room apartment they were assigned had a bathroom. Most refugee families were sent to the bombed-out Hongkew area, which had been leveled during the fighting in both 1932 and 1937 between the Chinese and the Japanese. Families crammed into single- or two-story houses that ran along alleys off the main streets, airless and dark, each with ten rooms and primitive bathrooms—often no more than "honeypots" or buckets that had to be emptied several times a day. One newly arrived refugee wrote: "For people who are used to incomparably better conditions, this seemed so hopeless, the surroundings so sordid, that many grown men . . . were overcome with such hopeless despair, that they sat down on the dirty floor and wept like children."

By February 1939, the number of refugees had surged past Victor's estimates. More than 6,000 Jewish refugees were living in Shanghai, and they were arriving at the rate of 1,000 a month.

LIVING CONDITIONS WERE GRIM, but the refugees faced no legal barriers or restrictions. Erich's father began to look for work. In Vienna, he had run a wholesale fruit import business. When it became clear that the Reismans would have to leave Vienna, Erich's mother had begun taking lessons from a Jewish agency to sew gloves. In Shanghai this became the family's lifeline. Like many men, Erich's father had trouble adjusting to the loss of his job and prestige. He began selling his wife's gloves to other refugees, then he and Erich's elder brother got jobs as auto mechanics at a Shanghai bus company owned by a German immigrant. Soon they had accumulated enough money to buy a small home in Hongkew and rent out part of it to tenants, earning a small side income.

A few months later Erich and his family walked a few blocks down the street and did something that in 1939 would have been impossible in Vienna or Berlin: Erich was bar mitzvahed, having turned thirteen. While the Jews pouring into Shanghai were overwhelmed and complained endlessly about crowded housing, poor sanitation, and the lack of jobs, they were also free. Their arrival in Hongkew launched another transformation of Shanghai. The city already had foreign neighborhoods such as the International Settlement and the French Concession alongside the Chinese-controlled parts of the city. Now it added "Little Vienna."

Unable to find work in their professions, many of the refugees began opening shops, restaurants, and cafés in Hongkew. They put up German signs and sold German food. They started up three different German-language newspapers supported by advertising from refugee butchers and tailors. Many of the refugees were amateur musicians. They joined together and started a chamber orchestra. Amateur theater groups sprang up across the neighborhood, with artists from Vienna and Berlin vying to put on the best productions of Bertholt Brecht's *Threepenny Opera* and works by August Strindberg, George Bernard Shaw, and Noël Coward. Almost 300 artists joined in the European Jewish Artist Society and organized exhibitions.

Amid his busy social calendar, Victor took time to eat with the refugees and attend theater productions put on by amateur refugee theater groups. He brought the British ambassador to tour the refugee workshops. "Busy helping with shows given for our Children's

Milk Fund and finding partners for some of the Refugee businesses which are doing well," he wrote in his diary. "Have a good ladies tailor, a leather man and a soap manufacturer all doing nicely."

One of the refugees Victor hired was Theodore Alexander, a young man who had fled Berlin for Shanghai with his determined mother, who sewed the family gold and stock certificates into a mattress and carried the mattress with her on board the ship that took the family to Shanghai. Theodore carried a Torah scroll from their neighborhood synagogue, which had been ransacked by Nazis during Kristallnacht. On the rough sea crossing, when the pitching and yawing of the ship sent other passengers to the outside decks to be sick, Theodore's mother refused to let her three children leave the table, declaring, "We don't know when we will eat again or when we will have fun again." She ordered a bottle of Chianti. On landing in Shanghai, she turned to Theodore, who had just turned eighteen, and said, "This is one of the wicked cities in the world. I can't stop you from seeing girls, but make sure the next morning you get a shot" against venereal disease.

Theodore, who had studied English in Berlin, was hired by Victor as a purchasing agent, buying supplies for the Cathay Hotel and Sassoon's other properties. After fleeing the chaos and anti-Semitism of Berlin, Theodore marveled at Victor's and the Kadoories' power in Shanghai. He was inspired to pursue a lifelong dream and began studying to become a rabbi.

IN FEBRUARY 1937, as the refugees first began arriving, Horace Kadoorie decided to start a community group for Jewish refugee children, offering them food, medicine, and sports and recreation activities. The existing English-language schools in Shanghai couldn't accommodate them, and many were being left to fend for themselves. "Since their arrival in Shanghai the beauties of life were denied to them," an English-language newspaper in Shanghai reported. "Many children were living in alleyways . . . and some of them were bunked forty in a room. Their parents, being fully occupied trying to find work, had not sufficient time to take proper care of them and they were thus left to wander around the streets unattended."

By then in his midthirties, Horace had grown up in the shadow of his elder brother. Lawrence oversaw the family's growing investments in Hong Kong, leaving Horace to oversee the running of Marble Hall and assist his father in business. As the Japanese closed in on Shanghai and refugees poured off cruise ships docking at the Bund, Lawrence was riding out the crisis in the safety and calm of Hong Kong 700 miles to the south. Elly had put Horace in charge of some of the family's investments, like the Shanghai Gas Co., but Lawrence regularly chided his younger brother for his lack of business skills. "The staff are delighted at my appointment" as chairman of the Shanghai Gas Co., Horace wrote to his brother. To which Lawrence wrote back in the margin of the memo, "Good—I hope you will like your new job. You must learn something about gas."

As the crisis deepened, Horace was left behind to deal with his father and the increasingly menacing Japanese. If Horace was angry, he never showed it. The refugee crisis was his opportunity to establish an identity separate from his father and his brother, to establish that he was his own man. For years, Horace had taken such comments in silence, always responding politely to his brother and wishing him good health, bending to the will of his father and brother. Now he found his voice and responded to his brother with newfound assertiveness.

The plight of the refugees animated Horace in a way business never did. "A terrible catastrophe has come upon us all," he wrote to a friend in London. "I have lived amongst these poor refugees at Shanghai and have heard and seen for myself what they have and are going through." Concerned that the young refugee children arriving with their families didn't have any place to exercise, Horace started the Shanghai Jewish Youth Association, which sponsored recreation and sports as well as vocational courses in engineering, accountancy, stenography, and bookkeeping for young people. The group placed 300 young people in jobs. It provided medical exams and checkups, toys and books, a hockey league, and Girl Scout and Boy Scout clubs. When summer came, Horace funded an eighteen-day summer camp just outside Shanghai with swimming, tennis, and badminton, campfires at night, and a special dinner and party at Marble Hall. "It was a fine vacation for kids, most of whom had never been away from the hot, stuffy city," a teacher wrote. Horace visited every day with his secretary, inspecting the playground, dining room, and kitchen and meeting with doctors and teachers. "The average weight gained in 18 days during the first summer camp was 3.3 lb. per child," he noted.

In November 1939, Horace leased and renovated a building in Hongkew and hired teachers from the refugee community and from Shanghai's English-language community to staff what became known as the Kadoorie School. It included classrooms, a library, music rooms, and a gymnasium. He had Lawrence send him the guitar that had belonged to their mother, so teachers could use it in music classes.

He insisted all classes be taught in English using a British curriculum, because English was the dominant language of business and municipal affairs in Shanghai and would be more useful to the students than their native German. Aboard a ship sailing back to Shanghai from Europe, Horace met a Jewish refugee, Lucie Hartwich, who had been the principal of a school in Berlin. He hired her on the spot to be the school's principal. By 1940, 700 students were enrolled in the Kadoorie School, with several hundred additional students receiving vocational training in the evenings. Erich Reisman enrolled and in six months was fluent in English. Horace kept close track of the students. If a child became sick and had to be hospitalized—a frequent occurrence, given the poor sanitation and limited medical supplies in Shanghai—Horace sent the family a basket of fruit and flowers. He cosigned the report cards sent home. A reporter for a Shanghai English-language newspaper visited the school and pronounced it "a model institution." It was hard to believe, the newspaper wrote, that such a place existed "exclusively for refugee children."

"Many of the refugees literally cried when they saw what we were doing for their children," Horace wrote to his brother.

Writing to Horace from Hong Kong, Lawrence complained about the time Horace was spending at the school instead of running the Kadoories' gas company. "I feel that it will amply repay us if you are able to give your personal attention to" the family business, he scolded his brother. Horace shrugged off his brother's irritation, at one point responding to a lengthy memo from Lawrence on business questions by saying he was "kept so busy attending to refugees trying to explain local situation . . . that there was no time to write." His Shanghai office had become an "unofficial refugee center," but "it is a great life, anyway we are kept too busy to be worried," Horace said.

. . .

IN HIS MEETINGS WITH INUZUKA and the Japanese, Victor continued to play for time. "I now get pilgrimages from everyone from Tokyo," he wrote to a friend. "Yesterday an ex-minister of Finance and member of the House of Peers, today two members of the Diet.... I seem to be getting some influence in those quarters which is all to the good. But of course, there is always the danger of the army doing something foolish here if they get bloody minded." Japan hadn't formally joined Germany as an Axis ally, and Victor tried to persuade Captain Inuzuka and the other Japanese officials he met that doing so would be a mistake. "The line I have been taking," he wrote confidentially to a friend, "is 1) that the worst thing that could happen to Japan is an alliance between Germany and Russia; 2) the second worst thing would be for Japan to join the Axis and drive Great Britain into an alliance with Russia in the Far East against Japan."

Inuzuka was growing wary. He pressed Victor to intervene with Franklin Roosevelt and to steer American newspapers, which he believed the Jews controlled, to turn public opinion in favor of Japanese goals. The Jews, Inuzuka wrote, were like *fugu*, the Japanese puffer fish delicacy that was lethal unless prepared and served the right way: "It is very delicious but unless one knows well how to cook it, it may prove fatal to his life."

BY THE EARLY SPRING of 1939 there were 10,000 refugees in Shanghai. Victor and the Jewish leaders were overwhelmed. They appealed to Jewish organizations in Europe to slow the torrent of refugees but were told that the Gestapo was encouraging Jews to flee to Shanghai and Italian cruise lines were advertising that Shanghai was the only place where refugees could go without any formalities. The businessmen overseeing the refugee efforts, none of whom had any background in relief efforts or social work, began to bicker among themselves. Victor sent his accountant to investigate how his money was being spent and set up his own committee to supervise spending. He pleaded with international refugee organizations for money. "TWO HUNDRED AND FIFTY THOUSAND DOLLARS FOR HOSPITAL AS CONDITIONS VERY BAD AND DANGER EPIDEMIC," he cabled the American Joint Distribution Committee, which was overseeing worldwide efforts to help Jewish refugees trying to flee Europe. "MATTER IS URGENT . . . SITUATION MAY BECOME DESPERATE."

The refugees kept arriving; by May 1939 there were more than 12,000. They clogged the tenements of Hongkew, many of them living three and four to a room. Some turned to prostitution to survive. Families waited in lines for food. Diphtheria, scarlet fever, tuberculosis, measles, and typhoid were appearing in dormitories that Victor's International Committee and other groups had built to house the overflow of refugees. Victor feared disease would spread to the wealthier parts of Shanghai. He contemplated cutting the free meals he was offering to one a day to cope with the rising numbers. He complained to his confidante Emily Hahn that many of the Jews arriving now represented the "leavings" of Europe, the poor and the desperate.

In a meeting with Victor, Inuzuka proposed accepting even more refugees and setting up a colony for them in Pudong, across the river from the Bund. The plan went nowhere, but the thousands of Jews arriving in Shanghai served Japan's purpose. Keeping the Jewish refugees "under our influence . . . has a sort of 'hostage' sense," Inuzuka cabled to Tokyo. "As the war in Europe develops, to obtain a place of refuge for Jews . . . is a pressing necessity and their desire to obtain a place of safety at any cost obviously becomes more and more earnest."

In Tokyo, some of Inuzuka's superiors began to suspect that Victor was conning them. The sincerity of Sassoon is "doubtful" and "in view of the intrinsic nature of the Jews," relying on him to help Japan "is not readily believable."

Fueling their skepticism, Victor refused to speak out publicly in support of Japan. In July 1939, on his way to Hong Kong, he stopped off in Tokyo, where he told an immigration official he blamed Japan for the growing tensions with the West. If the Japanese continued to harass his factories in Shanghai, he said, he and many others would relocate to Hong Kong. Japanese police followed him for the rest of his trip. On a trip to New York, Victor told a radio audience that the Japanese people must soon "revolt against a power-mad military clique." Newspapers in Tokyo called for his arrest. Some Jewish leaders in Manchuria, under direct Japanese rule, pleaded with Sassoon to stop speaking out. In New York, the FBI assigned him two bodyguards, fearing he might be attacked by Nazi or Japanese sympathizers.

Nevertheless, Inuzuka insisted to his superiors in Tokyo that his "fugu" plan—keeping the refugees as hostages—was the right approach. He had looked Victor in the eye and knew he was sincere. "The Jews are clever at bargaining by habit of 2,000 years standing and do not employ such a foolish policy as to show their real intentions on their face. The stronger their desire is, the cooler attitude they pretend to take. . . . This fact will be admitted by any person who has an experience of association with the Jews."

In the late spring of 1939, Sassoon met with Inuzuka and said he and his fellow businessmen were running out of money to help feed and house the refugees. The numbers were growing. Germany showed no interest in slowing the exodus. Inuzuka, too, was under pressure by Tokyo to bring the situation under control. Three months later, in August 1939, the Japanese announced that no more Jews would be allowed into the city. There were 15,000 refugees in Shanghai, with 3,000 more en route. Those 18,000, Inuzuka and the Japanese agreed, would be protected.

IN SEPTEMBER 1940, Japan formally joined Germany and Italy to form the Axis powers, strengthening the hand of Japanese hardliners who were suspicious of Inuzuka's negotiations with Victor. The Nazis were turning their attention to the Shanghai Jews. Japanese officials demanded that Victor and the Jewish leaders give them a list of all the Jewish refugees—the same tactic the Nazis had used before rounding up Jews in Europe. "They are afraid of German Jews from Spain joining the Chinese, of German poison gas experts joining the Chinese," Victor confided to his diary. "They want [the] committee to find records of all German Jews in Hongkew!"

The Japanese-language newspapers in Shanghai, controlled by the military, began printing articles warning that the proliferation of Jewish merchants in Little Vienna undermined Japanese stores and businesses. Japanese officials invited members of the German Gestapo to Shanghai. The Gestapo visited Little Vienna and shut down a play written and performed by refugees that described the sufferings of Jews after the Nazis occupied Austria. Unless the play were stopped, "reprisals would be taken against Jews living in Germany and against Jewish émigrés here," a Shanghai newspaper reported.

The Japanese army "is behaving just as gangsters did in America during the days of Prohibition," Victor wrote to a friend. "Everyone has to pay for protection." A contingent of Japanese soldiers appeared at a cotton mill south of Shanghai that Victor owned and instructed him to sell them cotton at 40 percent of its value. They announced that if Victor rebuffed them, they would issue an order preventing him from selling his cotton to anyone else. "The Japanese here are queer," he wrote from his office in the Cathay Hotel. "The army are very annoyed with me and talk of having me 'dealt with,' which means kidnapped or bumped off whereas I am very popular now with the Older Government crowd and the Bankers and Industrialists in Tokyo who say that I have a clear mind, am absolutely correct in my views as a Britisher and must be cultivated as one likely to be a good friend of Japan when all the trouble is over."

At the Cathay, Victor tried to keep up spirits by showing spy movies to the dwindling foreign population. In Berlin, Hermann Goering denounced him as a "mischievous Hollywood playboy." Victor kept up hope that Germany wouldn't start a war and was disconsolate when Germany invaded Poland. A few months later he listened on the radio as France surrendered. "Bad news of French asking for terms," he wrote in his diary. In July 1940 Inuzuka demanded several meetings with Victor. He insisted that Victor invest in Japanese factories to show his good faith and ensure the safety of the refugees. "Told him no funds available," Victor recorded in his diary.

Inuzuka and the Japanese increased the pressure. They suggested that Victor merge his vast property holdings with a Japanese company to "safeguard" his real estate. Victor demurred and delayed a formal response. Finally, a Japanese officer arrived at Victor's office in the Cathay Hotel with two armed sergeants. Sassoon gave them a

ME VOILA THEREFORE WALKING A TIGHTROPE

proposed list of properties—rat-infested tenements and derelict houses. "This is an insult to Japan," the officer declared, jumping to his feet. "We will never forgive you."

A few weeks later the Japanese gave a private dinner for Victor at the Cathay. Over brandy, a Japanese officer warned that the mighty Sassoon empire would soon collapse unless Victor became more co-operative.

"Tell me, Sir Victor," he asked in a low voice, "why exactly are you so anti-Japanese?"

"I am not anti-Japanese at all," he replied. "I am simply pro-Sassoon and very pro-British."

Inuzuka, hearing of these meetings, had had enough. Victor Sassoon has "obviously elected to disregard the sympathy and the generosity hitherto accorded Jewish refugees by Japanese authorities." He was engaging in "anti-Japanese propaganda activities."

Warned that if he remained in Shanghai and the Japanese took over the International Settlement he would likely be arrested, Victor boarded a ship bound for India and left in the fall of 1941—just weeks before the attack on Pearl Harbor.

HORACE, COMMITTED to the Kadoorie School, remained. He took the family Rolls Royce, removed the luxurious car body, and replaced it with a makeshift bus body on the wheelbase to transport children to the school. With more and more children coming to the school, Horace reduced the number of meals he could feed refugee children to one a day. "According to the doctors this will cause much sickness and death, but we cannot help it," he wrote to Lawrence. "I am very worried." Food was running low throughout Shanghai, and food riots were becoming a "daily occurrence" across the city, Horace reported. Law and order were breaking down. "At 5 am today there was a kidnapping just outside the China Club in front of our gate," Horace wrote Lawrence. "As far as I can gather three or four people were kidnapped. We are indeed living in a pleasant neighborhood." A few days later the Japanese blockaded the street in front of Marble Hall. "A little boy of six was crying lustily outside our houses; he could not get home," Horace reported. "So, we took him in and gave him shelter for the night."

In September, Horace and Lawrence agreed to send Elly, who was seventy-six and ailing, to stay with Lawrence in Hong Kong, which both brothers considered safer. They sent Elly's doctor along as well and installed Elly in a suite at the family-owned Peninsula Hotel. "Should war be declared it may be that we will be separated for a long time and we will each have to act on our own discretion," Horace wrote to his brother.

IT WAS VERY EARLY Monday morning of December 8, 1941, in Shanghai when Japanese planes attacked Pearl Harbor, crippling the American fleet. Shortly before 4 A.M., Japanese soldiers armed with samurai swords boarded the one American gunboat on the Huangpu River, the USS *Wake*, and overpowered the crew. The Japanese shelled and destroyed the British ships nearby. Unopposed, Japanese marines in tanks and armored cars drove down the Bund. Trucks with loudspeakers drove past the Cathay Hotel blaring the news of Shanghai's capture. Soldiers distributed leaflets with caricatures of Roosevelt and Churchill clinging to each other in terror as Japanese bombs fell. British and American citizens were told to report to Hamilton

House, Victor's luxury apartment complex. It had been turned into the headquarters of the Kempetai—the Japanese equivalent of the Gestapo. "Enemy aliens" were issued bright red armbands to be worn in public. "A" stood for Americans, "B" for British. In the harbor off the Bund, in front of the Japanese consulate, a Japanese warship dropped anchor. It was the *Izumo*, one of the ships that Jacob Schiff's loans had helped build thirty-five years earlier.

Japanese army officers showed up at the Kadoorie School. They told Horace lessons would no longer be taught in English but in German. They evicted Horace from Marble Hall, placed him under house arrest, and took him to a private home owned by another foreigner, where he was told to look after two sick foreigners.

At the Cathay Hotel, Sassoon executives called Theodore Alexander and other clerks and ordered them to come in early to the company's business offices and start shredding and destroying business records, so they wouldn't fall into Japanese hands. As the clerks pushed files through paper shredders, they heard the stomp of boots in the hallway. The doors were flung open. Japanese soldiers entered and seized the offices, detaining the clerks. Captain Inuzuka arrived at the Cathay Hotel, took the elevator to the ninth floor, and strode into Victor's abandoned suite. As Japanese soldiers pored through Victor's papers, Inuzuka stepped behind Victor's desk and settled into his chair. He ordered Japanese photographers to snap a picture. He was the boss of Shanghai now.

Emaciated prisoners greet American soldiers liberating the
Japanese-run Chapei Internment Camp in Shanghai,
where the Kadoories were held prisoner.

7

War

As the Japanese troops occupied the Cathay Hotel in Shanghai and seized his brother Horace and put him under house arrest, Lawrence Kadoorie crouched in a military rescue boat cutting across Hong Kong's harbor.

Kowloon, the rural peninsula attached to southern China, lay behind him. Ahead lay Hong Kong Island, its waterfront bristling with office buildings and docks. Above the waterfront loomed Victoria Peak, 1,800 feet tall, a landmark. It was December 8, 1941. Near the top of the peak that emerged from the clouds, in Hong Kong's most exclusive neighborhood, lay Lawrence's house, exposed to Japanese artillery fire and incendiary bombs. Inside huddled his wife and two small children. In a surprise attack coordinated with their December 7, 1941, bombing of Pearl Harbor in Hawaii and their attack on the International Settlement of Shanghai, Japanese planes were dropping bombs on Hong Kong's airport. Japanese troops and artillery swept into the colony from China across the frontier border a few miles away.

Lawrence hadn't seen the attack coming.

In April 1940, the British Hong Kong colonial government had urged British women and children to board ships and evacuate to Australia. Lawrence's wife, Muriel, refused to leave and petitioned for an exemption. She was a young mother and pregnant with a second child. She wasn't going to abandon her husband. By early 1941, observers near the border with China could see Japanese columns positioning ammunition and supplies. British army reinforcements arrived in Hong Kong and began to prepare for an invasion. Lawrence and other British men were conscripted for military training. But Lawrence, like most of the British, considered Hong Kong impregnable and war unlikely. Unlike Shanghai, Hong Kong was a British colony. It was like India, part of the empire. Britain would never let it surrender. Unlike Victor, who had grown to mistrust and dislike the Japanese, the Kadoories still admired Japan. As children, Lawrence and Horace had vacationed in Japan for two months almost every summer with their parents. They admired the serenity of Japan, the delicacy of the scenery, the art and the architecture—such a change from raucous Shanghai. Their mother, Laura, had marveled at how rapidly Japan was modernizing. "Everyone agrees that Japan is coming on," she wrote in her diary in 1919. Elly had done business with Japanese companies, importing timber and helping beautify gardens around several Japanese temples, which won him the appreciation of the Japanese royal family. Like many British in Hong Kong, the Kadoories thought Japan more civilized and elegant than China, and even as they worried about Japan's expansion, they grudgingly admired the way Japan had defeated the Russians in 1905 and conquered Manchuria.

Throughout the 1930s, the Kadoories had become wary of Shanghai and poured more and more of their money 700 miles south into Hong Kong. Lawrence had been groomed by Elly to take over the business, and at forty-two he was by any measure a success. For more than ten years, ever since his father had named him chairman of China Light and Power, he had worked to bring electricity—and modernization—to Kowloon, the area north of Hong Kong that Elly had invested in with Robert Hotung and José Pedro Braga. For Lawrence, electricity—or as he preferred to call it, power—was the key to Hong Kong's future. "There are those who will remember the days when Kowloon went lightless by night" and roads were lit by kerosene lamps, he declared in 1940. But now, "industries ranging in size from the manufacture of joss sticks to the building of ocean-going steamers, as different in their nature as the preserving of ginger and the mining of lead ore, are today dependent on the power supplied by" the Kadoories. Lawrence designed and built a country home along one of Hong Kong's remote inlets, outfitting it with the latest technology imported from Europe, including an air conditioner that took up a corner of the living room and blasted cold air against the ninety-degree heat and humidity.

If Lawrence had a monument in Hong Kong, it was the Hok Un Power Station, the largest electrical generator in Asia. At a grand opening in February 1940, Lawrence told an audience of dignitaries and British officials that he had built the new power station "with an optimistic view of the future."

Twenty-two months later, Japan invaded Hong Kong.

Japanese troops surging across the border headed directly for Lawrence's pride: the new power plant. British officials had warned Lawrence that if Japan invaded, he would need to blow up the plant to keep it out of Japanese hands. China Light engineers living near the plant rushed over and set off an explosive charge, destroying the turbines. They stripped key parts and dumped them into the harbor to make the power station inoperable. Lawrence, who had been given military status and training in the weeks leading up to the invasion, was given passes and a small boat to rescue his father and the China Light personnel. As they finished their work, Lawrence hustled them back to the harbor, jumped into the launch, and headed back to Hong Kong Island to escape the advancing Japanese.

Stepping onto dry land, Lawrence drove in his Sunbeam Talbot up the switchbacks to his house on the Peak while a shell landed ahead of him. Two bullets ripped through the back of the car as Lawrence accelerated. "You saw everything happening, there was no means of stopping, you just went right up through it all," he recalled later.

Lawrence pulled up to his house, but it was empty. Panicking, he began pounding on doors of nearby homes, finally discovering his family hiding in the home of an aunt. Muriel greeted him at the door with their two young children: Rita, one year old, and Michael, still in his mother's arms. Muriel refused to leave the house. A Japanese artillery shell exploded close by. The Kadoories' Chinese nanny, carrying Rita, collapsed to the ground bleeding, hit in the face by shrapnel. The curtains of the house caught fire. An incendiary device singed Rita's clothes. The Kadoories piled back into the car and fled down the road to the home of a friend. They were the last family to leave the exposed Peak. On Christmas Day 1941, Hong Kong surrendered.

Eleven days later, on January 5, 1942, the Japanese ordered Lawrence and his family, along with all British nationals, to assemble in Statue Square, a small park in front of the headquarters of the Hongkong and Shanghai Bank along the Hong Kong waterfront. It was the same place where, almost fifty years earlier, a Hongkong and Shanghai Bank executive had come up to a forlorn Elly on a park bench and persuaded him to shift his money to the new bank in exchange for a generous line of credit that would allow him to keep his incubating business empire afloat. As he was hustled out of his suite at the Peninsula Hotel, Elly grabbed his morning coat as protection against the winter chill.

From Statue Square, the Japanese paraded the captured civilians in a "humiliation parade" to buses that would carry them to internment camps. Barbed wire lined the roads; dead bodies hung from the wire, shot by the Japanese. Emily Hahn, *The New Yorker* writer who had been Victor Sassoon's lover in Shanghai, witnessed the scene. "Think of it," she wrote later. Hong Kong's British elite "who behaved like kings, sitting as they did on that heap of coolie labor. Remember this. And then, suddenly, this!" Lawrence, his wife and two children, and his father were pushed onto a bus and driven to a group of college buildings hastily converted into an internment camp next to Hong Kong's prison at Stanley, on the other side of Hong Kong Island. The family's other great luxury hotel, the Repulse Bay, was just three miles away.

More than 2,000 prisoners were packed into Stanley Camp. Conditions were grim. The buildings making up the camp had been shelled during the Japanese invasion, and many were missing roofs or had holes in the walls. In the "married quarters" assigned to the Kadoories, thirty people shared a single shower. There were few beds. On a good day, Lawrence recalled, the rations were "one cigarette, a small tin of watery rice, some boiled lettuce and a little soup." The prisoners, who had always relied on servants, learned to cook, and to make, mend, and wash clothes. They gardened, put on plays and concerts, held religious services, and played cards. Lawrence joined a group of imprisoned government officials who tried to keep up morale by laying plans for a postwar government and budget.

Because of Elly's age, the Japanese excused him from many of the chores required of other prisoners. He walked around the internment camp in his morning coat, occasionally sitting under a tree and talking with other prisoners seated around him. One day an agitated British prisoner—a police inspector—ran up to Lawrence.

"I'm not going to Shanghai with your father," the police inspector announced. "Damn you! I am staying here."

"What on earth are you talking about?" Lawrence responded, bewildered.

"I understand your father is taking the whole camp to Shanghai with him," the inspector said.

Lawrence strode up to his father under the tree, demanding to know what was going on. Was he losing his mind? Elly said he had just been joking.

"If they are prepared to believe that I can do this, even under these circumstances, in the middle of a war, then my credit is still good."

The truth was that no one was going anywhere, and his credit no longer mattered.

BACK IN SHANGHAI, though the Japanese placed Horace Kadoorie under arrest as an "enemy alien," they still took no action against the Jewish refugees. Lucie Hartwich, the German Jewish refugee Horace had hired to be the principal of the Kadoorie School, was still considered a German citizen. Ironically, since Germany was an ally of

Japan, Hartwich could continue to run the school day to day. Nevertheless, with Victor Sassoon now in India and Horace under arrest, the refugees needed another champion. An American woman from Buffalo took on the role, and it turned out that her most important job, like Victor's, was to charm Captain Inuzuka.

After years of pleas from Victor, Elly, and others, the American organization overseeing worldwide efforts to help Jews fleeing the Nazis, the Joint Distribution Committee, finally agreed in the spring of 1941 to help in Shanghai. Seven months before Pearl Harbor, they sent American Laura Margolis to Shanghai to determine what they could do. Margolis was a left-leaning social worker from Buffalo. She didn't have much time for rich benefactors; in Buffalo she had often clashed with rich donors, believing they were just giving money to ease their conscience and always interfered with the work done on the ground by social workers like herself. Charities weren't run like businesses, she believed. The businessmen never understood that. In 1939, the Joint Distribution Committee had sent Margolis to Cuba to help Jewish refugees landing there. She was in Havana when the transatlantic liner *St. Louis*, carrying more than 900 Jewish refugees from Europe hoping to reach the United States, was turned away and forced to return to Europe, where many of the refugees were killed. It was an incident that became known as "the voyage of the damned." Shanghai had almost twenty times as many refugees—18,000. Margolis was determined that the tragedy that had befallen the Jews of the *St. Louis* wouldn't be repeated.

Margolis arrived in Shanghai in May 1941 after a two-week ocean voyage. The city appalled her. "I hated it," Margolis recalled later. "It was glittery, it was crowded, and it was Chinese dead on the street." She had arrived in Shanghai with a suitcase of practical work clothes and low-heeled shoes. She was told to buy new dresses, so she could attend parties at Marble Hall and meet the Kadoories, who were funding the refugee school. Victor Sassoon put her up in a room at the Cathay Hotel but then left on a business trip. "Nothing can ever touch them; nothing can ever happen to them," Laura said of the Kadoories and the Sassoons. Leaving Marble Hall one evening she almost stepped on a dead Chinese man in the street. "I would go to my hotel, put down the blinds, and go to bed, just to get all of the horror out of my head." Victor Sassoon, the Kadoories, and the Jewish businessmen trying to help the refugees had made a mess of things, Margolis concluded. Like the rich donors in Buffalo, they didn't know how to run a welfare agency. They were a "committee of billionaires." At several cocktail parties held at the Cathay Hotel, Margolis met Captain Inuzuka, who struck her as quiet and polite. With her assistant, she made plans to formally take over refugee efforts.

The Japanese invasion of Shanghai's International Settlement on December 8, 1941, woke Margolis in her Cathay Hotel room at 4 A.M. She looked out her window. The harbor was aflame. Margolis swiftly tore up her most important papers and flushed them down the toilet. She went down to the lobby of the Cathay Hotel and saw the Japanese guards with their bayonets. They shooed her back up to her room. Americans weren't allowed outside. They were prisoners.

After a few days, Margolis learned that Inuzuka had installed himself in Victor's office and penthouse. She asked to see him. He greeted her cordially and offered her tea. Margolis handed him a telegram she had received just before the Japanese invasion from the Joint Distribution Committee informing her that money had been deposited in a Swiss bank for her to use to feed and clothe the Shanghai refugees. With the banks closed and Margolis confined to the hotel, she was unable to get the money.

"You're an occupying power now," Margolis told Inuzuka. "Occupying powers don't like riots. Hungry people riot. You and I and our countries can be fighting out there, but I think it would be to your benefit to let me use the credit I have." Inuzuka agreed but told Margolis she couldn't seek help from Victor Sassoon, the Kadoories, or anyone who had worked with them. It was clear to Margolis that Inuzuka was "furious" at Victor now that his betrayal had been exposed. He had already arrested one of Victor's deputies who had stayed on in Shanghai. As Margolis prepared to leave the meeting, Captain Inuzuka made another request, reflecting his enduring belief that the refugees in Shanghai, and the Jews trying to help them, had influence over the U.S. government. He asked Margolis if she was Jewish. She said she was. He told her to contact Robert Morgenthau, the Jewish U.S. secretary of the treasury, and ask him to ease regulations that were freezing Japanese money in the United States. Margolis said she didn't know Morgenthau. She added that she appreciated Inuzuka's humanitarian help and quickly left his suite.

BY THE SUMMER OF 1942, Lawrence and his family had been in the Hong Kong detention camp for five months. His fellow prisoners turned to him for encouragement, and he prided himself on keeping up everyone's spirits, focusing on the future when, he was sure, the Japanese would be defeated. But the war was taking its toll. He was losing weight. Elly's health was deteriorating. An interned British doctor told Lawrence that Elly likely had prostate cancer. Lawrence sat with his father and helped him compose a letter to the Japanese camp commandant. Citing his "advanced age" of seventy-eight and his "weak state," Elly requested that he and his family be allowed to return to Shanghai and Marble Hall and spend the rest of the war there. He listed his "many important business connections with important Japanese interests both in Shanghai and Hong Kong" and noted that he had visited Japan many times. He described the honors he had received and the people he knew, including King Faisal of Iraq and Haile Selassie of Ethiopia. A few days later Lawrence was summoned to the camp commandant's office and was told he was being released. He should consider himself a "Canadian newspaperman." He was to buy tickets for himself and his family on a ship to Shanghai.

With no cash, and the banks under Japanese control, Lawrence borrowed money from an Indian friend and bought passage on a small ship carrying diplomats, their families, and other foreign nationals to Taiwan and then Shanghai. The ship had room for 600 passengers; more than 3,000 jammed aboard. The five Kadoories—three adults and two small children—squeezed into one cabin. They gave one berth to Elly, who was becoming sicker and weaker. A journey that should have taken three days took nine, as the ship zigzagged to avoid American submarines. Passengers weren't allowed on deck except in the evening. Lawrence changed his baby son's diapers outside on the deck and washed them out in saltwater.

Now that they were at war, the Japanese put up barriers and checkpoints across Shanghai. Initially, Chinese and foreigners alike believed that the occupation would be short-lived. The Japanese would be no match for an enraged America. But as the war dragged on and Japan won a series of victories, the Japanese tightened their grip. The Japanese issued the Westerners ration cards. Food was expensive, and a black market soon sprang up. Rich foreigners like Horace could get the food they needed. The Japanese were especially cruel to Chinese at the checkpoints. They made the Chinese get on their knees and extend their hands in front of them and hold that position for hours before they would let them pass—whether they were going home or going to work.

Lawrence's hoped-for "release" turned out to be a ruse. When the Kadoories arrived in Shanghai, Elly was taken to Marble Hall—which had been taken over by the Japanese—and was locked up along with Horace in the stables behind the house. Lawrence and his wife and two infant children were imprisoned in the Chapei internment camp, two sprawling three-story dormitory buildings in an abandoned university next to a chemical factory, seven miles from the Bund. Unmarried detainees were placed in one building, married families with children in the other. The Kadoories were placed in a dormitory room with another family, eight people jammed into a space designed for two students. Rain came through the broken panes of the windows. The families dragged in eight beds and shared them at night, propping them up against the walls during the day. Every morning and night they lined up for a count in the hallway. Showers—cold showers—were down the hall in a communal shower room. In a large, unheated room, the Japanese guards doled out small portions of rice—the size of a cigarette pack—and rotten vegetables. Inmates boiled the weevils they found in the rice and ate them for protein. One inmate recalled his father "coming in with a bowl of tomato peel, broken eggshells and rice" and offering it to his children for dinner. For meat, the Japanese scavenged from Shanghai's dog track the carcasses of dogs that had died or were too old to race. The prison cooks turned the dog meat into stew, piled it with garlic, and doled it out for lunch. The weight of one of the women sharing a cell with the Kadoories fell from 135 to 85 pounds. IF YOU DON'T WANT TO EAT THE FOOD DON'T EAT IT, a handwritten sign on the wall of the dining room read, BUT LEAVE IT FOR THOSE WHO MUST TO STAY ALIVE.

Muriel Kadoorie, Lawrence's wife, was twenty-six when she was imprisoned. She had been part of Hong Kong's upper class, the daughter of a well-to-do member of the extended Sassoon clan whose father was a well-known scholar. She played the piano and loved music. While she and Lawrence were courting in the 1930s, Muriel, strikingly pretty and lively, traveled frequently to Shanghai, staying at Marble Hall, going horseback riding in the morning and dancing with Lawrence at parties and nightclubs at night. She met the British businessmen who ran Shanghai, including one man who had a peculiar way of organizing his wardrobe. Every morning he would ask his manservant the temperature. If his servant answered "seventy-five," he would open a cupboard in his closet marked with that number, and there would be a complete set of clothes suitable for that temperature. With no delay, he was able to don suit, shirt, tie, and bowler hat.

Muriel was twenty-three when she married Lawrence in 1938; he was thirty-nine. She refused to leave Hong Kong and abandon her husband when the British ordered an evacuation of women and children on the eve of Pearl Harbor. Her mother, who had become a nurse, died in Stanley while caring for other detainees. She had been sharing her meager rations with sick patients, and Muriel believed that her mother's malnutrition had hastened her death. All the ambitions she harbored when she was younger were being wiped out by the war, Muriel told the other inmates. She saw her role starkly: "[T]o look after your babies, to do everything you possibly could and try and live as normally as possible."

The Japanese frequently punished the Kadoories and other inmates by denying them water for two days—a punishment that was especially cruel to the infants Michael and Rita. Bullying Japanese guards dished out fearsome punishments for minor infringements. A Chinese man who sneaked into camp to sell the prisoners food was caught, tied to a tree, and beaten there for three days in full view of the camp prisoners. Inmates could not sleep because the man moaned all night.

Lawrence became a leader of the prisoners, organizing meetings to discuss the future of Hong Kong to keep up spirits. He taught himself shorthand, so he could take notes at the meetings. Several times a week Lawrence joined the female inmates in the courtyard of the family wing of the prison to wash his family's clothes, nailing an empty perforated can to the top of a mop handle and using it like a plunger to wash his son's dirty diapers in a bucket of soap and water. He was the only man who took on wash duty. He told Muriel it was a good way to hear the gossip and news of the camp.

IN JULY 1942, several refugees living outside the Chapei camp approached Laura Margolis in a panic. German members of the SS had arrived in Shanghai, they said. They were planning to exterminate the Jews.

Their fear was justified. Captain Inuzuka had been abruptly transferred from Shanghai to Manila, a sign that the hard-liners in the Japanese military had gained the ascendency and were preparing to toughen treatment of Shanghai refugees. SS colonel Josef Meisinger, who had earned the moniker "the Butcher of Warsaw" by sending thousands of Jews to their deaths in Poland, was dispatched to

Shanghai accompanied by another SS officer. In August, Meisinger met the Japanese officials at the Japanese Naval Headquarters in Shanghai and laid out several options to "deal with" the "problem" of the 18,000 Shanghai refugees. The Japanese could send the Jews to Manchuria and elsewhere to perform hard labor to help the Japanese war effort. They could set up a concentration camp for "medical experiments" on a nearby island in the Yangtze River. Finally, Meisinger spread out a large map of Shanghai and outlined his preferred plan. In a few weeks, on the first night of the Jewish New Year, German SS units would round up Jewish refugees attending services with their wives and children at Shanghai's synagogues. They would seize the rest at their homes. The Jews would be marched through the streets to the harbor, loaded onto ships slated for demolition, towed out to the ocean, and sunk.

Japanese officials were appalled. After an internal debate they offered their Nazi allies a compromise. The refugees were still valuable hostages, but they needed to be kept under tighter control. They decided to create a ghetto in the Hongkew neighborhood—the poor, crowded district of row houses, outdoor toilets, and filthy alleyways that had become known as Little Vienna—where 10,000 refugees seeking cheap housing had settled. Over the radio and on the newspaper front pages, the Japanese announced the plan. "Due to military necessity," all Jews were ordered to move to a one-square-mile area in Hongkew. The terms "Jew" and "ghetto" were not used. The Jews were referred to as "stateless refugees" and the ghetto as a "designated area." Laura Margolis was put in a prison camp; her efforts to help the refugees ended abruptly.

Erich Reisman and his family, who had bought a house outside the "designated area," were notified that they had to move and that their home was being confiscated and turned over to a Japanese general. Erich had been attending the Kadoorie School, taking boxing lessons on the side. He and his brother, mother, and father moved into a single room in the new ghetto. More than 18,000 Jewish refugees now lived in Hongkew alongside 100,000 Chinese. The only greenery there, the refugees joked, was the green-painted benches on the sidewalk. Food rations were cut; the food and milk provided by the Kadoories and the Sassoons and then by Margolis and the Joint Distribution Committee were drastically cut back. Japanese sentries rolled out barbed wire across the streets and guarded the entrances and exits to the ghetto. Refugees needed a properly stamped pass to enter and leave. With Inuzuka gone, control over the refugees passed to another anti-Semitic Japanese officer, Sergeant Kano Ghoya. Ghoya referred to himself as "King of the Jews" and enjoyed making refugees wait in line in the broiling sun for hours to apply for a pass. He attended refugee soccer matches at the Kadoorie School and made the players parade in front of him. He slapped refugees whose behavior annoyed him. "He could be very mean, and if he caught anyone disobeying even the smallest rule, he would punish them harshly," one refugee recalled.

To help feed his family, Erich's father opened a vegetable stand in the ghetto and sent Erich and his brother to wait in line every day for passes so they could buy vegetables from Chinese markets outside the ghetto wire and bring them back for resale. The Kadoorie School remained open. Erich graduated and got a job working in a pharmacy, filling orders and delivering medicine. The money he made kept his family alive. No one knew what fate awaited them.

. . .

ALTHOUGH THEY HAD LOST most of their possessions and were now crammed into tiny rooms in the Shanghai ghetto, the refugees were better off than their Chinese neighbors, some of whom were also refugees from war zones farther north. The Chinese and the Jews couldn't communicate well with one another. Few of the refugees learned more than a few words of Chinese, and the Chinese didn't know German or English. But the simple fact that they could live openly astonished many of the refugees. Gerhard Moses, a refugee from Vienna, recalled: "In Europe, if a Jew escaped, he or she had to go into hiding, and here in Shanghai we could dance and pray and do business." He was amazed at "how people that were even more badly off than I was could feel sorry for me." Josef Rossbach, another refugee, kept a toy bamboo rickshaw he played with. A Shanghai rickshaw puller would come home several nights a week, bundle Josef and his own children into his rickshaw, and pull them around the streets laughing. "They don't know anti-Semitism," an amazed Leo Roth, a refugee, told his family.

VICTOR SASSOON WAS IN INDIA, beyond Japan's military reach. He raised money to help wounded British soldiers and traveled the world to speak on behalf of the Allied cause. Han Suyin, a left-wing writer sympathetic to the Communists, met him on board a ship sailing from Bombay to New York and dismissed him as haughty and arrogant. "He came on board with a limp, a monocle and that Shanghai brand of arrogance that now seemed almost a parody," she wrote later. With "monocled haughtiness" he announced to her, "We'll be back in Shanghai next year."

In a speech in Boston, Victor was more realistic, recounting the string of defeats suffered by the Allies in Asia since Pearl Harbor, the way in which the British and Americans had underestimated the Japanese military, and the capitulation of Singapore and Hong Kong. "They seem to know exactly what was going on in our territories, what we were doing, what we proposed to do and what problems they had to solve. We, on the other hand, seemed to know very little, if anything at all, as to what they were doing."

Victor predicted that the Allies would eventually win the war and the world would be ruled by a "Russian empire," a United States–dominated Europe, and an Asian empire "which will probably be run by the Chinese." The Chinese, Victor argued, having seen the success of Japan, would say to themselves, "If just learning a few Western tricks enables Japan to almost beat the United States and Great Britain, what a chance for China with 400,000,000 people. We used to rule the world and why shouldn't we rule again?"

"I think the Chinese are changing in their mentality," he concluded. "I think they have awakened, and I think the Chinese are going to base themselves on Japanese methods."

For now, however, the Japanese controlled Shanghai and had imprisoned Victor's top deputy and political adviser, Ellis Hayim, a member of the Baghdadi Jewish diaspora brought to Shanghai by the Sassoons starting in the nineteenth century. Hayim played a crucial role in feeding and housing the refugees. Now he was jailed in what was once Victor's showpiece, Embankment House, lying sick and unattended. An American journalist imprisoned with Hayim was released and wrote to Victor of Hayim's suffering. He quoted Hayim: "I stood up under these hardships for sixty days but am now breaking up after eighty-two days. For days I have been trying to get a doctor to attend to my fever, but they won't move a hand. A lot of good all my money does me. I never dreamed I would be reduced to living like the filthiest coolie." Hayim was so weak he had to be helped to the toilet and held by other prisoners. "He was down with what he said was malaria and his limbs were cramped from lying in his corner so long," the journalist wrote to Victor. "He was inclined to blame you for his miserable lot." Meanwhile, the journalist wrote, "the Japs amused themselves in that studio-atelier of yours, poring over the things you left behind."

Victor, reading the letter from the safety of India, was mortified. His despair over the future grew. He asked his other executives who had joined him in India what he was worth. They ticked off the money still safe in banks, the millions invested in the American stock market, factories in India, and his vast real estate holdings and investments in Shanghai.

"You can forget China," Victor said gloomily. "It's lost."

BY 1944, the Kadoories had been imprisoned for two years inside Shanghai's Chapei internment camp.

Elly became sicker and sicker. Lawrence found an old typewriter and wrote a letter to the Japanese commandant, asking that his father be allowed to die at home, surrounded by family. "My father, who is 80 years of age, is dying, and to see his eldest son and grandchildren would give him the greatest pleasure." Lawrence asked that the Kadoories be allowed to move back to Marble Hall and "be permitted to live together with my father during the last days of his life so that we may care for him and comfort him."

Lawrence was given permission to return to the house, where he saw his father for the last time in a small room above the stables, alongside their former servants. In August 1944, Elly died. Lawrence was permitted to bring his father's body into the house before burial. Shortly thereafter, the Japanese allowed the family to leave the Chapei camp and live under house arrest in the stables while the main house was prepared to become the residence of the puppet governor of Shanghai.

Before the Japanese invaded, Horace had bought a large piece of furniture that had a shortwave radio built into it. After moving back to Marble Hall, Lawrence would slip down to the drawing room late at night and, out of earshot of the Japanese guards, listen to the American Armed Forces Network. It was there he followed the progress of the American forces and, in August 1945, learned of the dropping of the atomic bomb that the American announcer said "would change the course of humanity."

A few weeks later, on August 20, 1945—his wife Muriel's birthday—American soldiers showed up at the entrance to Marble Hall. For the first time in nearly four years, Lawrence turned on the lights in Marble Hall. The war was over.

IN THE HONGKEW GHETTO, Erich Reisman realized the war was over because the Japanese guards manning the gates abruptly disappeared, leaving the barbed-wire gates open. Refugees and Chinese civilians spilled into the streets of Hongkew in celebration. "It was like Sleeping Beauty awakened from her sleep," recalled one refugee.

Erich and the other refugees ran through the streets, tearing down the signs that marked the borders of the "Designated Area," dancing alongside the jubilant Chinese. The American army marched into the city and hoisted American flags atop the buildings lining the Bund.

As the American soldiers headed north to what they had been told was the Jewish ghetto, they braced themselves for the horrors they had heard about in the ghettos and concentration camps in Europe. But in Shanghai, miraculously, they found more than 18,000 Jews who had survived. They had lived in filthy conditions and had eaten poorly, but no Jews had been intentionally murdered. Cut off from information for the past four and a half years, the refugees surrounded the Americans, clamoring for news of their relatives in Austria and Germany. Most of the refugees had not heard from their families since the Japanese takeover of Shanghai in 1941. "After Germany invaded Poland . . . letters from my family would come less and less frequently. The last communication I received was a Red Cross letter from my sister, dated November 8, 1942," one refugee recalled.

From the radio, from cinema newsreels, and from Red Cross officials, the Shanghai refugees now learned of the fate of European Jewry. Newspapers published alphabetic lists of survivors every week, which the refugees then took and posted throughout Hongkew. Each week, the refugees gathered to examine the lists, hoping that the names they sought would appear. "We sat lost in our thoughts, our own grief," one wrote. As the grim news rolled in, one of the Reismans' neighbors in Hongkew learned that nearly every single one of his relatives on both sides of his family, more than forty people total, had been killed. Two other women had lost every family member. "Everything we'd been through suddenly paled in comparison," a refugee wrote. "The hunger, the disease . . . the poverty, none of it mattered anymore. We were lucky. Nobody gassed us. We had our lives, but that was no cause for celebration."

AFTER ISSUING more than 4,000 visas to Jews from his office in Vienna, Ho Feng-Shan was recalled by his superior, the Chinese ambassador to Berlin, in May 1940. With Nationalist China trying to maintain ties with Germany and buy arms to fight the Japanese, the Chinese ambassador feared that Ho was antagonizing the Nazis. He accused Ho of making money by selling the visas. Ho denied the charge; nothing was ever proved. Ho was criticized for "insubordination." When the Communists took over China and the Nationalist government fled to Taiwan, Ho remained loyal to the Nationalists and subsequently served as Taiwan's ambassador to Egypt, Mexico, Bolivia, and Colombia. He never talked publicly about the Jews he had saved. After he died in 1997, his daughter pieced together the story and persuaded Yad Vashem, the Israeli Holocaust memorial, to honor him as one of the "Righteous Among the Nations" for his courage and humanitarianism.

Erich Reisman and his family left Shanghai after the war and settled in the United States, where he married and worked as an aircraft mechanic. His brother, Paul, married a Jewish refugee woman he met in Shanghai and settled in Israel, then South America.

After being arrested and interned in a Shanghai prison camp, Laura Margolis was sent back to the United States in a prisoner-of-war exchange in September 1943. She wrote a scathing report for the Joint Distribution Committee criticizing the efforts of Victor Sassoon, the Kadoories, and the "committee of billionaires." Years later, she acknowledged that she had been too harsh and that they had done the best they could under enormous pressure.

Victor Sassoon sent all his Jewish employees checks for three years' salary—the three years they had been unemployed and forced to live in the ghetto. Despite being forced to move to a small apartment in the ghetto, Theodore Alexander completed his rabbinic study and was ordained as a rabbi by a panel of Jewish refugee rabbis in Shanghai. He married a refugee he met in Shanghai, and the couple held their reception at the Kadoorie School with a band and dancing. In 1947, Theodore used the windfall Victor sent him to book passage on a ship to California. He took with him to San Francisco the Torah he had rescued from his destroyed Berlin synagogue and brought to Shanghai.

Captain Inuzuka was arrested by the American military in Manila, and preparations began to try him as a war criminal. But refugees in Shanghai and Jews in Manchuria stepped forward to defend him, arguing that he had protected them against efforts by more radical Japanese military officers and the Nazis to harm them, and had provided a haven for 18,000 Jews fleeing the Nazis. In his defense, Inuzuka produced a cigarette lighter inscribed to him by a group of Jews in Manchuria during the war, thanking him for his help. The Americans decided not to prosecute him. Inuzuka married his Japanese secretary, who had accompanied him to Shanghai and to meetings with Victor, and lived out the next fifteen years in a Tokyo apartment. In the hallway, near the entrance, he kept a framed photograph taken by Victor Sassoon of Inuzuka and Japanese military colleagues clowning and laughing at the Cathay Hotel.

Communist soldiers celebrate the conquest of Shanghai, 1949

8

"I Gave Up India and China Gave Me Up"

When World War II started, the British oversaw Shanghai's International Settlement. Now, as across Europe, the Americans were in charge. General Albert C. Wedemeyer, the American commander in China, moved into Victor Sassoon's suite at the Cathay Hotel. A delegation of twenty American soldiers appeared at Marble Hall asking that the Kadoories put them up. At Marble Hall, Lawrence's four-year-old son, Michael, pedaled his tricycle along the mansion's 220-foot veranda making airplane noises. An American GI carried him up to bed on his shoulder, shouting, "I am your B-29!" As the Kadoorie servants went to warehouses around Shanghai to reclaim the furniture the Japanese had put in storage, the Kadoories ate K rations with the Americans while Lawrence's wife, Muriel, played the piano and promised them a "curry lunch" once things got back to normal. Another relative would tap the barometer that showed the weather outside, look out at clear skies, and announce, "Now, boys, it is time to exercise your airplane!" On

September 28, 1945, Horace's forty-third birthday, the Americans sent 200 planes roaring over Marble Hall in salute, a way of saying thank you to Horace for his hospitality, and a reminder of why it was expected. "I feel it is most important to cooperate with the Americans in any way possible, as the more they become interested in China, the more they will understand the problems which face all businessmen out here," Lawrence told Horace.

The British consul general protested that he and fellow Britons were feeling slighted, so Horace and Lawrence invited several Royal Air Force members to live in Marble Hall as well and turned over a wing of the house to the British Consulate to host visiting VIPs. They opened another house the Kadoories owned to be the British consul's residence. The British commanding general asked Lawrence to show him the Chapei internment camp, where Lawrence had been imprisoned, and invited him to witness the signing of the formal surrender of the Japanese troops in Shanghai.

At a dinner that stretched until three in the morning with officers drinking and swapping war stories in Marble Hall's massive dining hall, Lawrence asked if he could hitch a ride on a British military plane to Hong Kong. He needed to see what had happened to his power station and the Kadoories' homes there. The British commander agreed if Lawrence could be ready to leave in three hours, at 6 A.M. Lawrence shook Muriel awake, told her to please look after the children and the house, and headed off to Hong Kong, leaving Horace once again to deal with the uncertainty of Shanghai.

Over the next two years, the two brothers communicated almost daily in memos and letters between Shanghai and Hong Kong, their scribbled comments in the margins and increasingly urgent tone reflecting the panic setting in as the Communists conquered China.

. . .

THE AMERICANS HAD LIBERATED SHANGHAI but quickly turned the day-to-day governing of the city over to Chiang Kai-shek and the Nationalist Chinese. Horace was determined to be a good and politically astute host, but he drew the line at billeting Chinese troops. When eighty Chinese soldiers showed up at Marble Hall demanding beds, he and Muriel shooed them away, then offered to hire half of them as watchmen and guards to smooth over any hurt feelings. It was a carryover of the colonial mentality that had always defined Shanghai. But the city was changing. Little noticed in the drama of the war, the Americans and the British in 1943 had agreed to end extraterritoriality, the rule that put all foreigners and foreign businesses above Chinese law. The International Settlement—with its Municipal Council controlled by the Sassoons and other businessmen, its own courts and police force, and a British military force to protect it—ceased to exist once the war was over. The bubble the Kadoories and the Sassoons had lived in since the 1840s disappeared. The Kadoories were part of Shanghai now, and for the first time in more than a hundred years, the Chinese controlled the entire city. The Chinese had become "very anti-foreign," Horace reported worryingly to Lawrence.

At 10:30 A.M. on September 23, 1945, Horace left Marble Hall to go to the Shanghai Gas Co. for the first time since the end of the war. He was still listed as chairman. All that remained were some rotten desks; the Japanese had looted the office as they retreated. His Chinese employees confronted Horace. They blocked him from getting into his company car, saying he was no longer entitled to a car when transportation was in such short supply. Horace summoned the top

Chinese executive to his office. The executive refused to come. So, Horace went to the executive's office. "I am not too grand to enter your room," Horace declared. "If you do not wish to enter mine, I am big enough to come to you." Horace reminded the Chinese "that we had all fought the war together and must right postwar problems together." His gesture quelled the dispute, and he got his car back. Returning to his office, he sat down and wrote worried to Lawrence in Hong Kong: The Kadoories' Chinese employees "were losing respect for their foreign co-workers." Soon they "will have no respect for us."

Lawrence urged Horace to win over the Chinese by socializing with them at Marble Hall. "Cultivate the friendship of all classes of Chinese officials and businessmen with whom you come in contact," he advised his brother. "Ask them to lunch and give them Baghdad chow. Father made many good friends with the Chinese and others through his invitations to Marble Hall."

For all its new assertiveness, the Chinese Nationalist government was unable to govern the city. Fuel was in desperately short supply. The railway system had broken down. Inflation was rising. Horace wrote to Lawrence, asking that he send him cases of the jam and butter that were unobtainable in Shanghai. The aid the United States was pouring into China via Chiang Kai-shek and the Nationalist government was being siphoned off by corrupt Nationalist officials. "China is such an uncertain country: continual wars, dishonest government and corrupt personnel from top to bottom," Horace wrote to a friend. "I am preaching optimism to everyone but, sometimes, I wonder whether I should believe myself."

In February 1946 Horace reported that battles between the Nationalists and the Communists were raging just sixty miles from

Shanghai. Rumors were swirling that the British might be forced to return Hong Kong to China, and that the Americans were going to abandon the Nationalists' cause. During World War II and the Japanese occupation, the Communists and Nationalists had agreed to a cease-fire in the civil war that started back in 1927 in Shanghai. Japan's defeat signaled their resumption of that war; Nationalist troops held key cities including Beijing and Shanghai. The Communists controlled much of the countryside. The United States prodded the two sides to negotiate, but by the fall of 1945, just a few months after Japan's surrender, Nationalist and Communist forces were fighting around the country. The real danger to Shanghai and the Kadoories was not the newly emboldened Nationalist Chinese arguing with Horace about who should take possession of the company car. It was the Communists, led by Mao Zedong. Horace—shy, sweet Horace—was on the wrong side of history.

VICTOR SASSOON HAD FEWER ILLUSIONS than Horace about what lay ahead in Shanghai. Landing in Hong Kong soon after the Japanese surrender, Victor told newspapers that while Chinese governments would come and go—emperors, republicans, Nationalists, Communists—they all needed foreign businessmen like the Sassoons to survive. "The Chinese are a hard-headed race aware of their own limited experience in international business," Victor told reporters. Chiang Kai-shek and the Nationalists should now "take the lead from foreign business interests" and guarantee "safe investments for foreign business enterprise," he said.

The Communists, of course, had no intention of dealing with the likes of Victor Sassoon. Victor knew this. He told Horace that he was waiting to see "which way the wind would blow" before deciding whether to even return to Shanghai. He didn't plan to visit Shanghai for another six months and wouldn't make any plans about whether to invest for a year or two.

In fact, Victor had already decided to abandon Shanghai. He sent his cousin and right-hand man Lucien Ovadia to Shanghai to start unloading properties. Buyers were few. The Cathay Hotel was a shambles. The Japanese had ripped out carpeting and room fixtures as they retreated. The hotel faced at least a year of repairs before it could re-open. Ovadia sold one office building and had a deal to sell the brewery company that Victor owned to the Bank of China, but it pulled out at the last minute. He sold several other properties for a fraction of their appraised value. When Victor finally returned to Shanghai, he began looking for ways to smuggle foreign currency out of the country and evade the customs agents the Nationalist government had posted at airports and docks. One night, a friend of his was caught trying to smuggle $31,000 by plane out of Shanghai. "Unnecessary, unjustifiably stupid," he raged in his diary. Soaring inflation was destroying the economy and the confidence of Chinese workers in the Nationalist government. In 1944, twenty Chinese dollars had bought one American dollar. By March 1946, the ratio was 2,000 to one. A year later, it was 12,000 to one. Four months after that, the black-market rate was a million to one. Victor's Chinese employees, including the staff of the Cathay Hotel, refused to take their wages in cash, insisting instead on being paid in rice, pieces of cloth, or almost anything else edible or wearable. Those who accepted cash demanded to be paid every three days.

One payday, with Victor short of the bundles of banknotes he needed to pay staff salaries, angry workers demanded an emergency meeting in the Cathay's ballroom. Victor entered a room filled with hundreds of grim-faced employees. Wearing a light-colored suit, he climbed onto the stage. Chefs armed with meat cleavers flanked him to provide protection. He stood behind a wooden Chinese table, hanging his cane off the edge. He braced himself with both hands curled into fists and stood straight to address the standing-room-only crowd. He assured them they would be paid in a few hours. The workers dispersed; Victor obtained the necessary cash and had it distributed to the Chinese staff; another crisis had been averted.

THE COMMUNISTS LAUNCHED their major offensive in early 1947 soon after Victor returned to the city. The U.S. military estimated that the Communists had the momentum to win. In a report to the Chinese Communist Party's Central Committee, an optimistic Mao proclaimed, "This is a turning point in history."

News of the Communist advance rattled Marble Hall. "Conditions in Shanghai are deteriorating," Horace wrote to Lawrence. Garbage collectors went on strike for three days, then workers walked off the job at Shanghai's electricity company. The city's trams stopped running. Riots and looting broke out when the Shanghai police refused to report for duty for two days. Horace reported that workers stormed into the offices of the Sassoons' longtime rival Jardine, Matheson and refused to let the staff leave until they were promised higher pay to make up for the galloping inflation. Horace invited British embassy personnel to stay at Marble Hall to provide "good protection," since the embassy provided armed guards outside the house. He distributed 2 million Chinese dollars a day in "tips" to the household staff to make up for the collapse of China's currency. "Our financial position is terrible," he wrote to Lawrence. "I am sick of this place." He started carrying a Luger.

Another blow came when Horace learned that, contrary to what Victor had told him, the Sassoons were selling their properties. Indeed, Victor sold the building that housed the Kadoories' office—something Horace and his staff discovered only when they were told they would have to move out. "The Sassoons are trying their best to get out of as many of their interests as they can in Shanghai," he informed Lawrence.

The panic gripping Shanghai increased tensions between the brothers. From Hong Kong, Lawrence lectured his younger brother about managing their Shanghai businesses better: "If you organize your day properly and refuse to see people except at definite stated times, I think you will find that you can get through the work considerably faster and with less effort than if you just allow people to come in at any time, as they have been doing recently," Lawrence wrote. In another note, he criticized Horace's generosity and worried that Horace was being duped. When a local newspaper reported that one of Horace's guests had been staying in Marble Hall so long that she was telling people she was the new owner, Lawrence exploded: "I do not like the idea of having a hysterical and silly woman of this type in my house . . . causing us to be a laughingstock." In the same letter, he criticized Horace, who had once dreamed of becoming an architect and took great interest in the family's properties in Hong Kong as well as Shanghai, for spending too much on the family's country home in Hong Kong and on renovating the Palace Hotel in Shanghai. "I asked you not to leave things in a muddle but unfortunately you did so." Lawrence urged Horace to start selling stock and property. Horace agreed but moved cautiously to avoid attracting the Nationalists' scrutiny or starting a panic in the Shanghai stock market.

The pressure on Horace was showing. To Lawrence's increasing consternation, Horace, who had nursed their father in his dying months under Japanese house arrest, began spending several hours a day searching for a tombstone for Elly's grave. He researched tombstones that could be imported from Scotland and the United States and sent Lawrence sketch after sketch of what the stone could look like, its design and inscription. With the Communists advancing, Lawrence—always less sentimental than his brother—told Horace to abandon the search and arrange instead for Marble Hall's staff to buy a local tombstone in Shanghai and place it on the grave. Horace bristled and continued to send sketches until it became clear that he wouldn't be able to import a tombstone and he turned the task over to his Chinese staff. He began to worry about what would happen to the Shanghai home he had shared with his father and brother since the 1920s.

The Nationalists' military position was collapsing. Thousands of Nationalist Chinese troops defected to the Communists; hundreds of thousands surrendered, and the Communists seized their American-made rifles and trucks. By the end of 1948, the Communists were massing in northern China, preparing to move south across the Yangtze River, and to Shanghai. Horace turned his attention from the fate of the Kadoorie companies to the risks facing Marble Hall and the Kadoories' museum-quality possessions. Horace owned one of the most valuable ivory collections in the world, which, prior to the outbreak of hostilities, he had entrusted to a French judge living in the Vichy French Concession. This judge, near the end of the war, turned up surreptitiously in the middle of the night asking Lawrence to hide a gold ingot on his behalf. Lawrence buried the gold in the garden. After the war ended, the gold was retrieved and returned to the judge. Horace inquired about his ivories. The French judge looked uncomfortable and said it would be very difficult to find them. Subsequently they turned up in an antique shop. Horace offered to buy the collection back but was rebuffed.

It seems, however, that the Kadoories' Chinese servants likely had contacts among Shanghai's powerful underworld. When Lawrence visited Shanghai, one of the Chinese servants came to him, agitated, telling him that a strange man was at the front gate asking for a Kadoorie. When Lawrence went out to see who this was, he was confronted by a large, muscular Chinese man with scars on his head and face.

"Are you Kadoorie?" he barked.

Lawrence nodded.

"You have an ivory collection in the city and your family has been very good to China. You will have the ivory collection back in the morning and we will kill the man who has them."

Lawrence said such an extreme measure was unnecessary. The next morning, the collection of six hundred ivories minus six pieces showed up on the veranda. An American naval rear admiral who was staying at Marble Hall offered to take the collection out of Shanghai on his flagship.

Horace's secretary, citing her own "intelligence sources," told Lawrence that Chiang Kai-shek and the Nationalists had "no control whatever over the people" and "the Communists have covered too much ground in China, and the early fall of Shanghai into their hands is more than possible." With Communist troops a few hours' march from the city, Lawrence ordered his brother to destroy their correspondence and all their business records for fear they might fall into Communist hands.

Horace attended a speech given by Victor Sassoon at the Shanghai Rotary Club. Victor was particularly gloomy. Not only were the Communists on the verge of victory in China, Victor declared, but the Soviets were eyeing the Manchurian territory that bordered the Soviet Union and China for a possible takeover. "If Russia declared war [on Manchuria] today she would have a walk-over" because the United States and Great Britain couldn't respond fast enough, Victor predicted.

"Sir Victor's speech was excellent, but I personally feel it would have been better not to make it," Horace told his brother, who was back in Hong Kong.

A few weeks after hearing Victor's pessimistic speech, Horace left Shanghai on a plane to Hong Kong. He brought his Chinese butler with him. "I need some summer clothes as I have nothing," he wrote to Lawrence on the eve of his departure. "Please choose something nice so that I can have it made immediately and not boil in my winter clothes." He assured Lawrence that his butler could quickly return to Shanghai when it came time to host parties again in Marble Hall.

Horace never made it back to Shanghai again.

VICTOR STAYED ON, and the bitterness he felt spilled out as the Communists closed in. "The Chinese don't like foreigners and they never have," Victor told a reporter. "They'll do business with us but only to the extent that it suits their purpose." And, "The Chinese is like a woman," Victor said. "The more you give her the more she expects.

And if anything she does against your advice turns out wrong, she says, 'why didn't you stop me?'"

By this point, many Chinese were fed up with Victor as well. A letter in a Shanghai newspaper written by a Chinese-American businessman declared: "It is in China that he made so much money. Instead of expressing gratitude to the Chinese people he curses us as a whole. . . . If we don't like foreigners, as he said, how could he stay in China for most of his life? The most unpopular person in China is not the American but is the person who never appreciates the kindness of others."

On November 28, 1948, Victor left Shanghai with a Pan American World Airways round-trip ticket, the return flight scheduled for the spring of 1950. He told reporters that he expected that Shanghai would be controlled by the Communists by then, but insisted, "the Reds will be doing business with the United States and the British Commonwealth" because they will need Western products. Of course, he would like to liquidate his own holdings, he told the reporter. "But who would buy them with the state China is in today? If you can sell any of my assets there, I'll pay you a tremendous commission."

FROM HONG KONG, Horace followed the deteriorating situation in Shanghai and the advance of the Communists through daily letters from his Shanghai secretary and the caretaker of Marble Hall. A few months after he had left, his secretary wrote to him that the tombstone he had fretted over for so long had been placed over the graves of his parents. Since neither Horace nor Lawrence was there to pay respects, some of the Chinese servants and office staff placed flowers on the grave.

Otherwise the news was grim. The Chinese servants at Marble

Hall frantically packed up furniture, carpets, and silverware, hoping to ship it to Hong Kong. The Communist People's Liberation Army launched their artillery attack on the city. "Dull thuds could be heard all over the city," Marble Hall's caretaker reported to Horace. Two pieces of shrapnel struck Marble Hall.

"There may come a period, before and immediately after a new regime comes in, when food may become very scarce," Horace wrote back. "Our thoughts are very much with you all in Shanghai. . . . I doubt very much whether this letter will reach you but anyway I can try."

On the Bund, Chinese Nationalist troops swarmed into the Cathay Hotel and set up machine gun emplacements in rooms overlooking the street, vowing to defend Shanghai "to the death." Three weeks later, Communist troops entered the city to little resistance. The Nationalists forced a few shots from the Cathay's windows, then surrendered. The Communist troops—mostly peasant recruits from the countryside—entered the lobby and gaped at the marble walls and elaborate furnishings.

Victor, living at the Ritz in London, was sitting in his lawyer's office in that city when word came over the news ticker that Shanghai had fallen to the Communists.

"Well, there it is," he said quietly. "I gave up India and China gave me up."

A few days later, Victor was attending a play in London when a man came up to him in the lobby during intermission.

"I stayed at your Hotel Cathay during my last visits to Shanghai," the man said.

Sir Victor smiled sadly and corrected him: "My former hotel, you mean."

. . .

SHANGHAI BEGAN ITS NEXT TRANSFORMATION. Contrary to Victor's prediction that the Communists would work with him and other foreign businessmen, the new rulers of Shanghai began a slow, inexorable takeover of the Sassoon and Kadoorie businesses. They seized immediate control of companies crucial to the functioning of the city, like the Kadoories' Shanghai Gas Co. Then, rather than immediately seizing private property and expelling foreigners, the Communists decided to squeeze as much as they could out of foreign businesses. They presented them with a never-ending series of tax bills, regulations, and worker demands. They refused to allow foreign executives to leave China until they met the demands. China had undergone a "century of humiliation" at the hands of capitalists like the Kadoories and the Sassoons. Now it was the foreigners' turn to be humiliated.

As he had when the Japanese were closing in on Shanghai, Victor Sassoon had fled the city and left subordinates in charge—this time his cousin Lucien Ovadia, who had been trying with minimal success since 1945 to sell Sassoon properties. Soon after the Communists declared the founding of the People's Republic of China, the Communist police informed Ovadia that even though he was a British citizen, he couldn't leave China without a police permit. That couldn't be issued until the Cathay Hotel and all of Victor's companies had paid all their corporate liabilities, including taxes, wages, and pensions. Ovadia was a prisoner.

First came the tax bills. The buildings Victor had built that defined Shanghai's skyline—the Cathay Hotel, Hamilton House, Embankment House—were assessed new tax bills of several hundred thousand British pounds (several million dollars in today's money), payable immediately, with interest of 1 percent a day. Ovadia said he couldn't pay it. The Communists said he should request foreign currency from overseas. Ovadia told Victor not to comply. Sending money was "out of the question," Ovadia insisted. It was "only just a matter of time before all foreign assets would be taken over." Ovadia proposed that a Chinese or another foreign executive take his place, so he could leave Shanghai. The Chinese refused.

Next came labor demands. The Sassoon companies employed 1,400 people—1,100 worked at the Cathay Hotel and at Victor's many luxury apartment buildings. Another 300 had worked for him as office staff. In the first few weeks after the Communists took power, the Cathay lost most of its guests. Within a few months, the tenants of the large apartments and office buildings—mostly foreigners—left as well. The company had no rent coming in to pay its workers. Under new regulations, the Sassoon companies were prevented from laying off any workers. Ovadia offered to turn over all of Victor's properties to the Communist government, essentially abandoning them so he could leave. The Communists refused Ovadia once again.

The stalemate dragged on. The foreign businessmen who had once lorded over Shanghai lived in fear. A British executive at Jardine, Matheson was put in prison for six days without a word of explanation. Two Communist secret policemen visited Ovadia in his apartment in the middle of the night and had him fill out a detailed questionnaire about his background and work history. Ovadia was forced to meet his Chinese lawyer in secret because the lawyer feared being seen with him.

·   ·   ·

IN THE WEEKS LEADING up to the fall of Shanghai, the caretakers of Marble Hall kept assuring Horace of the loyalty of his household staff and of the Chinese tenants in their other properties. Like Chiang Kai-shek's claims of approaching victory, these were illusions. Soon after the Communists marched into Shanghai, the Kadoories' twenty-two servants—cooks, gardeners, maids, coolies—formed a union and presented demands for higher wages. Tenants in several of the Kadoories' properties refused to move out. More than forty relatives of the Kadoories' servants moved into Marble Hall. "Conditions are not very bright, and one meets with nothing but pessimism from all people, both Chinese and foreign," the caretaker wrote to Horace in Hong Kong. The Chinese seized the building that had housed Horace's beloved Kadoorie School and turned it over to a Chinese textile company, removing the Kadoorie name from the facade.

Communist government inspectors descended on the Kadoories' remaining hotels—the Palace and the Astor House—and produced lists of "repairs" and "renovations" that would have to be made to avoid fines. The new tax bill on Marble Hall was five times larger than under the Nationalists. The Chinese manager of the Astor House Hotel berated Horace in letters, asking him to send him money to pay for the growing number of Communist government–ordered repairs, fines, and demands for back taxes. The manager then slipped a message through an intermediary to Lawrence Kadoorie in Hong Kong apologizing for his "rude telegrams and letters." He was "forced to do so," he said, otherwise he would be accused of "sympathizing with foreigners."

"Do not pay the money, as it will be money thrown away," he

warned Lawrence. "They will try to squeeze more money. Eventually they will confiscate your property."

The Kadoories had maintained contact with Madame Sun Yat-sen as the Communists closed in on Shanghai. She was sympathetic to the Communists, and Lawrence believed she could be helpful in a takeover. She declared herself "a member of the Chinese Revolution" and denounced the Nationalists and Americans as "reactionaries." As Horace scrambled to pack up Marble Hall, Madame Sun approached the Kadoories, asking them if she could hold a charity event at Marble Hall. Lawrence ordered Horace to accept. It was important, he felt, to keep channels open to Madame Sun until it became clear where she stood.

That became apparent in October 1949 when Mao appeared on the rostrum of the Forbidden City to declare the founding of the People's Republic of China to the crowds below. Madame Sun stood at his side. Any hope that she might look kindly on her three-decade relationship with the Kadoories evaporated two years later when a woman representing Madame Sun appeared at the front door of Marble Hall.

Madame Sun, her representative announced in 1951, wanted to "lease" Marble Hall for her Child Welfare Fund. She would turn it into a children's theater and clinic. The amount of the lease would conveniently cover the fivefold increase in taxes that the Shanghai government was planning to impose on Marble Hall. Marble Hall's caretaker sent news of the request to Horace and Lawrence in Hong Kong. Five days later, Madame Sun's representative returned demanding an answer. That same week, all foreigners on a nearby street were told to move immediately and given a few hours to clear out. In another part of the city, a group of German properties was seized. "I hope you have reached a decision," the caretaker wrote, noting that Madame Sun was "taking over many valuable properties in and around Shanghai and I am afraid unless you volunteer to consider a lease you may find the property more or less expropriated."

Horace rejected the offer. "Definitely against taking such a step," he wrote. "In view of the long association of our family with Shanghai, we should keep the building for as long as this is possible. Should conditions change for the better and we return to Shanghai, the premises would be invaluable to us."

Victor Sassoon harbored no such illusions. After almost two years of being harassed and prevented from leaving the country, Ovadia turned over all the buildings Victor Sassoon had built to the Communist government—almost half a billion dollars' worth—with no compensation. He was given an exit permit and a railway ticket to Hong Kong and ordered to leave the country within forty-eight hours.

The Jewish presence that had once shaped and enlivened Shanghai was being erased. In the old Hongkew neighborhood, Communist troops marched into the synagogue where Jewish refugees had worshipped during the war, and where Erich Reisman had been bar mitzvahed. There were just a few elderly Jews left in all of Shanghai; the rest had left for Israel, the United States, or Australia. The troops took out the Torah that sat in a cabinet on the wall facing east, toward Jerusalem, and carefully hung a portrait of Mao on the wall. The building was turned into a mental hospital.

The Kadoories were only delaying the inevitable. Madame Sun, now firmly on the side of the Communists, was determined to teach the Kadoories a lesson. "The eyes of the nation are on Shanghai," she declared in a speech. "We have become a symbol of the struggle against the dead weight of imperialism" and capitalism that had "ridden the backs of our workers and citizens." In 1954, after years of resisting Madame Sun's demands, Lawrence acknowledged that the fight to save Marble Hall was over. He agreed to "donate" the property to Madame Sun Yat-sen and her children's fund. Madame Sun said she wouldn't need any of the staff or furnishings that the mansion came with. The Communists put the Kadoories' furniture into storage and charged the Kadoories far more in storage fees than their belongings were worth.

Lawrence wrote a memo to his brother: "I feel we must consider everything we have in Shanghai as lost."

PART THREE

Exile and Return

Lawrence (left) and Horace Kadoorie in Hong Kong

9

The Reckoning

Lawrence Kadoorie watched the collapse of Shanghai and of his family's business empire from the safety of Hong Kong.

In September 1945, just weeks after the Americans liberated the city, Lawrence had left Shanghai and flown to Hong Kong on a British Royal Air Force plane. He was desperate to see what had happened to his home and to the China Light and Power installations. In Shanghai, he spent weeks pleading with British and American military officers to fly him to Hong Kong. He made it as far as Kunming in southern China and was catching a ride in a British army jeep to the British consulate when he snagged his trousers on a nail sticking out of a seat cushion. A group of U.S. soldiers driving by spotted him standing on the steps of the consulate holding his pants together, looking embarrassed and uncomfortable.

"Say, buddy, what's wrong?" one called out.

"If you had only one pair of pants, you'd know what's wrong," Lawrence shouted back.

"Oh, come on, get into our jeep."

Three-quarters of an hour later Lawrence was dressed in tan U.S. army fatigues. He made his way to the British air force base. The commanders were adamant. Borrowed uniform or not, Lawrence was a civilian and they weren't flying civilian passengers to Hong Kong.

"Could I be classified as freight?" Lawrence asked.

So, they sat him down in the back of a plane, in his American GI uniform, atop piles of Hong Kong's crisp new currency that would be used to replace Japanese occupation banknotes. It was a fitting entrance for the man who would help rebuild Hong Kong's economy.

Before the war, when they were young and single, Lawrence Kadoorie and his friends had joked that compared with Shanghai, with its all-hours nightclubs and dance halls and rounds of extravagant parties, Hong Kong was "the best-illuminated cemetery in the world." In September 1945, Lawrence wrote to his wife, Muriel, that Hong Kong was now the "most looted city in the world." The Japanese had stripped and burned all the wood for fuel. Piles of rubbish lay heaped in the streets. The buildings were shorn of window frames, doors, and floors. Lawrence walked past a grand piano abandoned in the road, its wooden casing gone, just its metal strings and inner workings remaining. When night came, he told his wife, Hong Kong turned "black"—the lights worked in only a handful of buildings, one of which was the Kadoories' Peninsula Hotel, which the Japanese had used as their occupation headquarters. The Kadoories' business headquarters in the St. George's building overlooking the harbor had been used by the Kempetai, the Japanese secret police. The courtyard had bullet holes where the Japanese had executed prisoners. Feral dogs wandered the streets. Hong Kong was filled with "thin and tired people." Thousands of homes were uninhabitable. In 1941, before the Japanese occupation, 1.25 million people had lived in Hong Kong. The population had shrunk to 600,000.

The war had battered Lawrence, too—four years of imprisonment in two prison camps, house arrest in a single room above the stables of Marble Hall, watching his father die without medical care. Attending a wedding in Hong Kong hosted by an Indian businessman, he told Muriel he hadn't seen "so much food for many years."

Yet the war was also a liberation for Lawrence. Now forty-six, married with two young children, he had lived his life under the shadow of other men: his father, Elly, who had derailed his career as a lawyer, brought him to Shanghai, then dispatched him to Hong Kong to run his companies; and Victor Sassoon, who loomed over Shanghai's business world with his wealth, connections, and parties. Now, in the aftermath of the war, Elly was dead. Victor was diminished, unable to sell his Shanghai properties and embittered by the way China, and history, had turned against him.

Lawrence still had assets. Thanks to his father's foresight, he owned a controlling interest in China Light and Power, the major electrical company in Kowloon. The Japanese hadn't looted Hong Kong's banks, so the Kadoories' Hong Kong money was still safe. Lawrence had acted heroically in the defense of Hong Kong. He realized now that his family had been wrong about Shanghai. They had been blind like other foreigners to the inequality, to the advance of the Japanese, to the rise of the Communists, to how it could all be taken away. If they were going to make Hong Kong work, Lawrence would need to be different from his father, different from Victor Sassoon, different from how he himself had been in Shanghai.

Victor provided a model for success in Shanghai—the brash and flamboyant wheeler-dealer. As a young man, Lawrence had enjoyed that life as well, relishing parties at Marble Hall, visiting nightclubs, horseback riding. His family had profited enormously from colonialism. In those days in Shanghai, for most foreigners, the Chinese didn't really matter. What mattered was success. Now the situation was different. China was no longer prostrate. A new and united Communist China was emerging across the border, able to send in troops and take over Hong Kong whenever it wished. The British Empire was in retreat. The future was uncertain. Staying in Hong Kong, close to China, would take fortitude. Victor had fled. The Kadoories had retreated, too, their grand mansion Marble Hall seized by a woman, Madame Sun Yat-sen, they had once considered an ally. The plight of the Jewish refugees—many of whom were now staying in a makeshift dormitory in the Peninsula Hotel ballroom as they prepared to sail to Palestine or Australia—and his own imprisonment reminded Lawrence how vulnerable his family was.

If he was to have any hope of rebuilding the family fortune and one day returning to Shanghai, Lawrence knew he had to operate differently—more low-key, more mindful of the politics that had almost destroyed his family. In Shanghai, Lawrence had lived with his father and brother in a mansion staffed with forty-two servants. Here in Hong Kong, he would pass up a chance to build a mansion on the Peak and move instead to a modest house in Kowloon—albeit one surrounded by homes and apartment buildings he also owned. He would save the Shanghai excess for the family country home tucked out of sight in the remote New Territories, a home so large that when the son of a family friend visited, he exclaimed, "What is this—a hotel?"

"If we sit down and worry, not only will no progress be made but everything will get worse," Lawrence wrote in a letter to Horace in mid-1946 after several months in Hong Kong. "If we go ahead optimistically, and in the belief that Hong Kong has a great future before it, we may be wrong and lose out; but on the other hand, if we are right, and I think the chances are we shall be right, we shall recover our losses and progress." For the two sons of Elly Kadoorie, Hong Kong, Lawrence declared, "may become another Shanghai."

AFTER HIS FLIGHT to Hong Kong in a British Royal Air Force plane, Lawrence moved into room 444 of the family's Peninsula Hotel. On Christmas Eve 1945, he sat down at his desk in his room and wrote a memo to the British colonial authorities with suggestions on how to rebuild Hong Kong, starting with how to revamp the tax system. He remembered how he had battled boredom in the internment camps during the war by drawing up plans for a postwar Hong Kong with a group of imprisoned colonial officials and businessmen. "Whilst interned I prepared a memorandum on this subject but unfortunately circumstances rose which rendered it advisable for this to be destroyed," he wrote dryly.

The British colonial government embraced Lawrence's offer to help rebuild the city. Together they embarked on a dizzying array of projects to get the city back on its feet. Lawrence was named head of a business-government committee cataloging Hong Kong's destruction and what it needed to rebuild: how many feet of lumber would be required, how much wiring, down to thousands of missing doorknobs—the world's largest shopping list. He counted bathtubs and water pipes that had been destroyed and needed to be replaced. He reported that 160,000 Chinese—10 percent of the Chinese population—had been displaced and lost their homes, along with 7,000 Europeans, including Lawrence, whose home on the Peak overlooking the harbor had been destroyed by Japanese artillery fire.

Three and a half years in a Japanese prison camp and the stunningly swift advance of the Communists on the mainland of China had changed Lawrence. Shanghai's powerful foreign millionaires, he concluded, had erred in ignoring the suffering of the city's Chinese residents and the gross economic inequality that was fueling revolution. It was perhaps the realization that he himself had lost so much, and that so much of the family fortune now stood at risk as the Communists advanced on Shanghai. The radical free-market outlook Lawrence had embraced in Shanghai yielded to one that at times looked more like the New Deal, with government stepping in to repair and rebuild the city. He backed government rent controls to stop Hong Kong landlords from profiteering and chaired a committee that drew up plans to build a new fire station for Kowloon, a new police headquarters, an immigration office, a new post office and mail-sorting station, a new abattoir for slaughtering pork, and a new mental hospital. Next, he tackled transportation. He oversaw the distribution of 300,000 questionnaires to Hong Kong's Chinese citizens asking them how to improve ferry service—the first time Chinese residents had been asked their opinion. He lobbied for construction of a bridge to connect Hong Kong Island with Kowloon. He raised money for a new business school at Hong Kong's university. He lobbied to hire better civil servants, paying higher wages than before the war to avoid the corruption that had eroded the support of the Nationalists in China. Few details escaped him. When schools resumed classes but faced a shortage of furniture, Lawrence tracked down a factory run by Chinese owners that could manufacture 200 to 300 school chairs and desks a day. "More got done in six months than in six years," he boasted.

The *South China Morning Post*, the local newspaper tied closely to the British establishment and colonial government, praised the willingness of the British administrators "to bring in men of different backgrounds and talents" like Lawrence. No longer considered an outsider, Lawrence was "born in Hong Kong and must be associated more positively with the 'local' men . . . responsible residents of all races and creeds . . . who regard Hong Kong as their home." A top British official clapped Lawrence on the back and in clubby tones declared: "It is nice to know that we have a voice like yours at the top of the tree." Muriel and the children moved down from Shanghai to rejoin Lawrence. They moved into a house built on land they had bought in the 1930s as they shifted money out of Shanghai. Their new address: Kadoorie Avenue.

While Lawrence was making Hong Kong his new home, he was assuring that the remaining fortune would never be imperiled again. He met with an Australian official looking to accept some of the Shanghai Jewish refugees to China. Lawrence took the official aside. "Australia's a young country," he said. "I'd like to make a modest investment." He handed the official, Alex Maisel, a parcel of Australian banknotes. "Would you invest this for me?" Lawrence urged Maisel to buy stock in growing companies and real estate near city centers and register the purchases under the Kadoorie name. He told Maisel he was especially fond of apartment blocks on street corners and small shops with apartments above. Industrious shopkeepers, he reckoned, would rent both so they could lock up their shops at night and go straight up to bed and open early in the morning.

Never again, Lawrence decided, would the Kadoories keep more than half their assets in China or Hong Kong. If the Communists ever threatened Hong Kong the way they were threatening Shanghai, Lawrence wanted to be able to "cut the umbilical cord" that tied the family to China and begin again somewhere else.

THE SASSOONS AND THE KADOORIES weren't the only business-men who realized that Shanghai was near collapse. Wealthy Chinese who had made their fortunes in Shanghai were similarly panicked. As China in the 1920s and 1930s struggled with how to defeat the foreigners who occupied portions of its major cities and dominated its economy, these ambitious young Chinese had turned their anger inward toward China itself rather than outward toward the foreign-ers. They seethed at the stagnation of traditional China and saw in Shanghai and the success of foreign families like the Kadoories and the Sassoons a blueprint for their own rise.

The Rong family, moguls of the flour and textile industries, were typical of this subset of the population. Their wealth had already made them targets of the Nationalists and the Japanese, but they knew that their circumstances could only get worse under the Com-munists.

The family was originally from the city of Wuxi, seventy-five miles to the west of Shanghai. In the nineteenth century, they had owned a company engaged in the traditional trading of silk cocoons. Rong Zongjing, a son of the family, decided to move to Shanghai in 1887, coincidentally a few years after Elly Kadoorie was sent by the Sassoons to China. Like Elly, Rong was a young man, just fourteen when he left home. For him, like Elly, Shanghai was a city of eco-nomic and business opportunity. Rong followed the path expected of him as the eldest son of a successful Chinese businessman. He apprenticed at local Shanghai banks and sent money back to his family. He then opened his own bank in Shanghai in partnership with his father and his younger brother. Four months later, his father died. At that point, Rong, twenty-three, stepped off the beaten path. Rather than return to Wuxi to take over the family business, Rong insisted on staying in Shanghai, where he believed his prospects were greater. One of his relatives was working as a comprador with this new British firm, Jardine, Matheson. Rong formed a business venture with him and began learning about Western technology and business practices. He expanded into flour mills and cotton manufacturing. In 1921, he moved the family company to Shanghai.

His brother urged Rong to choose a location based on "feng shui," the Chinese belief that a building should be constructed and sited in a way that harmonizes with the surroundings and brings good luck. Rong refused, choosing instead to put his headquarters in the International Settlement near the banks and Western companies lining the Bund. At another location, "the feng shui might be good, but the telephone service is no good," he told his brother. He started taking out loans with the Hongkong and Shanghai Bank, the bank founded by the Sassoons and bankers to the Kadoories, and continued to expand. To ship his products to China's interior, he negotiated bulk rates with the China Merchants Steam Navigation Co., which had been started with the help of Elias Sassoon. Taking his cues from the Sassoons, he opened a school in his hometown of Wuxi to train boys to work in his offices and factories, providing them with vocational training and then apprenticeships in Shanghai. A decade after starting his business in Shanghai, Rong was the city's richest Chinese businessman. Newspapers dubbed him the "Flour King" and the "Cotton

King." His industrial empire included ten textile mills and sixteen flour mills. He employed 31,000 workers. To signal his arrival, he moved into a large European-style mansion initially built by a Western tycoon and began to mingle with the Western business elite. On the floor of a hallway in their new home, the Rongs noted a decoration in mosaic tile installed by the previous European owner. It was unlike anything they had ever seen before: a Jewish Star of David.

As the Communists advanced on the city, the Rongs divided—as many Chinese families did. Several members announced plans to flee the country with what money they could and start up businesses in Thailand and Brazil. But Rong Yiren, the thirty-two-year-old in line to take over the family business, decided to stay. He believed that the Communists would need businessmen to rebuild China. He would be a patriot.

One of Rong's relatives came up with a third plan. He could lead an exodus to Hong Kong and establish business there. Though it was a British colony under British rule, it was next to China and would offer the chance to return if the Communists turned out to be reasonable. Hong Kong was in ruins, of course. It barely had electricity. But the Rongs knew Lawrence Kadoorie.

A representative from the Rongs led a group of Chinese businessmen from Shanghai to Hong Kong and approached Lawrence for a meeting. They explained how panic and disarray were sweeping through the community of Shanghai businessmen.

The Rongs and the other textile manufacturers had ordered new equipment from Europe in the optimistic days after Japan surrendered. Now they were prepared to divert delivery to Hong Kong and build a new textile industry there. They faced two problems. Hong

Kong was more humid than Shanghai, and the cotton-spinning mills would require reliable electricity to run air-conditioning to keep down the dampness that could ruin the cotton threads. The Chinese businessmen also worried whether China Light and Power, still recovering from the Japanese destruction, could supply enough power to run the mills. They had just scuttled plans to move to Taiwan because Taiwan didn't have enough electrical power.

"Will you give us electricity if we come to Hong Kong?" the Shanghai textile factory owners asked Lawrence.

"Definitely," Lawrence declared.

Lawrence was bluffing. He didn't have enough turbines even to supply his existing customers with electricity. Lawrence's engineers had destroyed many of the generators as the Japanese invaded; the buildings housing them had been abandoned and overrun with rats. But Lawrence recognized the boon that bringing the textile industry would represent for Hong Kong and for his own balance sheet. He contacted a heavy industry manufacturer in London and persuaded it to divert a turbine it had sold to a company in South Africa to him instead. Within three days, Lawrence persuaded the British military government that was still running Hong Kong to donate several sites in Kowloon for textile factories. He formed a joint venture with the Rong family. Lawrence would serve as chairman of the board of what would be known as Nanyang Cotton Mill, giving the company a British partner and access to banks and credit. Lawrence was betting on his Shanghai contacts at a time when it was unclear how Hong Kong would weather the Communist advance on the mainland. The bet paid off. By 1949, Lawrence was supplying electricity to 249 factories. The next year, he added 367 more, setting China Light and Power on its way to becoming the dominant—and the most wildly profitable—electricity producer in Hong Kong. Ultimately 100,000 people from Shanghai would arrive in Hong Kong, providing—along with the local Cantonese—the skills and economic infrastructure that would drive the city forward.

In Shanghai, Rong Yiren, scion of the flour and textile fortune, watched helplessly as the Communists seized his family's factories and property. He had decided to stay in China while his older brother went to Hong Kong and joined in partnership with the Kadoories. "One stays in China; one goes overseas. If there are no problems, then I can return," his older brother had written to him. But soon after taking over the city, the Communists began a series of political campaigns against Chinese businessmen. They targeted business owners for the "five evils"—bribery, tax evasion, theft of state assets, cheating, and theft of economic information. In first four months of 1952, more than 200 former factory and business owners committed suicide.

On a spring afternoon, Rong Yiren lined up in the ornate lobby of Victor Sassoon's old Cathay Hotel with dozens of other business owners gripping thick envelopes that held their confessions to economic crimes. The line stretched across the lobby to the bar where Victor had once held court and served his signature cocktails. Instead of white-clad waiters serving drinks, behind the bar stood soldiers in beige army uniforms and Communist officials in blue "Mao jackets." A banner above them read: LENIENCY FOR THOSE WHO MAKE THOROUGH CONFESSIONS AND EXPOSE OTHERS! SEVERE PUNISHMENT FOR THOSE WHO REFUSE AND THREATEN WORKERS!

A Chinese writer who witnessed the scene as a child recalled later: "People in that procession were in immense fear, eerily like the Jews in WWII"—a striking image considering the work Victor had done to save Jewish refugees.

The Communists were determined to erase the foreign presence that had humiliated so many Chinese and produced such poverty and inequality. The British-built Shanghai Race Club, where Victor raced his horses and entertained his friends, was razed and turned into a People's Park where workers rowed boats on a man-made lake. The buildings along the Bund, denounced as a "springboard for economic imperialism," were now occupied by Chinese officials and bureaucrats. Tourists no longer danced to the latest music from New York or London at Victor's showpiece nightclub Ciro's; they listened to traditional Chinese ballads and ethnic songs. Almost 200,000 residents of Shanghai were sent to the countryside to help farmers—and purge themselves of the stink of foreign and capitalist influence. The number of foreigners living in Shanghai shrank to fewer than 3,000—most of them African, Asian, or Latin American students from regimes sympathetic to the Communists.

At the Cathay, Rong confessed to illegal profiteering and pledged to help the Communists build socialism. Mao invited him to a meeting in Beijing and presented him with a slogan inscribed in Mao's own calligraphy: SEIZE LAW OF SOCIAL PROGRESS; TAKE DESTINY INTO YOUR OWN HAND. Rong was named a vice mayor of Shanghai in charge of industry. He had given up a family fortune but survived to begin again in Communist China. "He was like a brightly lit steamer in the darkness on a rough sea set on a course for its chosen destination," a Chinese writer recalled. If Victor Sassoon were still in Shanghai, the writer speculated, he would have appreciated Rong's instinct for survival and would have wanted to befriend him.

. . .

BY THE TIME A BEDRAGGLED and exhausted Horace arrived in Hong Kong from Shanghai in 1948 fleeing the Communists, Lawrence's fusillade of reforms and study groups had transformed the city. An American magazine declared that in contrast with inflation and shortages and civil war in Shanghai and mainland China, Hong Kong was now a "boom town."

Safe in Hong Kong after flying out of Shanghai with the family butler and a few clothes, Horace settled into the relative isolation of Boulder Lodge, the Kadoories' weekend home in the New Territories, rather than in the cluster of homes on Kadoorie Avenue in Kowloon. Lawrence named his brother chairman of the Peninsula and Repulse Bay hotels, where his experience overseeing the family's hotels in Shanghai and his fondness for design and fine food could be put to good use. Horace's last decade in Shanghai had exhausted him. Lawrence was clearly the leader of the family and enjoyed the spotlight. Government officials who met with the brothers believed that Horace wasn't as clever as Lawrence. Yet Lawrence insisted that he never made a business decision without consulting his brother, and the two shared a checkbook and breakfasted together most mornings, when Horace drove from Boulder Lodge to meet with Lawrence in his house on Kadoorie Avenue.

One morning in 1949, Horace stepped out of Boulder Lodge and spotted a new gardener working the flower beds. He called over his Chinese maid.

"Who is this?" he asked in his rudimentary Chinese.

"That's my nephew," the maid replied nervously. "He is a refugee from China." As the Communists consolidated power across China, more than 10,000 refugees a month from southern China were pour-

ing into Hong Kong, fleeing the Communists' takeover: businessmen, landowners, rich capitalists, supporters of the Nationalists. From
being the "most looted city in the world," Hong Kong became one of
the most crowded. The refugees crammed into squatter huts without
plumbing or electricity in the countryside and hillsides. They badgered relatives to hide them and protect them.

The new gardener working Horace's flower beds was named
Leung Chik. He had arrived the day before with his wife, two children, and some rabbits in a cage. Their aunt—Horace's maid—was
hiding them in Horace's garage. A farmer in southern China who
owned several small plots of land, Leung had fled the advancing
Communist armies with his family and six dollars in cash. Leung
Chik looked anxiously at the tall, shy foreigner in front of him—Horace
wearing walking shorts belted awkwardly above the waist, pale white
skin showing above black kneesocks, and black shoes.

Horace took a step toward him and motioned to his maid to translate. "I am a refugee, too," he said.

Just as the plight of Jewish refugees in Shanghai energized Horace,
so the plight of this new group of refugees fleeing China unlocked
a purpose that matched Lawrence's drive for business success. The
Hong Kong government, fearful that Communist agents were slip-
ping into Hong Kong with the refugees, were sending police to houses
around Boulder Lodge to make sure Chinese families in the area
weren't secretly harboring refugees. When the police stopped by on
one of their routine checks asking if Horace had seen any refugees,
Horace waved them away. "No, nobody ever comes here," he said.
Leung Chik moved out of Horace's garage and into a lean-to hut
nearby. He scoured the surrounding fields for cast-off vegetables to
feed his family. He arranged to become a tenant farmer, renting land

for ten years so he could grow vegetables on his own. When Horace heard of this, he summoned Leung Chik and his aunt and asked why Leung Chik hadn't just bought some land. Leung Chik pointed out that he had no money. Horace offered to lend him the money. "You can pay it back slowly, gradually, I don't care," Horace said. Visiting Leung Chik's farm, Horace scolded him for using charcoal for heat, saying it was too dirty. He ordered China Light to come out and wire the house for electricity. He gave Leung Chik a discarded table from the Peninsula Hotel, so his four children would have a place to study.

Leung Chik began bringing Horace other refugee farmers seeking help. Horace gave them money so they could buy farm implements and seeds. One Christmas Eve, Horace was driving along country roads when he spotted a fire that destroyed a nearby farm. The next day he visited the farm and offered the owner, named Fu, an interest-free loan to build a new house. He arranged to buy him pigs, chickens, and pigsties and paid workers to build a path to the village, so Fu could walk or bike there to sell his vegetables. Fu began a tradition of visiting Horace on Christmas Day to discuss how the year had gone and to pay his respects, as he would to a Chinese relative.

Horace began writing to British administrators about rural problems and was so persistent that they placed him on a commission to address the issues facing farmers in the New Territories. His letters reveal a steel that his shy demeanor never showed in public. Behind the scenes, Horace became a fierce advocate for farmers and refugees in the New Territories. He kept track of meetings between government officials and farmer organizations and scolded the government when it canceled meetings. He refused to be a rubber stamp approving agricultural policy. No matter was too small. He would go to government officials about dumping he saw on rural lands, about pollution produced by industrial waste, about cars driving too fast on country roads.

In 1951, Horace went to Lawrence saying he wanted to do more to help the tens of thousands of refugees trying to scrape out a living in the New Territories. He proposed a project to support farming. Lawrence didn't know anything about agriculture, but he knew that Horace had always been fascinated by the science of planting and that he preferred life outdoors to that in an office. Lawrence agreed to start with an investment of $1 million in Hong Kong currency—about $170,000 today. "If that makes him happy, I am OK," Lawrence told friends.

Horace formed the Kadoorie Agricultural Aid Association—the KAAA. Armed with the initial funding, Horace approached the Hong Kong colonial government with a model, known as microloans, that would become popular decades later. The Kadoories would give farmers loans of a few hundred dollars, enough to buy a plot of land, seeds and farm implements, plus two pigs and stones to build a pigsty. The colonial government would provide experts to teach the farmers efficient farming techniques like terrace farming that turned rocky soil running up the hillsides into productive land. The farmers would use the money the Kadoories loaned them to grow and sell their products, then pay back the loan with some of their profits or in seeds or food. The approach, Horace insisted, wasn't charity; it was the farmers helping themselves. The Kadoories would give each farmer enough money to get going. The government would provide expert knowledge. The farmers would do the work.

Politics fueled the urgency behind the program. The Communists had halted their advance at Hong Kong's border but could take over Hong Kong any time they wished. The surge of refugees meant that families and clans now lived on both sides of the border, which meant the Hong Kong–controlled New Territories were ripe for infiltration, spying, or political discontent. Helping the farmers could improve the political stability of Hong Kong. Tasked with rebuilding the center of the city, the government had no resources left to help. As he had in Shanghai during the war, Horace stepped into the breach. Soon signs were sprouting across the New Territories announcing roads built by the Kadoories, so farmers could commute to villages to sell their products and children could walk to school. The KAAA built dams and water tanks in scores of villages. Horace funded orchards and encouraged farmers to diversify by raising chickens.

Typical of the families Horace was helping were the Tsangs. They lived on remote Lantau Island, miles from the development of Hong Kong's business and factory districts. Their mother still rose at 4 A.M. to walk an hour to hand pump water from a well and then bring it back to the house for washing and to prepare breakfast. Before school, the children made the same trek to haul back water to irrigate the fields. The Tsangs claimed they didn't care about politics—but in fact they had been sympathetic to the Communists and had hidden Communist guerrillas during the Japanese occupation of Hong Kong. In the years after the Communists took over, the Tsangs said nothing to the British authorities as Communists moved back and forth across their fields, infiltrating Hong Kong from across the border. They adopted a studied neutrality. "We all drink the same cup of tea," the family's grandfather told his clan.

One day in the 1950s, Horace showed up at the Tsangs' farm. Accompanied by a Chinese staffer who translated for him, he asked: "What do you need? Do you need pigs?"

"No," the grandfather responded. His granddaughter stood shyly by his side.

"Do you need chickens?" Horace asked.

"No," came the reply.

"Do you need a cow?"

Again, "No."

Horace's assistant interrupted in Cantonese and asked Grandfather Tsang what was the matter. Why was he being so hostile?

"We don't know this *gweilo* [this foreigner]," Tsang responded. "I don't trust him. What does he want from us?"

"He doesn't want anything," the assistant continued in Cantonese as Horace looked on. "He is a very rich man. He owns a lot of things—the Peak tram that goes up and down the mountain, a cement company. He wants to help you."

"OK," Tsang said. "We will take some cement." He paused. "And some water pipes so we can connect the stream to our fields."

Horace gave the Tsangs a letter authorizing them to pick up cement from the Kadoories' cement company and a check for several hundred dollars so they could buy pipes to divert water from the stream to their fields. Over the next few years, the Tsangs borrowed money interest-free from Horace's KAAA to buy fertilizer and seeds, paying back the interest-free loan in six months with money they were now making from vegetables. They agreed to let the KAAA build a dam to improve irrigation of their fields. They began raising chickens. Before, they had often had to feed their children sweet potatoes because they couldn't afford enough rice. Now they had enough and joined a cooperative started by the Kadoories that shipped their vegetables on boats to market to be sold. Veterinarians from the

Kadoories' group visited their farm to examine their chickens and offer advice and antibiotics to increase their yield. "The Kadoories changed our lives," said the granddaughter who had witnessed Horace's visits.

Then came the pigs. Pork was the staple diet for the people of Hong Kong, and a booming market as the population grew. Horace and his agricultural experts believed that breeding pigs was the quickest way to prosperity. If each farmer were given four six-month-old pigs and kept them for eight to nine months, he would soon have piglets and could begin selling the pigs for meat, earning a steady income. Horace believed the farmers were clever enough to manage their farms and make money if given technical support and access to better-quality fertilizer, seeds, and animals. Raising pigs, Horace reasoned, literally allowed the farmers to see their investment grow.

Horace also launched research into eliminating the "swayback pig." Decades of malnutrition and poor feeding habits had led Hong Kong pigs to develop a deformity—a swayed back that reduced the amount of meat and made the pigs die prematurely. Horace funded research that led to a new strain of Hong Kong pig that yielded more meat. By 1962, Horace's KAAA had helped 300,000 refugees and lent $60 million, all of which was being repaid by the farmers on a steady basis and lent out again as microloans. Leung Chik built a company that processed 20,000 pigs a year. He then opened a Chinese restaurant down the road from his farm that served a variety of dishes—including pork from his pigs—and named it after Horace. "Horace doesn't eat pig—he is Jewish," Leung Chik told his family. "But he is very smart about pigs."

The farmers developed a saying: "The Kadoories know everything about pigs except the taste."

The Kadoories understood how the politics of their world had changed. The British Empire was in retreat. India had been granted independence. That wasn't an option for Hong Kong; the Communists had made it clear that they intended to reclaim it. "China has enough trouble on her hands to try and clean up the mess in her own country . . . for us to clamor for the return of Hong Kong," Mao declared as the Communists conquered the mainland. "Perhaps ten, twenty or thirty years hence we may ask for a discussion regarding its return." The Cold War pinned Hong Kong between communism and capitalism, the "Free World" and "Red China." The Korean War, which pitted American and Chinese troops against one another, showed how volatile the region could be.

Hong Kong's solution was to adopt a policy of wary neutrality when it came to the mainland. "The strength of our position in Hong Kong depends largely upon non-involvement in political issues," Hong Kong's governor declared. "This can be achieved only by maintaining strict legality and impartiality in any issues with a political tinge."

At the same time, there was a battle unfolding for the hearts and minds of Hong Kong's Chinese population. Many, like the refugee Leung Chik whom Horace befriended, had fled communism. The KAAA offered them a capitalist alternative to the land redistribution and persecutions taking place in their former homes. The British colonial government didn't want to provoke China. But officials could work quietly with the Kadoories to push programs that showed the benefits of capitalism and improved Hong Kong's self-reliance. "The best protection against Communism is to provide living conditions that are better than those in China proper," Lawrence declared.

Electricity became another battleground, and here Lawrence took charge. As Hong Kong's economy recovered and then began to grow in the 1950s, hundreds of thousands of Chinese residents still lived lives that often felt as if they hadn't changed in fifty years. Factory workers went home to villages and neighborhoods where darkness descended as the sun set. Electricity ran only along the main roads. Water had to be hauled by hand for laundry, cooking, chamber pots. The lack of electricity shortened the day, increased the risk of fire, made getting water harder, limited the hours children could study, and cut people off from the news or even exposure to the outside world. What few street lamps existed were lit by gas. Every evening at 5 or 6 P.M. men with long bamboo poles with flames at the top walked along the streets to light the gas lamps, returning in the morning to snuff them out, much as they had when Lawrence first moved to Hong Kong with his parents at the turn of the century. Fortune-tellers spilled onto the streets and told fortunes by kerosene lamps; children huddled around kerosene lamps to study. The leading cause of house fire was kerosene lanterns tipping over. So desperate were people for electricity that they stole it constantly, running wires from main power lines to their homes. Electricity was so expensive that those who had it often had a single five-watt bulb that they turned on only when necessary. Kwok Keung, a Chinese doctor, ran a popular herbal drugstore in the Yau Ma Tei neighborhood of Kowloon that was spacious but dim; the only bright area lay under a single naked bulb where he examined and treated patients. The torrent of refugees worsened the problems brought by lack of electricity. In 1953, a fire started by a kerosene lamp raced through a massive squatter settlement, making 50,000 people homeless in one night.

Lawrence had wired and brought electricity to the factories that were filling the streets of Kowloon and transforming Hong Kong's economy, producing textiles, toys, and cheap electronics. Now he brought electricity to the residential neighborhoods and villages that stretched from the busy industrial districts north to the border with China. Under the Communists, China was aggressively pushing a rural electrification program. Connecting to the electrical grid in Hong Kong meant its residents could use electric fans and better lights, refrigerators and other appliances like electric rice cookers. The Tsangs, whose remote farm Horace had helped a decade earlier, were still hand pumping water every morning from a well to irrigate the fields and cook and clean. Their nine children gathered around a single kerosene lamp at night to study. After Lawrence and China Light wired Lantau Island, the Tsang children could study anywhere, and the family expanded its pig operation. Four of the Tsangs' nine children went on to receive college degrees; the family grew up to include two doctors, a teacher, three farmers, and two businessmen. Lawrence's decision in the 1950s and 1960s to relentlessly increase the generation and distribution of power paved the way for air-conditioned movie theaters and well-lit shopping malls, elevators and escalators that climbed the city's ever-taller buildings, a dazzlingly bright skyline and bustling streets. It turned the wrecked and depleted city Lawrence returned to after World War II into "a neon-emblazoned outpost of capitalist modernity on the edge of monochromatic China."

Horace and Lawrence Kadoorie, declared an Australian publisher after meeting them, were the two most effective anti-Communists Asia had produced.

Lawrence called himself the last Victorian. He had been born in 1899, in the final years of Victoria's reign. He shared with the

Victorians the optimism of empire—that he knew what was best for Hong Kong and for the Chinese. Colonialism might have been in retreat and discredited—leaving a legacy of ethnic conflict and war in India, the Middle East, and Africa—but here in Hong Kong, Lawrence believed, the last outpost of the British Empire was succeeding. "There's a lot of good in colonialism," he told a magazine reporter. "It brought in education, it brought the post office, the banks. It brought in law and order. Take India: which is better, everybody killing themselves?" Lawrence was formal and courtly; he often came across as paternalistic and arrogant. Colonialism suited him. "There is no doubt that Hong Kong is run by an elite; it is," Lawrence declared. "I believe in this elite, and I think it's far better than Western democracy." When the Shanghai industrialists he had helped right after World War II were joined by a new generation of Hong Kong entrepreneurs and complained that Lawrence was using his monopoly position to charge higher rates than in other cities, he beat back calls to nationalize his electricity company. Many Hong Kong colonial officials were sympathetic to the protests. They complained that Lawrence was profiteering, that he badgered them with requests and lobbied them for concessions that benefited only himself and his companies. They pointed out that the farmers Horace helped in the New Territories soon became paying electricity customers of China Light. The Kadoories, one colonial official wrote, act like "Shanghai people in big limousines" operating with the "squeals of the privileged." Lawrence negotiated a compromise that permitted the government some regulation of electricity rates in exchange for a guaranteed rate of profit. To many who visited Hong Kong, Lawrence, like the city, was an anachronism. But it was an anachronism that seemed to be working.

Recognizing Lawrence's influence, the Hongkong and Shanghai Bank, the most powerful institution in Hong Kong, rivaling the colonial government itself, put him on the board of directors. It was the seat previously held for generations by the Sassoons. Lawrence's appointment represented the ascent of the Kadoories past their longtime rivals. Lawrence Kadoorie, too, had lost a fortune in Shanghai. But in Hong Kong, he was making it all back—and then some.

In China, by contrast, after a decade of rapid growth following their seizure of power, the Communists were embarking on a series of politically driven economic experiments designed to push the Chinese economy past Great Britain and rival capitalist countries. The Great Leap Forward, initiated by Mao in the late 1950s, aimed to turn every backyard shed and outbuilding into a factory and dramatically increase grain production through central planning. It caused a countrywide famine that killed millions. The full extent of the disaster wouldn't be revealed for decades, but refugees who escaped China for Hong Kong told horrifying stories of starvation and poverty to Chinese friends and relatives whose own economic lot was improving.

VICTOR SASSOON NEVER USED the return portion of his ticket to fly back to Shanghai.

As China fell under the control of the Communists, Victor traveled the world staying in hotels and at his new headquarters in Nassau in the Bahamas, where there were no personal or corporate taxes and where the mild climate, he hoped, would ease the now constant pain in his hips. Once one of the richest men in the world, he had lost an estimated half a billion dollars in buildings and companies when the Communists seized Shanghai. His cousin Lucien Ovadia saw the success Lawrence

Kadoorie was having in Hong Kong and advised Victor to keep the lucrative Sassoon properties he owned in Hong Kong and buy more. But Victor refused and sold his properties. He was done with China. "Victor always made the wrong decision at the wrong time in the wrong place," observed Maurice Green, who had worked for Victor in Shanghai and had moved to Hong Kong to start his own business.

In the Bahamas, Victor built a scaled-down tropical version of his one-time Shanghai empire. He bought a five-story pink office building he called "Sassoon House." He established an insurance company and other investment vehicles just as he had in Shanghai. Several of his former employees settled in the Bahamas to work for him. He often visited a camera store in Dallas, Texas, where he indulged his fascination with the latest gadgets and photography equipment. He spent tens of thousands of dollars visiting stud farms, attending horse sales, and studying breeds. He kept horse racing stables and trainers in London and in Ireland and spent the May-to-September racing season in England.

Now in his seventies, he stayed in touch with the two Soong sisters who had sided with the Nationalists. He met his old lover Emily Hahn for lunches when he was in New York, at the 21 Club or the Four Seasons. They talked about the changes they were reading about in China. "The Chinese are hating the Communists more every day," he wrote to her.

On one trip to New York, he suffered a slipped disk and was hospitalized, then forced to use a wheelchair. He persuaded the American nurse who had cared for him in New York to move to the Bahamas. Her name was Evelyn Barnes. Originally from Dallas, she was thirty, a petite blonde whose brisk efficiency impressed him. She described herself as a "Southern hillbilly" and described Victor to friends as younger than his years. They became a couple and gave parties for friends. Sitting on his huge terrace at his Nassau house from which half a dozen stairs led down to the beach and pool, he personally mixed the cocktails and always seemed in high spirits.

Victor rarely spoke about China, and when he did it was laced with bitterness and loss. One of Barnes's nieces, named Evelyn Cox, took a gap year before college to spend time with her aunt and Victor. The Chinese had put a bounty on his head, he told Cox. He could never go back. He spoke of the anti-Semitism he had encountered. He had given the best parties, he said, but he wasn't always invited to the parties thrown by others. Over dinner, he talked about friends who had escaped the Communist takeover by boat, with soldiers firing machine guns at them. Victor had escaped before the Communists arrived, but the Communists had seized his properties, and even those he sold hadn't fetched nearly what they were worth. Cox sensed Victor's melancholy. "His world had changed so much," Cox recalled. "He didn't have the kind of influence he used to have. I cannot imagine how he felt leaving Shanghai for the last time. . . . For all your hopes and dreams, what you had built, this whole thing you had thrown your life into."

In his late seventies, Victor married Evelyn Barnes, his nurse. Her family thought it was his way of thanking her for taking care of him and making sure she would be financially secure. Victor characteristically tossed it off with a joke: "I had to disappoint so many other women," he said.

Shortly before he died, Victor visited his lawyer in New York to adjust his will. As he walked out, he told his niece, "Darling, I want to tell you, I've left you some money, but I want you to make me two promises. First, don't ever put all your eggs in one basket. Second, don't ever invest in any get-rich-quick deals."

Later he added a third: "Promise me you will never go to China."

In August 1961, Victor suffered a heart attack and died at eighty. He was in the process of building a new house in Dallas. It had a gallery overlooking the front entrance hall, modeled on the one he had once built in his summer home in Shanghai.

LAWRENCE'S FATHER, ELLY, had built Marble Hall to underscore his power and prestige in Shanghai. Lawrence already owned the two best hotels in Hong Kong—the lavish Peninsula and the Repulse Bay—along with his enclave on Kadoorie Hill and a country mansion with its own beach. For his monument, he appropriately planned an office building. It would replace the old four-story colonial building with verandahs on the Hong Kong waterfront, where his father had started the business seventy years earlier and which had been the Kadoorie headquarters ever since. The new skyscraper would be Hong Kong's tallest building and sheathed in reflective bronze. It would have a private museum for the Kadoories' jade and ivory collections and a top-floor penthouse apartment for Lawrence's son, Michael, who, after being sent to Europe to finish his education, was returning to Hong Kong to be groomed to take over the business.

Construction started in the mid-1960s—just as chaos was enveloping China.

The Shanghai millionaire capitalist Rong Yiren initially fared well after confessing to his economic "crimes" in the lobby of the Cathay Hotel in the 1950s. The Communists had appointed him a vice mayor of the city in charge of industry. But starting in the late 1950s Mao toppled Rong and many others as he launched a radical attack on his opponents and all vestiges of "old China." Landlords were punished; intellectuals were humiliated. Shanghai itself became a target. Though it was China's richest city and its factories produced more than half the country's gross domestic product, the Communist leaders remained suspicious of the people who had grown up in the shadow of Marble Hall and the Cathay Hotel. At one point they even discussed moving the entire population to the countryside for "reeducation." When Mao launched the Great Leap Forward, it was a disaster, producing widespread famine. Many Chinese in the south survived only because relatives in Hong Kong smuggled them packages of food. Communist officials later admitted that 100 million people suffered from some form of persecution in the first three decades of Communist rule.

The Cultural Revolution was even worse. Following the disaster of the Great Leap Forward, China's other leaders sidelined Mao and began introducing economic reforms. Mao decided to strike back, unleashing the Cultural Revolution, which was designed to topple his opponents by mobilizing radicalized young people. Paradoxically, he chose Shanghai to headquarter his new struggle. It was away from his rivals in Beijing. His wife, Jiang Qing, had built a power base there with several radicals who supported Mao. They pushed aside and banished Rong Yiren and even cherished political figures such as Madame Sun Yat-sen.

The young Cultural Revolutionaries renamed streets and buildings. Nanjing Road, built by Silas Hardoon and home to the best shopping in China, was renamed Anti-Imperialism Road. The Huangpu River, which had brought ships carrying the Sassoons and other foreigners to the Bund, was renamed Anti-Imperialism River. Radical Red Guards scraped away the Cathay logo from the front of the hotel. They marauded through the city's cemeteries, including the Jewish cemetery where Elly and Laura were buried, destroying the tombstone that Horace had spent months designing. Demonstrators attacked the British consulate down the Bund a few blocks from the Cathay Hotel, storming into the compound and painting anti-British and pro-Mao slogans on the walls and the Queen's portrait. Around Shanghai, swarms of Red Guards, often middle school and high school students, attacked and beat more than 10,000 people, eleven of whom died. Another 707 committed suicide.

The Cultural Revolution spread to Hong Kong. It began as a strike at an artificial flower factory. Demonstrators surrounded the government administration building and recited lessons from Mao's Little Red Book. A general strike was launched in June. Rioting broke out; in total, fifty-one people were killed. There were 250 bomb attacks, and another 1,500 devices were defused.

Lawrence Kadoorie naturally sided with Hong Kong's British establishment and colonial government. When leftists called for a strike at China Light and Power to cripple the city, Lawrence kept his power plants open and fired the strikers. Construction of a new power plant continued without interruption.

The Kadoories' house in Kowloon sat up the hill from a school whose teachers supported the Red Guards. Lawrence and his family heard the demonstrations and chanting students every morning. The neighborhood was considered so dangerous that American embassy personnel living nearby were moved across the harbor to Hong Kong Island. People nervously eyed Hong Kong's border with China, wondering whether the Red Guards would come across the border and seize the colony. As the rioting escalated, Britain mobilized its army troops. British officials warned Lawrence that if Chinese troops crossed the border, British troops would be unable to defend Hong Kong for more than eight hours. Leaving the office one day in his Rolls Royce, Horace ran into an angry crowd of pro-Communist demonstrators blocking the street and waving flags. Shrewdly, Horace leaned out the window and offered to buy some of the flags. The protesters agreed and let him through.

Was history repeating itself? Was Hong Kong, like Shanghai, about to fall to the Communists?

Lawrence convened a meeting of the family, including his son, Michael, who flew in from Europe. They met in the family's temporary offices next to the still-unfinished skyscraper overlooking the harbor that was going up to house the Kadoorie headquarters. Twenty-four stories tall, it was already visible across the city. Two Boeing 707s stood ready to bring the bronze aluminum panels to Hong Kong that would sheath the outside of the building. But with the riots breaking out across Hong Kong and in China, Lawrence wondered whether construction should proceed. The specter of the Kadoories' flight from Shanghai and the millions they had lost hovered over them. The expensive cladding could be canceled, and the building finished in steel and concrete like other buildings.

"We can go to a normally clad building with a very much reduced cost," said Lawrence. "Look, I can't see the future, we don't know it any more than others. I have confidence here. But it's not enough just for me to have confidence." The decision would have to be unanimous.

The family agreed to go ahead. "Hong Kong is like a rubber ball," Lawrence said. "The more it drops, the more it bounces back." Construction had been taking place during the day. Lawrence ordered it to continue into the night. The cladding would need to be welded on, which meant arcs of sparks now flew from the building and the roof throughout the night. All of Hong Kong, Lawrence declared, will see that "Kadoorie is still building."

A few weeks later, Lawrence learned that the Americans had taken satellite photos of the border with China and spotted the Chinese People's Liberation Army advancing toward Hong Kong. The soldiers paused at the border. Rumors swept Hong Kong that China was preparing to invade. Michael contacted a friend at the American embassy and was given a closer look at the photographs. He reported quickly to his father. The Communists were building military installations, but they were facing the wrong way—not toward Hong Kong, to prepare for an invasion, but away from Hong Kong, to prevent rogue troops or Red Guards from trying to invade the city.

Hong Kong was safe, for now.

Chinese leader Deng Xiaoping (left) and Lawrence Kadoorie

10

The Last Taipan

As China fell, Hong Kong rose.

Every weekday at 8 A.M., two foreign luxury cars swept down the street from Lawrence's house on Kadoorie Avenue. After driving his Jaguar in from his country home at Boulder Lodge to have breakfast with his brother, Horace sped to his beloved Kadoorie Agricultural Aid Association up in the hills of the New Territories overlooking China or to his office at the Peninsula Hotel, where he examined new furnishings and decorations and discussed additions to the international menu. Lawrence's chauffeur drove the taipan in his MG sports car to the pier where Lawrence boarded the Star Ferry. He crossed the harbor and strode to the bronze-clad St. George's Building, the now-completed beacon of stability that had reassured Hong Kong during the 1967 riots. From his paneled, green-carpeted corner overlooking the harbor, he presided over the family empire of electricity, real estate, factories, trading, and finance. The Kadoories were Hong Kong's first billionaires. The packets of money they had sent abroad in the late 1940s with refugees to invest in Australia, the United States, and South Africa had blossomed into overseas office buildings and shopping malls. In Hong Kong, Lawrence had expanded the city's power grid and pushed projects as diverse as a harbor tunnel and, at Horace's urging, the importation of a hardier strain of pig. "Apartments are lighted by a Kadoorie-controlled utility and are often carpeted by the products of Kadoorie looms," *The Wall Street Journal* wrote in 1977. "The tunnel under Hong Kong harbor (linking Hong Kong Island and Kowloon and the New Territories) is a Kadoorie idea. And through a Kadoorie-funded agricultural program, much of the pork and chicken here bears the Kadoorie mark." Powered by Lawrence's electricity, spared any further political turmoil, Hong Kong boomed. It joined the "Asian tigers" of economic growth, embracing a mixture of free-market economics and colonial rule that improved education, expanded housing, and kept unemployment low. By the 1970s Hong Kong's per capita income was ten times higher than China's. It had the fifth-busiest port in the world; if it were a country, it would rank twenty-fifth globally among trading economies. Television, radio, and a vibrant press fed a creative and increasingly globalized population, a burgeoning tourist industry, and pacesetters in global fashion and film. Lawrence boasted that he effectively controlled 10 percent of Hong Kong's economy, as almost every factory relied on him for electricity, as did millions of residential customers.

Throughout the turmoil in China, even during the Communist-inspired riots in Hong Kong, Lawrence was careful never to say a bad word about China. China refused to recognize the "illegal treaties" from the Opium Wars that had turned Hong Kong over to the British, leaving open the threat that it could take over Hong Kong at any time. It didn't, because Hong Kong was useful. Like Shanghai earlier in the century, Hong Kong had become a window on the West. It offered a way for China to do business with Western companies and earn foreign exchange without capitalism infecting China. China needed a place where it could "do things which it cannot allow its people to do," Lawrence believed, such as deal with Western bankers and invest in property. "Our future relies on our being useful to China and that is the only reason we're here." He warned his fellow taipans against the arrogance businessmen showed in the 1940s. It was that kind of attitude in Shanghai that "brought down the Bamboo Curtain."

Lawrence kept alive what contacts in China he could. He continued to send money to the elderly servants in Shanghai who had once served the Kadoorie family in Marble Hall. He also sent representatives to informal meetings with officials at the New China News Agency, which was the unofficial Chinese embassy in Hong Kong. Publicly, Lawrence was unrelentingly optimistic about the future of Hong Kong and his belief that he would one day return to Shanghai. Among friends and people who visited him on weekends at Boulder Lodge, he sometimes dwelled upon the war years, the humiliating death of his father above the stables of the family mansion. Lawrence's favorite piece of music came from those war years imprisoned in Shanghai: Beethoven's Fifth Symphony, with its famous opening notes of "da-da-da-*dum*." Lawrence had listened to those notes almost every night in the waning days of the war, sneaking down from the room above the stables to the parlor of the Marble Hall. They were the notes the BBC used to announce its hourly broadcasts. The notes and the powerful music that followed, Lawrence believed, were the sound of fate knocking. The war, he believed, had been his fate and taught him how little he could control. In 1970, a newspaper asked Lawrence if it were true that he owned a computer the size of a room, and that after feeding into it all the relevant historical and political data, he already knew to the month when China would take back Hong Kong—or if that would ever happen. "I fear you have been misinformed about my powers and those of a computer," he replied. "Neither of us tell fortunes."

In China, the country lay in waste after the Cultural Revolution. The average per capita income of Chinese peasants, who made up 80 percent of the population, was $40 per year. Less grain was produced per person than in 1957. The technology in factories hadn't been updated since the 1950s. Colleges had been shut for a decade. From this rubble emerged a diminutive man in his sixties—just a few years younger than Lawrence Kadoorie—already hard of hearing and a chain smoker: Deng Xiaoping. A tough, veteran Communist revolutionary, Deng had climbed to the top of the Chinese leadership after 1949 and then been hardened by a purge in the Cultural Revolution that banished him to the countryside. There he nursed his son who had been paralyzed after being tossed out a window by Red Guards. Determined to rise again, Deng saw the economic "tigers" of Asia surpassing China—Japan, South Korea, Taiwan, Singapore, and even Hong Kong. Deng and his allies were determined to unleash China's potential and end their country's isolation by developing good relations with other countries that would share their technology and expertise with China. The thaw began in 1972, when President Richard Nixon visited China and began restoring diplomatic and economic relations. At the end of his visit, the Chinese looked for a place to sign the Shanghai Communique normalizing U.S.–China relations. They chose one of the few elegant places left in Shanghai—a ballroom of the old Hamilton House, a luxury apartment building built by Victor Sassoon in the 1930s.

By 1973, Deng was back in power and began rehabilitating many of the old Shanghai capitalists who had also been purged and sent into exile away from Shanghai during the Cultural Revolution—including Rong Yiren, scion of the Rong family, who had remained behind in Shanghai, risen in power, then been purged by the radicals. Meanwhile Rong's family members had fled to Hong Kong and set up business with the Kadoories. Deng tapped Rong to lead China's efforts to woo foreign investment and rehabilitate China's industry. He became known as Deng's favorite "Red Capitalist." Reemerging as well was Madame Sun Yat-sen, a living link to Shanghai's cosmopolitan past who had held charity balls in Marble Hall and then seized the mansion when the Communists took over. She noted approvingly that Lawrence had agreed to turn over Marble Hall without a legal fight or public battle and had always withheld criticism of China while other foreigners had denounced the Communist government. Suddenly the Kadoories had two friends in the leadership in Beijing.

Soon after Nixon's breakthrough visit to China, Lawrence was approached by a representative of the Chinese government asking if he would help them negotiate the purchase and construction of two nuclear reactors for China's first commercial nuclear power station. "You are familiar with building power plants with your work in Hong Kong," the representative told Lawrence. "We would value your help." A few years later, Deng would unveil the "Four Modernizations," a staggeringly ambitious program to rejuvenate China's economy with foreign help and to modernize agriculture, industry, national defense, and science and technology.

Lawrence had long dreamed of selling electricity to China. In the 1930s, he and his father had proposed building high-voltage electrical wires from Hong Kong to Canton, but China's political instability and the invasion of the Japanese had killed the plan. China now faced a stark reality. It didn't have enough power to run all the factories it planned to build. The phone call from Beijing opened a door for Lawrence. In February 1974, he held a secret meeting with the British governor of Hong Kong, Sir Murray MacLehose. He unveiled his plan. The Kadoories, who had first come to China on steamships and brought electricity to the rural New Territories, would now bring China into the nuclear age.

For Lawrence, this was fate knocking. For all his loyalty to Great Britain and his lifetime in China, Lawrence had never felt fully at home in either Shanghai or London. The Communists, of course, had driven him from mainland China. He thought he had found acceptance in Hong Kong in the 1950s as he made it his home and helped rebuild the city and was named to the board of the Hongkong and Shanghai Bank, the apex of the colony's business and social establishment. No British businessman in Hong Kong was as rich as Lawrence or owned a company as influential as China Light and Power.

He was wrong.

In 1967, as Communist-inspired riots raged in Hong Kong and imperiled its future, the Hongkong and Shanghai bank decided to diversify and broaden its base by buying an Arab bank, the Bank of the Middle East. The Middle East, too, was in turmoil; Israel's victory in the Six-Day War unleashed intense anti-Israel and anti-Jewish feeling among Arab governments and businesses. Fueled by this growing anti-Semitism, the Bank of the Middle East demanded that Lawrence—the prominent Jewish businessman—be removed from

THE LAST TAIPAN

the board of their new owners. The Hongkong and Shanghai bank had been founded by the Sassoons, and the Kadoories had long been customers and advisers, culminating with Lawrence's appointment to the board. But some in the bank had never stopped mocking the Kadoories' Judaism and venting anti-Semitic comments.

When the head of the bank approached Lawrence, who was the senior member of the board of directors, he agreed to resign, saying he didn't want to become an impediment to the bank's business. Privately, some officials at the bank referred to Kadoorie as "that dirty Jew."

Though his staff urged him to retaliate by pulling all his business with the bank, Lawrence closed only some accounts. He started a competing bank, but he continued to keep China Light's connections to the bank, arguing that if he shifted to another it would inconvenience millions of customers who weren't involved in the dispute.

Now with China opening, he saw an opportunity to prove his worth, expand his power, and restore the Kadoories as a bridge between China and the West.

Nearing eighty, the old lion prepared for one final act.

ON MAY 26, 1978, just five days before turning seventy-nine, Lawrence sat down in his room in Beijing in the Peking Hotel—the best hotel for foreign guests—and wrote in flowing script to British prime minister James Callaghan on Peking Hotel stationery. He had returned to China after more than thirty years.

"In the short time we have been here, and as an old China hand, I am impressed by the improvement in the standard of living," he wrote. "One senses that the people have a purpose and objective. Of course, given China's tremendous population, one cannot expect too rapid a change from what is now a bicycle economy into that of the jet age." Nevertheless, Lawrence predicted that there was a "good chance" the Chinese would indeed meet their targets by the year 2000 and be on the verge of becoming a major world economy.

Lawrence then made his way to Shanghai. He was uncharacteristically nervous. He had continued sending money to several Kadoorie servants, even after Shanghai fell, though it was unclear whether they had received the money during the Cultural Revolution. He had heard that several had been badly treated because they had worked for "foreign colonials." Lawrence asked to see Ling Ying, the servant he had been closest to as a young man, who had served as the Chinese caretaker of Marble Hall after Horace left. The Chinese brought Ling Ying, now an old man as well, to meet Lawrence, and the two fell into an embrace. Ling Ying was cautious. The two could meet privately, but everyone assumed the meeting was being secretly recorded. "Everyone is singing from the same hymn sheet," Lawrence told his son, Michael, later. Ling Ying was too scared to talk openly.

Lawrence was then taken to see the graves of his parents, Elly and Laura. He knew that the old Shanghai Jewish cemetery where he had buried Elly in 1944 no longer existed. The Red Guards had ransacked and destroyed it during the Cultural Revolution. Instead Lawrence was taken to a new "foreigners' cemetery." There was the gravestone that Horace had designed as Shanghai was being encircled by the Communists—or perhaps it was a replica. Neither Horace nor Lawrence had ever seen it, because Horace had fled Shanghai before it was erected. Genuine or not, the gravestone showed that someone in the Chinese government, even during the Cultural Revolution, and certainly now under Deng Xiaoping, cared enough to preserve the Kadoorie grave, believing that the connection with the Kadoories was worth preserving as well. Like Lawrence's order to continue construction on the St. George's Building in 1967 that sent a shower of sparks visible across Hong Kong, the gravestone sent a signal.

LAWRENCE RETURNED TO HONG KONG brimming with plans and ideas. He wrote to Callaghan renewing his plea for an ambitious plan to sell electricity to Guangdong Province, the Chinese territory adjacent to Hong Kong, and get British firms the contracts for the transmission lines. Callaghan's private secretary was cautious, writing to his boss that Lawrence "has proved to be an invaluable friend to this country. . . . However, we also need to avoid giving him carte blanche to commit the United Kingdom to schemes entirely of his own devising." Another official agreed, scrawling on a letter that "anything to do with China seems to develop irresistible momentum." But China was moving quickly to restore its ties to the West. It restored through-train service from Canton to Hong Kong and began direct plane and hydrofoil service between the two cities. Deng invited MacLehose, the Hong Kong governor, to Beijing. He reassured him that China was committed to reform and to opening the economy to foreign investment, and that Hong Kong investors should "put their minds at ease." The stock market soared. British officials might have been skeptical; Lawrence, the "old China hand," was convinced. "If Mr. Deng is able to hold the country to its present course over the next five years, I feel confident the impetus created will be such as to enable China's modernization program to continue under its own momentum," Lawrence declared.

But a bigger issue loomed. With China opening to the West and seeking to join the global economy, the 1997 expiration of the lease of the New Territories suddenly seemed very close. Hong Kong could become less of an alien threat—"a capitalist pimple on China's backside," as the Communists used to call it—and instead a lucrative addition to an economic superpower. China could take over Hong Kong peacefully and without fuss simply by waiting until 1997 when the lease ran out and Britain had to—legally—turn the New Territories back to China. It was impossible to imagine transferring back to China the 4 million people living there, the land that accounted for 80 percent of Hong Kong's territory, and all the infrastructure the Kadoories and others had built and expect the rest of shrunken Hong Kong to survive. The clock was ticking on Hong Kong, just as it had once on Shanghai.

As LAWRENCE PLOTTED IN BEIJING and Hong Kong, in London Margaret Thatcher led her Conservatives to victory and was elected prime minister.

It was a fortuitous turn of events for Lawrence. He was Thatcher's kind of businessman—direct, down to earth, an outsider who liked to think big. After meeting Soviet president Mikhail Gorbachev, Thatcher famously declared that Gorbachev was someone she could "do business" with. Lawrence was someone she could do business with as well. Thatcher admired the free-market economic policies that drove Hong Kong. She had first visited it two years earlier; it was a model of what she wanted Britain to be—low-regulation, low-tax, secured by the rule of law, and run by honest and efficient British administrators. Lawrence wrote Thatcher a congratulatory letter soon after she was elected, and they planned to meet three months later in her office at 10 Downing Street. Her aides prepared her for the meeting by describing

Lawrence as a "remarkable octogenarian who is thought to be one of the world's richest men . . . an Anglophile and a great China watcher. . . . He is a grand strategist. . . . He sees China becoming a major world political and economic force." Lawrence's plan was indeed a grand strategy. He wanted Great Britain to subsidize construction of a nuclear plant that would provide power to both Hong Kong and southern China. With the handover still eighteen years away, the plan would begin connecting the two and show China Hong Kong's value. The proposed contract would run well into the next century, long after the lease expired. It would show concretely that Hong Kong could be "a part of China under British administration" just as the International Settlement in Shanghai had once been a thriving commercial enclave in China run by the British. "If ping pong diplomacy can bring about a rapprochement between the PRC and the United States, then why cannot a nuclear power station . . . be a major factor in solving the problem" of Hong Kong, Lawrence mused.

Thatcher responded to Lawrence enthusiastically. In contrast to the caution of Callaghan, she slashed through with a pen a draft letter written by her aides, replacing polite and noncommittal language with enthusiastic support. She crossed out sentences characterizing the discussion as "most useful" and wrote that she had "enjoyed" it. She changed "as I have said before, the Department of Industry will continue its commitment to support your efforts" to "the exciting prospects . . . and opportunities which China offers us must be grasped. You have an inside track and I know you will not lose the initiative." Within months, Lawrence was in Guangzhou, the old Canton, which his father had dreamed of electrifying in the early part of the century. In negotiations, the Chinese brought out records of meetings Chinese officials had had with Elly in the 1920s. Lawrence signed an agreement to allow China to tap into the electricity generated by China Light and Power. In three months, electricity was flowing across the border. The idea "has been cherished by me for the past 50 years, and it is particularly pleasing that this has been achieved in my 80th year," Lawrence declared.

In some ways, the timing of Lawrence's nuclear gambit couldn't have been worse. United States investigators were looking at the accident at Three Mile Island, a partial meltdown of a reactor at a nuclear power plant in Pennsylvania in 1979, and halted construction of nuclear plants. A million Hong Kong residents would ultimately sign a petition opposing construction of a nuclear plant near Hong Kong on safety grounds. Lawrence dismissed the concerns. "Some people feel that a nuclear power station is dangerous, and that it should not be used near cities," he wrote in a memo. He disagreed. The proposed nuclear plant located along Daya Bay in China, just over the border with Hong Kong, would be the biggest foreign investment ever in Communist China, and powerful encouragement to keep China on a modernizing path. Thatcher then invited Lawrence to London to attend a state dinner in honor of Mao's handpicked successor, Hua Guofeng, who was visiting Europe for the first time. Lawrence was "very well impressed" meeting the titular Chinese leader, though Deng Xiaoping was already maneuvering to replace him. Lawrence found Hua "very well informed as to what is going on in the world" and eager to "preserve and maintain the prosperity that we now have, and to enlarge and help it to grow." At a private meeting with a senior Chinese leader in Guangdong, Lawrence was told that the entire Chinese leadership, including Deng Xiaoping, was eager to see the project succeed. "It could be the future of Hong Kong we are talking about," Lawrence told Thatcher.

In 1981, formal talk began between China and Britain about what would happen in 1997 when the lease on the New Territories expired. MacLehose, Hong Kong's colonial governor, believed that Hong Kong needed stronger representation in London. He suggested to Thatcher that she name Lawrence, already a knight, to become Hong Kong's first member of the House of Lords. It was a chamber with limited power. But the appointment would give Lawrence enormous stature in the eyes of Hong Kong residents and the Chinese government, and a platform to advocate for Hong Kong as the 1997 handover approached. Lawrence had won Thatcher's favor by placing huge orders for electrical equipment with British factories. She agreed to the idea, and in 1981 Queen Elizabeth made Lawrence "Baron Kadoorie of Kowloon in Hong Kong and of the city of Westminster." At the same time, the Chinese government named Lawrence to the "consultative committee" that would draw up the laws that would govern Hong Kong after 1997. Lawrence stood at the apex of both the Chinese and British governments as they negotiated the fate of Hong Kong below. "If it's in my interest then it's in Hong Kong's interests because if Hong Kong went wrong I couldn't stay," Lawrence declared. "I'm therefore working for Hong Kong to preserve the conditions that made it good for me to stay here." A Hong Kong Chinese newspaper dubbed Lawrence "King of Kowloon."

As China opened, more and more of its Shanghai history began to reappear.

In 1979, United States treasury secretary Michael Blumenthal stunned officials he was meeting in Beijing when he began to speak to them in Chinese—in Shanghai dialect.

"We know you are Jewish," an official blurted out. "But this is a surprise."

Blumenthal explained that he had been a refugee in Shanghai during World War II. He had attended the Kadoorie School and had learned Chinese from neighbors and in the odd jobs he had as a teenager.

"I can say more old Shanghai words than you," Blumenthal told his hosts in Shanghai dialect.

The Beijing officials quickly contacted officials in Shanghai. The story of the Shanghai refugees and the ghetto in Hongkew had been buried by the Communists. The Kadoorie School had been turned into a factory, the synagogues into mental hospitals or warehouses. Chinese families had moved into the apartments once occupied by the Reismans and others. Some of the doorposts still had shadows of the mezuzahs the refugees had nailed there—the small ornamental rectangular boxes containing a Hebrew prayer. But that was the only sign of what had happened forty years earlier. Blumenthal told Chinese officials in Beijing he wanted to visit his old house in Shanghai. That would be impossible, the Chinese said. The Chinese didn't know where it was; even most buildings on the Bund were still closed to foreign visitors. "I will show you where it is," Blumenthal announced. And so, on a side trip to Shanghai, Blumenthal walked a group of Shanghai officials down Chusan Road to number 59, through a dark hallway, and out into a dingy courtyard. He pointed to the second floor, a two-room apartment he had shared with his father and sister from 1943 to 1945. "It's been a long road from here," he said. Outside the building he took the Chinese officials to the site of an old movie theater nearby. "I used to go to the movies a lot, and dream," he said.

Peter Max, the American illustrator, returned to Shanghai and said he was hoping to find his Chinese "amah," or maid, who, he said, had first taught him how to draw. Michael Medavoy, now a Hollywood executive, announced that he wanted to make a movie about the Shanghai refugees.

Other refugees and children of refugees began to return, too, signing up for rigidly structured official tours of China and ducking away to visit their old tenement apartments in Hongkew. As part of the "Four Modernizations," Shanghai city planners had ambitions to redevelop the city and were considering leveling the Hongkew neighborhood and replacing it with skyscrapers and new housing. But with more and more refugees and tourists coming and asking to see the neighborhood, the Chinese realized the value of its history and laid plans to put up historical markers at Blumenthal's house and build a Jewish refugee museum in the old Hongkew synagogue.

Behind the scenes, China was also using the refugees to build an important military connection. In 1979, as China was opening to the world, it initiated a twenty-seven-day border war with Vietnam over a disputed boundary. Despite having a far larger army than Vietnam, China was beaten back and humiliated. The Chinese realized they needed to improve their ability to destroy Vietnam's Russian-made tanks. In meetings with the American secretary of state Henry Kissinger, the Chinese raised the possibility of buying American anti-tank weapons. Kissinger said that was impossible. But he pointed out that another country had had great success in defeating Soviet-made tanks—Israel, which had defeated the Arabs and their Russian tanks repeatedly in wars in the Middle East in 1967 and again in 1973. As the Chinese rediscovered the history of the refugees, they learned that Shaul Eisenberg, the billionaire head of one of Israel's largest companies and an international arms dealer, had been a refugee in Shanghai. Late one night in February 1979, an unmarked Boeing 707 took off from Ben Gurion Airport in Tel Aviv for Guangzhou, China, and then to a military base on the outskirts of Beijing. It carried a delegation of Israeli defense officials and manufacturers, led by Eisenberg. After a series of preliminary meetings with the Chinese, he returned to Israel with a shopping list—missiles, radar, artillery shells, and armor. He often traveled on Israeli air force planes, which had their blue Star of David insignias removed to keep their missions secret. Over the next decades, Israel became one of the top arms suppliers to China, and China became Israel's biggest trading partner in Asia.

IN HIS NEW POSITIONS in London and Beijing, Lawrence continued to push his vision of Hong Kong remaining under British control even if the Chinese formally took over sovereignty. He was careful to praise China's leaders, showing his preference for strongmen who could deliver stability that would be good for foreign investment and growth. "I think it's wonderful the way they have managed to control the country," Lawrence said in 1983. "That mass of people has to be controlled by a very tight hand if it's not to split into all sorts of factions." Hong Kong, he argued, could be useful to the new, emerging China. "China is at that period of its development in history when it wants the West close by," he told the Chinese. "It might not need it in 50 years but now it does need it and will for some considerable time." In a show of loyalty, Lawrence continued to invest in Hong Kong even as negotiations between China and Great Britain deadlocked over Hong Kong's future and many companies began switching their headquarters out of Hong Kong. That prompted the stock market and the value of the Hong Kong currency to fall. His company invested billions in construction of a new power plant in Hong Kong and continued negotiations to build the Daya Bay nuclear plant. He met regularly with Li Peng, an engineer and government minister who would soon be named China's prime minister, and other top leaders. Taipan-like, Lawrence pressed his political case to keep Hong Kong under British control even as he negotiated the terms of the largest foreign investment ever in China.

But Deng Xiaoping had other ideas, and so did the British.

Deng was flexible about economic reform and eager to have the country do business with Lawrence. But he was adamant that China would reclaim Hong Kong by 1997. In preparation for a crucial meeting with Deng about Hong Kong's future, Thatcher received advice from Lawrence and other business leaders. But when Thatcher met with Deng in Beijing and floated the idea of Hong Kong continuing under British administration, Deng dismissed it immediately. He bluntly informed her that if China wanted, it could seize Hong Kong later that day. Leaving the talks, the normally composed Thatcher stumbled on the stairs—a sign many in Hong Kong took to mean that she had been rattled and upset by Deng's obstinacy. The Hong Kong stock market plunged and the Hong Kong dollar, the bedrock of the city's economy, fell in value. Ultimately, the Chinese imposed a plan they had developed for Taiwan years earlier. Known as "one country, two systems," it preserved British legal and economic rules for fifty years, as Lawrence wanted, but made it clear that Hong Kong would be ruled by China. Indeed, while the British consulted Lawrence regularly about how to deal with China, the Chinese placed him, as a foreigner, only on the "advisory" commission that was drafting the official document that would govern Hong Kong. The actual drafting was done by Chinese businessmen loyal to Beijing whom the Chinese saw as the future of the city. Lawrence was a useful conduit to British businesses in Hong Kong, the Chinese felt, and the Chinese relied on him to pass along concerns of the foreign business community. But the power was firmly to be in Beijing's hands and in the hands of the Chinese politicians, officials, and businessmen who would be running Hong Kong after 1997.

In London, Lawrence faced defeat as well. Fearing an influx of Hong Kong Chinese after the 1997 handover, Britain's Parliament passed a bill restricting the ability of Hong Kong residents to immigrate to Britain. Chinese residents of Hong Kong had traditionally been considered British subjects, as the city was a colony. In 1981, however, Parliament effectively turned them into second-class citizens who, in 1997, would become Chinese nationals. The British passports that millions of Hong Kong residents carried when they traveled were to be stamped with the gold letters "Hong Kong" on the front; their rights to immigrate to Britain or even seek help from British embassies overseas were sharply curtailed. It was an issue that was far more important to the Chinese residents of Hong Kong than to the British residents like Lawrence who already had British citizenship. But Lawrence—whose own father had faced opposition when he tried to get British citizenship in the 1920s—was enraged by the changes.

Donning the ermine cloak of a member of the House of Lords, the new "King of Kowloon" rose in Parliament in London and spoke passionately against the new rules. They give "an impression of rejection; a feeling that—at this important stage of our history—Britain is 'distancing' itself from Hong Kong—that we are losing our 'Britishness.'" The Chinese residents of Hong Kong are "not seeking refuge or the right to live and compete with your working population," he told the House of Lords. The only thing Hong Kong citizens were seeking was "the assurance that Great Britain, a country they have come to trust, will not let them down."

Lawrence listed all the Hong Kong companies forming joint ventures with China. He emphasized that he himself, when building the biggest power station in Hong Kong, had created 7,000 British jobs by ordering British equipment. "Great care must be taken," Lawrence warned, otherwise Hong Kong would become "a dead city buried in the pages of history."

Despite Lawrence's pleas, the bill passed.

As he had in 1949 when he lost everything in Shanghai, and again in 1967 when Hong Kong was threatened by the Cultural Revolution, Lawrence faced a choice: Stay or leave. He decided to stay and adapt. With many still nervous about the agreement turning Hong Kong over to China, Lawrence welcomed a top Chinese official to his Castle Peak Power Station and hoisted the Chinese flag. He abandoned his long-cherished belief in Hong Kong's unique importance as a bridge between an advanced West and a developing China. Instead, Lawrence embraced China's emerging self-image in a speech that could have been written in Beijing: "Europe has reached a plateau. The United States and Russia face each other with long-range ballistic missiles." China, by contrast, "offers a new field for development, a world power in the making." Hong Kong could be regarded as "the child of China, the son sent to Western school to absorb a foreign education." Now, he said, "That son returns to his parent with learning gathered from Western contacts. He is a good son and desires to help his father and his father has that understanding necessary to bridge the cultural gap existing between two civilizations."

Lawrence believed he was following prudent business strategy, no different from so many other foreigners who were flattering China in the hope of getting a piece of China's business. When Lawrence had returned to Shanghai in 1978 after thirty years, China's economy and wealth lagged far behind that of Hong Kong and the West. Now it was catching up. Soon the size of its economy would surpass Great Britain and would rank second behind the United States. For the Chinese, Lawrence's change in tone signaled what they had long sought—being treated as equals, discarding more than a century of colonialism and humiliation that had infected relations between China and the world. After the speech, Lawrence returned to his office, where he kept a tattered brown-and-white stuffed Humpty Dumpty doll on a leather chair behind his vast oval desk. It had been left behind years earlier by his son. He kept it around, he said, "to remind me that Humpty Dumpty took a great fall."

A MONTH AFTER giving his speech, Lawrence was invited to Beijing to meet Deng Xiaoping. It was only the second time Deng had agreed to meet a foreign businessman.

The two men joked about their ages. "Between us there is more than 160 years of wisdom," Lawrence said. "Hong Kong people should listen to us." Deng sought out Lawrence's son, Michael—age forty-four and next in line in the Kadoorie dynasty—and vigorously shook his hand.

In the formal part of the meeting, Deng praised Lawrence's billion-dollar investment in the nuclear power plant. "You had the guts to come and invest in China, to take the risks when other investors were afraid and hesitant," the Chinese leader told Lawrence. "That is a friendly act. We appreciate that."

Lawrence responded enthusiastically. "I am very pleased to do something for China," he said. "I hope that our cooperation will continue along the road we have established."

Deng turned to the aides seated beside him. "When I met Lord Kadoorie it is like meeting an old friend even though we have never met before."

The Daya Bay project, Deng said, "is a marvelous thing. . . . It is going to be an economic bond between the mainland and Hong Kong and contribute to stability and prosperity in Hong Kong and give confidence to the people in Hong Kong."

Deng paused and leaned toward Lawrence. "When will the plant be commissioned?"

"The first unit is planned for commissioning in October 1992," Lawrence responded, "and the second in July 1993."

"How old are you?" Deng asked Lawrence.

"I am eighty-six," Lawrence replied.

"I am eighty," Deng said. "You are six years older than me." Deng made a quick calculation. "By the time Daya Bay is commissioned, you will be ninety-three and I will be eighty-eight. I hope we will then hold a celebration party together."

Lawrence beamed: "Certainly!"

And yet despite Lawrence's wealth and status, the tremors of China's rise and reemergence began to buffet him. By 1989, Deng Xiaoping's post-Mao reforms were stalling. They produced high unemployment, high inflation, conspicuous inequalities, and a demand for political changes. University students began to protest, and hundreds of thousands gathered in Tiananmen Square joined by ordinary citizens calling for an end to corruption and more democracy. The Communist leadership was paralyzed.

Lawrence had learned not to underestimate the Communists or their determination, and his response to the 1989 Tiananmen massacre and its aftermath showed both his political savvy and his moral compromise—a dilemma that more and more Western businesses would face as China grew in power and retained tight control over its people. Lawrence met Pan Guang, an influential academic with close ties to the Chinese government, and asked him bluntly: "If I invest, and there are students in the streets, can the government keep control?" Pan assured him the government would keep control.

When Deng ordered troops into Tiananmen Square to crush the uprising and imposed martial law, hundreds of thousands of Hong Kong Chinese marched to protest the crackdown. As Western governments and many companies criticized the crackdown and halted trade and investment, Lawrence was uncharacteristically silent. Li Peng, the Chinese prime minister who encouraged the crackdown and was being reviled as the "butcher of Beijing," had been a key ally in approving the Daya Bay nuclear project. Work on the plant continued. When Lawrence finally spoke out, he defended Deng and the Chinese leadership. "Too much democracy is not the best thing for this area of the world," he said. "There must be controls." When the last British governor of Hong Kong, Christopher Patten, attempted to introduce political reform in Hong Kong that would leave the colony with a more democratic system before the Chinese formally took over in 1997, Lawrence criticized him: "In a large country, you must have a strong leader. One man, one vote, or Western-style democracy will not work.

You can't run a country or a business just by everybody saying, 'This is my idea and yours is no good.'" It was just what the Chinese government wanted to hear.

OCCASIONALLY LAWRENCE WOULD ASK his son, Michael, to take him up in a helicopter and fly over Kowloon and the New Territories, over the power plants he had built, the transmission lines now leading into China, the lights in the villages and on farms and spilling from the windows of apartment houses and from factories, from the Tsangs' Lantau Island house, which now had electricity, from Leung Chik's chicken business and restaurant, and from the animal pens of Farmer Fu, whom his brother had befriended—a bright, shining tapestry of light.

"I did that," he would say, looking down. Occasionally, he would direct his son to land the helicopter in a village where the Chinese residents would come out and greet the taipan.

Portraits of Victor Sassoon and his wife installed in his restored suite at the Cathay Hotel, renamed the Peace Hotel

11

Back on the Bund

Lawrence never made it back to China.

As he entered his nineties, Lawrence spent most of his days in a wheelchair with severe arthritis. His hands trembled, and his gait, when he did walk, was unsteady. He still attended board meetings of China Light and Power. "I keep my spirits up by attending the office regularly, taking interest in the many changes that are taking place in this area of the world and in being grateful for the many blessings that God has given me," he wrote to a friend. When the opening of the Daya Bay nuclear plant was postponed a few months for technical reasons, Lawrence wrote to Deng Xiaoping: "Though I regret to say that I am now in a wheelchair due to arthritis, I still hope to see you in Daya Bay at the opening of the nuclear power station" in six months' time.

A month after that letter, Lawrence was driven to Boulder Lodge for his usual Sunday curry lunch with his wife, Muriel, his brother, Horace, and several friends. He read the newspapers and talked about what the future held for Hong Kong after 1997. The following Monday, he attended a China Light and Power board meeting. The next day, he visited one of the company's offices, complaining in passing that he thought he was coming down with a cold. On Wednesday, August 25, 1993, at the age of ninety-four, Lawrence Kadoorie died.

Two years later, Horace passed away as well. He had been ill for years, but when he was in his eighties he had managed to attend a reunion in San Francisco of some of the Shanghai refugees he had helped save and the alumni of the wartime Shanghai Kadoorie School. More than 1,000 refugees attended, including Michael Blumenthal, the former United States treasury secretary who had learned English at the Kadoorie School, and Lucie Hartwich, the Berlin teacher Horace had met on a ship en route to Shanghai and whom he had hired on the spot to run the school. The refugees, many of whom had not seen one another in forty years, mingled in a large hotel hall decorated with signs of the Shanghai ghetto shops. They wore name tags with pictures of themselves as children. At a reception at a local synagogue that had been founded by Shanghai refugees, they dedicated a series of stained-glass windows to Horace, thanking him for saving them. Attending the service was Theodore Alexander, the Berlin refugee who had worked for Victor Sassoon, become a rabbi in Shanghai, and been married at the Kadoorie School. Thirty-five years after last seeing Horace, he mounted the pulpit. "Today we are respected citizens—Jews who have made a valuable contribution to the benefit of those countries in which we have made our homes," Alexander said as Horace looked on, beaming. "How fortunate we have been . . . in that the education provided to our younger generation was such as to enable them to take their place in the world. They inspired us all in a time of despair to prepare for a better future." The Torah

Alexander had carried as a teenager from Berlin to Shanghai and as a young man from Shanghai to San Francisco rested in the ark alongside him.

The two Kadoorie brothers were buried within a few feet of each other in Hong Kong's Jewish cemetery. The Chinese government sent official condolences on Lawrence's death. A government delegation from Beijing came to pay its respects to the family at Lawrence's home. The Chinese officials had dinner with Lawrence's son, Michael, and talked about the importance of family and raising children with strong values. The Chinese knew that Michael, now fifty, and his sister, Rita, were inheriting the company and that Michael would be taking over the reins. The Chinese wanted to continue to do business with the Kadoorie dynasty.

Michael and Rita had been born just before the Japanese invasion of Hong Kong and had been interned with their father and mother in Hong Kong and then in Shanghai. One of Michael's earliest memories in the days after the Americans liberated Shanghai was of being carried to bed on the broad shoulders of American soldiers. Lawrence was forty-two when Michael was born. "He could have almost been my grandfather," Michael later recalled. Just as Elly had focused on his business and left the running of his family to his wife, so Lawrence left the raising of the children to Muriel, a diminutive, soft-spoken woman who nevertheless was one of the few people who could influence and sway Lawrence. She was aided by a staff of servants. Horace, who had never married nor had children, became a large part of their lives, taking them around to the Peninsula Hotel kitchen, sneaking them treats, and on weekends piling them into his car to visit the New Territories and the farmers he was helping.

Few people expected much of Michael. He had had a reputation growing up as a playboy and rich dilettante who enjoyed driving fast cars, flew helicopters, and rarely worked past 7 P.M. Michael Kadoorie "is a man of many enthusiasms . . . unfortunately business isn't one of them," *The Wall Street Journal* quoted a friend saying in 1977. The newspaper predicted that he wouldn't succeed his father. He had returned to Hong Kong at age twenty-two after attending a private boarding school in Switzerland and working at several financial internships in London. Lawrence had put him on the board of the Kadoories' hotel company largely because Michael and Horace had always gotten along. Michael also considered China Light and Power, the electric utility that Lawrence ran, and which contributed the most to the Kadoories' profits, "boring." He enjoyed fussing over details of the hotel's furnishings, including even the spacing of the hangers in its closets, and relished adding the latest technology and gadgets.

Now, after Lawrence's death, the new head of the dynasty turned out to be deft in negotiating with and working with China's leaders. He left the day-to-day running of the company's operations to professional managers, but carefully nursed the Kadoories' growing relationship with the Chinese government. Michael attended the opening of the Daya Bay nuclear plant and then won agreements for the Kadoories to build other electric plants across China. As a new generation of Chinese leaders rose, Michael flew to Beijing to meet them, charming them with the way he would often discard prepared speeches and speak informally. Hearing of his penchant for flying helicopters and driving fast cars, Chinese Communist Party leader and president Jiang Zemin needled him at a meeting, asking which was safer. "Both are safe," Michael answered diplomatically. Under his leadership, the stock-market value of China Light and Power, the family's biggest investment, increased tenfold and the value of the Kadoories' hotel company tripled. The Kadoories were ranked the tenth richest family in Asia, with a fortune topping $18 billion.

As the 1997 handover to China approached, Michael expanded his alliance with the powerful Rong family, who had prospered in Shanghai in the 1930s and whom Lawrence had helped relocate and expand in Hong Kong after the Communists seized power. Rong Yiren, the "Red Capitalist" who had stayed in China to help the Communists, had been put in charge of a new company, China International Trust and Investment Corporation, to buy stakes in companies overseas. Rong sent his son to Hong Kong, where, with support of the Chinese government and its capital, he started new businesses and began buying stakes in many of Hong Kong's iconic companies as a sign of China's approaching takeover of Hong Kong. Michael invited Rong's son to buy 25 percent of China Light and Power. It was a form of insurance to protect the company as China took control of Hong Kong. When it became clear a few years later that the Chinese valued the Kadoories and wanted to continue to do business with them, Michael bought the stake back.

Michael had lived in Shanghai only briefly as a young child, but since China had opened again and the Kadoories had resumed doing business there, he visited regularly. He sought out his old servant who had taken care of him when he was an infant. The two had an emotional, tearful reunion. Michael met with the executives of his hotel company and told them he wanted to return to Shanghai and build a hotel. The Kadoorie-owned Peninsula was now one of the most famous luxury hotel brands in the world, with new hotels in Bangkok and Manila and plans for hotels in Beverly Hills, New York, Paris, and London. China Light and Power provided the bulk of Michael's personal fortune, but outside of Hong Kong, few had ever heard of it.

However, most people—especially among the rich and well-connected circle that Michael traveled in, whom China was trying to woo for investment and tourism—had heard of the Peninsula.

Along the Bund in Shanghai, there was one spot that every company in the world wanted—the old Hongkong and Shanghai Bank building with its regal bronze lions out front. But it became clear that the Chinese bank that now owned the building had no intention of selling the building to a foreign developer. Michael turned his attention to another parcel, farther down the Bund. It was the old British consulate. Margaret Thatcher had asked for it back in the 1980s when she met with Deng Xiaoping and was rebuffed. Jardine, the Kadoories' old rival, hoped to build there, and so did the Rockefellers in partnership with the Japanese. Michael swooped in, backed by the Chinese government, and nabbed it. The prestige of the Peninsula was part of the reason the Chinese government agreed to sell to Michael. But the Kadoories knew the other factors: Lawrence's decisions to turn over Marble Hall to Madame Sun Yat-sen, to never speak ill of the Chinese government even during the Cultural Revolution and Tiananmen Square, and to invest more than $1 billion in China when many investors were still unsure how reliable a partner China would be.

From the roof of his new hotel, Michael could look down the river to the spot where Elly had first docked in the 1880s as a young man. He could look along the Bund to the Kadoories' Palace Hotel, where Chiang Kai-shek had held his wedding reception and Baghdadi immigrants had kissed the back of Elly's outstretched hand seeking favors. Turning the other way, he could look out onto Hongkew, the old Jewish ghetto where Horace had built his school, and the Garden Bridge over which first the Japanese and then the Communists had marched, ending the reign of the British, and of the Kadoories, over Shanghai.

At the grand opening of the new Peninsula Hotel on the Bund, Michael hired acrobats dressed as bellhops to scale the façade. Costumed Chinese drummers beat large drums at the entrance as Chinese and British movie stars, officials, and a handful of royalty mingled in the marble lobby, posed for photographs, and sipped champagne. "We are proud to have come home," Michael declared. It was a party Victor Sassoon would have enjoyed.

For a century, the Kadoories had met with and advised every Chinese leader except for Mao. Now Michael met regularly with Deng's successors and with Xi Jinping, China's powerful new president. At a meeting with two dozen Hong Kong business leaders, Michael was the only Westerner present. Xi took a moment and sent an aide over to shake Michael's hand and deliver a personal message: "Your family has always been a friend to China."

IN 1979, when I first visited Shanghai, China was just opening to the world. There was no acknowledgment of the Sassoons or the Kadoories. China was still mired in communism. It was cold, programmed. Yet even then there was a spark in Shanghai: the elderly bellhop in the old Cathay Hotel speaking French, young people boldly coming up to tourists to practice their English, elderly couples waltzing at dawn on the Bund. On a street just off the Bund the manhole covers were still engraved with the English letters SMC—for the Shanghai Municipal Council, the British-dominated office that had run the International Settlement until the outbreak of World War II.

Just down the road, in the lobby of a 1930s office building—I learned later it had been built by Victor Sassoon—a torn Chinese poster obscured a glassed-in building directory listing European office tenants from 1949, just before the Communists arrived.

In the following years, workers started scraping off paint from the domed ceiling of number 12, the Bund—the former Hongkong and Shanghai Bank building. They discovered eight murals that depicted the historic skylines of Hong Kong, Tokyo, London, New York, Bangkok, Paris, and Calcutta—the cities Shanghai had started trading with in the nineteenth century. Shanghai was rediscovering that it was an international and cosmopolitan city. But it was not just an embrace of nostalgia. As the Chinese economy accelerated, the Communists overcame their suspicion of Shanghai and poured money into rebuilding the city; they allowed its citizens to enter business and finance and turn Shanghai into a business hub that rivaled and then surpassed Hong Kong, and then set their ambitions on joining the ranks of Tokyo, New York, and London. Now, in the twenty-first century, the Kadoories and Sassoons are lionized and celebrated. Victor Sassoon, who was too scared of being arrested to set foot back in Shanghai after 1949, is honored with a portrait in the restored suite where he plotted business deals, entertained Nationalist politicians, flirted with Emily Hahn, and outfoxed Captain Inuzuka. A few blocks away, the Kadoories have opened their new and lavish Peninsula Hotel, the two great families once again presiding over the river. To the north of the Bund, across the Garden Bridge, the Shanghai neighborhood of Hongkew, where the Sassoons and the Kadoories sheltered and protected 18,000 Jewish refugees and which the Chinese once planned to tear down, has been transformed into Jewish Disneyland, with a new refugee museum and a reconstructed café from the 1930s. Israeli prime minister Benjamin Netanyahu has sipped coffee at the café surrounded by Chinese television cameras.

History in China is fungible. When I first visited Shanghai, historians could talk about the "lost tribe" of Kaifeng Jews who settled in China a thousand years ago and kept some Jewish traditions alive—but not about the Sassoons and the Kadoories and their more recent and more transformative impact on Shanghai. Capitalism, in 1979, was still a forbidden topic. Forty years later, you could talk about Victor Sassoon and the Kadoories, but not about the Kaifeng Jews; the Chinese were cracking down on religion. At the Shanghai refugee museum, an exhibition panel was devoted to Ho Feng-Shan, who had issued visas to Erich Reisman's family and thousands of other refugees even though Ho was a Nationalist and opposed Communism. A few weeks later, an exhibit praising Japanese diplomat Chiune Sugihara, who had issued visas allowing Jews from Lithuania to escape the Nazis, had disappeared. China was in a diplomatic feud with Japan; Japanese heroes weren't welcome.

At the new Shanghai Peninsula Hotel, the Kadoories opened a rooftop bar they dubbed "Sir Elly's Bar," with a sweeping view of the Bund and its art deco towers, the same ones that had greeted travelers for almost 100 years. It also had a breathtaking view, across the river, of the futuristic towers of the Pudong district—the new China in steel and glass. Looking down from Sir Elly's rooftop bar, one sensed that the Bund was no longer a reminder of a disconnected past but a road that links new Shanghai and old. Viewed from a historical perspective, today's Shanghai is what one might have expected. Shanghai in the 1930s had more skyscrapers than most American cities; today its futuristic skyline features three of the world's ten tallest buildings. Two airports link Shanghai to the world just as passenger and cargo ships used to move up the river and deposit passengers and cargo in front of the Cathay. The Sassoons and the Kadoories were Shanghai's first billionaires. Now there were 100,000-plus millionaires in Shanghai and more than thirty billionaires—all of them Chinese. Lawrence Kadoorie called Shanghai in the 1930s the "Paris of the Orient." Now it preferred being compared with New York and London.

Cosmopolitan, sophisticated Shanghai had returned. When Lawrence Kadoorie's wife, Muriel, returned to Shanghai after her husband's death, she complained that she was continually disoriented. Everything had changed. The new Shanghai museum was where the racetrack had been. Marble Hall was now hemmed in by elevated highways. The French Club where she liked to dance in the 1930s was almost unrecognizable. She was always trying to get her bearings.

It was a common complaint by visitors to Shanghai, even those who visited the city frequently. Shanghai changed at a dizzying pace. Skyscrapers and shopping malls wiped out old neighborhoods. New shops and restaurants crowded the main avenues. Visitors to Shanghai marveled at the city's vibrancy: the Chinese thronging the expensive shops, lining up at Starbucks for coffee, rushing to work and to parties. This was the Shanghai that Western business executives and tourists embraced and at times grew apprehensive about, the Shanghai that hummed with energy, sophistication, and self-confidence. Some of its former residents wouldn't have been surprised at all by this new Shanghai: Elly Kadoorie, Horace Kadoorie, Lawrence Kadoorie, certainly Victor Sassoon. They would feel right at home in the city they helped create.

What had the Kadoories and the Sassoons meant for China? What does Shanghai's past tell us about China's future?

Certainly, both families were the beneficiaries of empire and colonialism. The opium trade that was the foundation of the Sassoon fortune had destroyed the lives of millions. The fortunes made by the Sassoons and the Kadoories were built on low wages and unfair competition. They exacerbated inequality that left Chinese dying in the streets of Shanghai even as the Kadoories danced at Marble Hall and Victor Sassoon presided over his extravagant parties at the Cathay Hotel. They fueled the rise of the Chinese Communist Party and its triumph. The Sassoons and the Kadoories exploited Shanghai, but they also ignited an economic boom that attracted the Rongs and millions of others who found in the city a place to pursue their entrepreneurial dreams as China wrenched itself from a sclerotic, feudal society into a modern industrial one. It was the Chinese who transformed Shanghai, and China. The Sassoons and the Kadoories helped light the fuse. At a time when much of the world, including China, is building up physical, political, and cyber walls to limit immigration and the free flow of people, ideas, and information, there is a lesson in Shanghai. The Sassoons were in many ways the first globalists. Their experience foreshadowed the problems and anger that globalization would bring in later decades. Inequality in Shanghai was a scourge that radicalized the Chinese, helped bring the Communists to power, and decimated the fortunes—and moral credibility—of both families. The Kadoorie family had long been active in charity. In the aftermath of the Communist revolution, Lawrence and Horace recognized even more the importance of education, health care, housing, and helping refugees, even when their chauvinism and paternalism masked for many the progressive impact of what they were doing.

The Sassoons and the Kadoories were good businessmen but often poor politicians. Victor Sassoon foresaw the rise of Gandhi in India but misjudged the hold the Nationalists had on China. His masterful effort to hold off the Japanese and protect 18,000 Jewish refugees was the moral high point of his life. Yet he could never extend the same empathy to the Chinese. The Kadoories were more attuned to China's politics and its needs, from Laura Kadoorie's early support of charity to Horace's creation of the Kadoorie Agricultural Aid Association. Lawrence and Horace refused to abandon China entirely, and their commitment paid off for them as a family and for Shanghai and Hong Kong. Yet when China rose and demanded Hong Kong's return, Lawrence clung to the idea of continuing some form of colonial rule over the city. And when China's resurgence was clear, they did not publicly condemn the Tiananmen massacre. They did not lobby to bring more democracy to Hong Kong. Perhaps commercial profit was prioritized over political freedom—a dilemma that many foreign companies from Google to Facebook to Apple must increasingly face.

The Sassoons and the Kadoories created essential strands of Shanghai's DNA. Victor Sassoon left Shanghai its most distinctive buildings—hotels and office buildings that withstood war and decades of Communist neglect so that they could reemerge as touchstones of Shanghai's history and its economic rebirth. Victor gave Shanghai its glamour, its frisson and mystery. The Sassoons and the Kadoories also created opportunity—for their fellow foreigners, but even more important, for those who poured into Shanghai seeking a better life. Not surprisingly, when China made its U-turn in 1978 and decided to open and embrace many capitalist institutions, it turned to Shanghai to establish its new stock exchange (which the Sassoons and Kadoories had first established in the 1890s) and a gold exchange, and to staff many of the economic ministries. Many of

China's most creative and economically savvy political leaders came from Shanghai—Prime Minister Zhu Rongji, who led China in the World Trade Organization, and President Jiang Zemin.

From the time Elias Sassoon donned the robes of a Chinese scholar and walked around his walled compound, and Laura Mocatta prodded foreigners to contribute to Chinese charities and supported education for Chinese girls, the Kadoories and the Sassoons showed an affection for and interest in China that the international business executives from oil companies, technology companies, and manufacturers—who poured into China after 1978—clearly lack. For them, China is just business.

The Kadoorie and the Sassoon families felt an emotional tie to China and a cultural debt. They collected Chinese art, assembling some of the most valuable collections in the world. Victor Sassoon broke down social barriers, inviting Chinese to his parties and his box at the racetrack, and left Shanghai only when the Communists conquered the city. Though they could have lived anywhere, the Kadoories returned again and again to Shanghai, and later Hong Kong. They made China their home.

The Sassoons and the Kadoories provided contrary lessons in their determination to build a family dynasty. David Sassoon, the family patriarch, held his family together even as he dispatched them around the world to build the Sassoon empire. One after another he sent his sons abroad, shuffling them from city to city, giving them opportunities to make individual fortunes but keeping the goals of the family at the forefront. The moment he died, the centrifugal forces of London society, sibling rivalry, and assimilation spun the family apart. The Sassoons rose to the top of just about every profession they chose and every city they settled in. But the family also quarreled over money and religious belief and split into factions. The Sassoons never regained the cohesiveness and focus of David and his eight sons. Elly Kadoorie, by contrast, perhaps seeing what had happened to the Sassoons, never allowed his sons to stray from the family business or his strict guiding hand. After his wife died, he forced Lawrence and Horace to abandon their studies in London and work for him in Shanghai. He groomed them for the next two decades. It was only after Elly died that Lawrence and Horace, in their forties, came into their own. They continued to work side by side. And Lawrence would repeat the same pattern with his son, Michael, bestowing on him the family business. The reward: a family today worth $11 billion.

Overlooked by history, and sometimes clashing with their male relatives, the women in the Sassoon and Kadoorie dynasties played a pivotal role in their success in business and in China. Laura Mocatta brought Elly connections to the British Jewish elite and an awareness of how China was changing. She opened doors for him among the Chinese with her charitable contributions to hospitals in China and schools that taught English and enabled Chinese students to get better jobs. Her decision to run back to save a Chinese governess from a house fire became part of the Kadoorie legend in China. Who knows what her influence might have been in Elly Kadoorie's role in civil war between the Communists and the Nationalists, the Japanese invasion of China, the refugee crisis, World War II, and the Communist takeover? Flora Sassoon was rewarded for her business acumen by being toppled in a boardroom coup. Rachel Sassoon, the most influential female newspaper editor in Britain, ended her life living alone and declared insane. In the 1930s there were rumors that Victor Sassoon would marry Emily Hahn, the adventurous and insightful *New Yorker* writer. What might her influence have been on him?

China in the twenty-first century had the country its leaders and people had yearned for ever since the British first arrived and defeated them in the Opium Wars: a proud, militarily strong country that is once again a global power. But Shanghai and the legacy of the Kadoories and the Sassoons illuminate an ongoing debate: the rivalry between Shanghai and Beijing and two different paths forward for China. Every visitor to China feels the difference between Shanghai and Beijing: Shanghai is open, diverse, cosmopolitan. It embraces innovation. Beijing, though a big city, is shaped by a different history. It is more inward looking and nationalistic, home once to the emperor and now the Communist leadership. Shanghai Chinese mock their compatriots in Beijing as unsophisticated, narrow-minded, and suspicious of the world. Those who live in Beijing scorn Shanghai people as caring only about money and fashion and still being slaves to everything foreign. Talk to the Shanghai people about money, they will say, but you can't trust them on politics. They still like the foreigners too much.

As China grows in global power and influence, such distinctions matter. They will shape the attitude China takes toward the world. Which will China choose?

A FEW BLOCKS DOWN the Bund from the new Peninsula Hotel, Victor Sassoon's niece Evelyn Cox sat in the tourist bus as it drove through the streets of Shanghai. She didn't want the other tourists to know who she was. Her uncle Victor's warning to her decades ago still stayed with her: promise me you will never go to China, he had said. He himself had never returned after the Communists took over, fearing he might be arrested on some trumped-up charge, detained like his cousin Lucian Ovadia, whom the Communists had kept in the country for more than two years while they demanded more and more money to pay Victor's Chinese workers and repair the buildings they had expropriated.

In 2007, a foreign company was hired to restore and manage the old Cathay Hotel, spending millions to bring it back to its former opulence in the new booming Shanghai. The new managers asked Cox for the details of Victor's favorite Cathay Hotel recipes, the ones that he had written down in his voluminous diaries: steak Diane, deviled chicken, spicy chicken made with Colman's mustard. What were the leftovers he asked the Cathay kitchen to use to turn into soups or stews?

Now Evelyn Cox, who had spent the last years of Victor's life visiting him frequently and traveling with him to Dallas, London, and New York, had been invited to Shanghai to see the restored hotel. A coffee shop renamed Sir Victor's Café served his old recipes. A small museum off the lobby featured pictures of Victor, and menus and silverware from the 1930s. Chinese tourists thronged the streets outside the hotel posing for selfies in front of the façade. As evening fell, the art deco building glowed, bathed in spotlights. "This is what the Westerners left us," a taxi driver said as he drove past. "Isn't it beautiful?"

Cox had brought with her oil portraits of Victor and his late-in-life wife "Barnsie"—Victor looking distinguished and statesmanlike in contrast to earlier photographs showing the younger, rakish bon vivant with a twinkle in his eye who was always ready for the next deal, the next party, the next turn in Chinese politics. In a ceremony attended by Chinese officials and shown on Chinese television, the hotel installed the portraits in Victor's renovated suite, which guests could now book for $1,100 a night. The Chinese had finally accepted

Victor for the positive things he did for Shanghai, Cox thought, no longer caricaturing him as "this horrible rich person who lived off the poor people." Victor had come home as well.

The Sassoon diaspora that had spread after David Sassoon's death in 1864 deposited family members around the globe, in London, Jerusalem, Washington, D.C., and New York, and in professions ranging from banking to government to arts to rabbinic studies. (Contrary to what many believed, it didn't place them in hair-cutting salons; Vidal Sassoon wasn't related.) The family fortune dwindled and dissipated. Much of Victor's wealth, which had made him one of the richest men in the world in the 1930s, was tied to the Cathay Hotel and scores of other buildings he owned in Shanghai, which the Communists seized. Over the years, family members made occasional efforts to get the Chinese government to compensate them. They were always rebuffed. The Kadoories, by contrast, had fled Shanghai for Hong Kong, remained committed to China's rise, and reaped the benefits. For the Sassoons, Shanghai had slipped into the nostalgia of family lore and memory. Hugh Sassoon, a London banker and descendant of the formidable Flora Sassoon, was being interviewed for a background check at one point before entering a deal. As part of the routine questioning, he was asked if he had ever engaged in money laundering. He chuckled. "My family used to be in the drug trade," he said.

One Sassoon who maintained the family connection to Shanghai was James Sassoon, Hugh's son, who traveled often to China for business and became head of the leading British business group that advocated for trade with China. In 2013, he became a top executive at Jardine, Matheson, the same company that his family had battled and outwitted in the opium trade in the 1870s.

In 2002, James Sassoon was named a senior official for the British treasury. He was sent to Beijing for economic talks and met with China's finance minister, Lou Jiwei. As often happened on these trips, the Sassoon name and its history preceded him.

"Your family's name is very well known in China," the finance minister began.

James Sassoon acknowledged that, and they talked a bit about his family's history and Victor's vast holdings. Then Sassoon added, impishly, "It is a shame that China has not implemented the policy that many countries in Eastern Europe adopted where they have allowed former owners to come back and reclaim their properties. If China did that, our family would be much better off."

Lou looked at him and broke into a smile. He switched to English and leaned forward. "Let's let bygones be bygones."

Acknowledgments

I received help and support from people and institutions around the globe in the research and writing of this book.

My first thanks are to the members of the Kadoorie and Sassoon families who shared their recollections and archives with me and connected me with family, friends, and business associates. The Kadoories have established the Hong Kong Heritage Project for many of their family and business papers along with oral histories of many others in Hong Kong. Under the guidance of Amelia Allsop, a historian in her own right, it was an invaluable resource, and I benefited from the assistance of Clement Cheung as well as Melanie Ho, and their staffs. Members of the Kadoorie and Sassoon families reviewed a draft of this book for accuracy while understanding that matters of interpretation and analysis—and any error—remained mine. I thank them for their time and the generosity of their cooperation.

Similarly, several members of the Sassoon family shared recollections and family papers with me: Isaac Sassoon in New York, Nathan Sassoon in Jerusalem, Joseph Sassoon in Washington, D.C., Hugh

Sassoon and James Sassoon in London. Evelyn Cox shared her recollections of Victor with me, as did her brother Christopher. James Sassoon reviewed the manuscripts and corrected matters of fact while acknowledging that the family's interpretation of events may sometimes differ with my own.

The 300-plus source notes document my debt to news reports, research, and scholarship on Shanghai, Hong Kong, and China. The work of several historians deserves special mention and thanks. Maisie Meyer pioneered the study of the Baghdadi Jews in Shanghai, and her books and conversations provided a rich portrait of their life in Shanghai. Stanley Jackson and Cecil Roth both documented the life of Victor Sassoon in the 1940s and 1960s. H. Parker James has researched Victor Sassoon's life extensively and generously shared with me his many insights. Taras Grescoe captured the world of the Cathay Hotel and the relationship between Victor Sassoon and Emily Hahn in his book *Shanghai Grand*. Peter Hibbard shared with me his research materials and insights behind his books on the Cathay and the Kadoorie hotels. Robert Bickers of the University of Bristol has vividly evoked the world of the International Settlement and documented the changing role of Shanghai and its place in China's worldview through the decades. Frank Dikotter persuasively analyzed the unique world of Shanghai in the 1920s and 1930s and its role in China's modernization. Leo Goodstadt gave me insight into the evolution of Hong Kong after World War II through today. My views were also shaped by conversations with Ezra Vogel, Roderick MacFarquhar, Jonathan Goldstein, Marvin Tokayer, Elizabeth Sinn, Steve Tsang, Patrick Cranley, Steve Hochstadt, James Ross, Yaron Ben-Naeh, Manli Ho, Meron Medzini, Chiara Betta, Harriet Sergeant, Dvir Bar-Gal, and Yuk Chui Kong.

I wish to thank the many people in Hong Kong who, in addition to those already listed, shared their recollections and insights about the

Kadoories and China: William Mocatta, Y. B. Lee, Susan Turner, Michael Green, Robert Dorfman, Elaine Forsgate Marden, David Zweig, Richard Margolis, S. J. Chan, David Akers-Jones, Leo Ou Fan Lee, Vaudine England, Elizabeth Sinn, Edmund Kwok, John Dolfin, Andy Brown, Zoe Yeung, Connie Yuen, Tsang Fan Kwong, and Dennis Leventhal.

Libraries and archives across the world opened their collections to me. My thanks to the Jardine Archive at the University of Cambridge Library, the special collections at the Hong Kong University Library, the collections at the British Library and the British government archives at Kew, and the Howard Gottlieb Archival Research Center at Boston University. Special thanks to Anne Peterson, who oversees Victor Sassoon's diaries at the DeGolyer Library at Southern Methodist University in Dallas. The Northeastern University library responded to all my many requests promptly, and Susan Conover helped keep my research and administrative responsibilities on track.

In Shanghai, Helen Yu assisted me with research and helped set up many interviews, and shared her own impressions of the Kadoorie and Sassoon families. Pan Guang and his colleagues at the Shanghai Academy of Social Sciences provided a great deal of insight both in meetings and in their research over the years, as did Xu Xin and his colleagues at Nanjing University.

In writing, I benefited from the friendship (and often accommodations) of Dave Arnold and Ann Moritz, Doug Tifft and Bonnie MacAdam, John Tagliabue and Paula Butturini, Lila Lu and Glenn McKay, Steve Stecklow, Laurie Hays, Harold Varmus and Connie Casey, and Dan Golden.

Several colleagues read drafts of this book and offered helpful critiques and suggestions, most of which I was smart enough to take. My thanks to Timothy Cheek, Mark Clifford, Lori Lefkovitz, Ethan Bronner, Amelia Allsop, Mei Fong, David Wessel, Tom Ashbrook, Doug Tifft,

Michael Carlisle, and Michael Mungiello. Julie Lipkin was my careful copy editor from the book's proposal through many drafts.

Andrea Schultz and her team at Viking offered enthusiastic support from the inception of this project. Georgia Bodnar read drafts with a careful eye. Her probing questions and editorial perspective improved the book at several key points. Terezia Cicel was a deft line editor, trimming repetitions and awkward phrases and making clearer what I meant to say. Her good humor and judgment made the book better. I also wish to thank the careful copyediting work of Cathy Dexter. In London I benefited from the support and insights of my British agent, Bill Hamilton, and my publisher, Richard Beswick, and his team at Little, Brown.

My agent, Michael Carlisle, was, as always, enthusiastic when it mattered, wise when it counted, an insightful editor, and a good friend. Go Patriots!

I first visited Shanghai when I was in my twenties, many years before I met my wife, Barbara Howard, and we had our family. She says she always knew we would go back to China. When we did, it was with our three children. They, too, fell in love with Shanghai. This book is for Barbara, and for Molly, Ben, and Nick. I couldn't be luckier, or happier.

Notes

CHAPTER ONE: THE PATRIARCH

3 **"Only his eyes showed between the turban and a high-muffled cloak":** Stanley Jackson, *The Sassoons* (London: Heinemann, 1968), 8.

4 **Baghdad was a crossroads of cultures:** For a description of the richness of life in Baghdad, see Jackson, *The Sassoons*, 2–3; Cecil Roth, *The Sassoon Dynasty* (London: Robert Hale Limited, 1941), 17–24.

5 **Presiding over this dynamic, self-confident community:** Details of the Sassoons' role in Baghdad and David Sassoon's Baghdad years are drawn from Jackson, *The Sassoons*, 1–9; Roth, *The Sassoon Dynasty*, 24–36; Maisie J. Meyer, *From the Rivers of Babylon to the Whangpoo: A Century of Sephardi Jewish Life in Shanghai* (Lanham, New York: University Press of America, 2003), 31–32.

8 **turned toward the disappearing shore and wept:** Jackson, *The Sassoons*, 8.

9 **offered him an interest-free loan:** Jackson, *The Sassoons*, 12–13.

10 **David Sassoon joined the British Empire at the height of its political and economic power:** Details of David Sassoon's success in Bombay drawn from Jackson, *The Sassoons*, 17–22; Roth, *The Sassoon Dynasty*, 37–62; Thomas A. Timberg, "Baghdadi Jews in Indian Port Cities," in *Jews in India*, ed. Timberg (New York: Advent Books, 1986), 273–81;

Joan Roland, *Jews in British India: Identity in a Colonial Era* (Hanover: Brandeis University Press/University Press of New England, 1989), 14–57.

10 **"great object of the Government":** John Darwin, *The Empire Project: The Rise and Fall of the British World-System, 1830–1970* (New York: Cambridge University Press, 2009), 36.

11 **proposed in Parliament bills to end all discrimination against Great Britain's Jews:** Jackson, *The Sassoons*, 19.

11 **a just and kind government:** Interview with Prof. Yaron Ben-Naeh of Hebrew University's Department of Jewish History and Contemporary Jewry and director of the Center for Research and Study of Sephardi and Oriental Jewish Heritage. Ben-Naeh reviewed hundreds of letters from David Sassoon to his family, written in Judeo-Arabic.

12 **"God Save the Queen!":** Jackson, *The Sassoons*, 19.

12 **"tall, spare, hard of muscle, with an El Greco face":** Jackson, *The Sassoons*, 10.

12 **needed to think creatively:** Jackson, *The Sassoons*, 20–22, 39–40.

15 **David set up the equivalent of a Sassoon company town:** Jackson, *The Sassoons*, 333–34; Meyer, *From the Rivers of Babylon*, 15–16.

17 **"We possess all things":** The emperor's letter to King George III has been widely reprinted; for example: https://sourcebooks.fordham.edu/mod/1793 qianlong.asp.

17 **"an old, crazy, first-rate Man of War":** Helen Robbins, *Our First Ambassador to China: An Account of the Life of George, Earl of Macartney—With Extracts from His Letters, and the Narrative of His Experiences in China, as Told by Himself* (London: John Murray, 1908), Google Books, 386.

17 **The opium trade became the flashpoint:** Meyer, *From the Rivers of Babylon*, 57–68; Jackson, *The Sassoons*, 22–24. For an excellent overview of the Opium War, see Julia Lovell, *The Opium War: Drugs, Dreams and the Making of Modern China* (New York: Overlook Press, 2015).

18 **"selling products injurious to others":** "Lin Zexu (LinTse-hsu) writing to Britain's Queen Victoria to Protest the Opium Trade, 1839," University of Southern California Annenberg, USC US–China Institute, accessed November 2019, https://china.usc.edu/lin-zexu-lintse-hsu-writing-britains-queen-victoria-protest-opium-trade-1839.

21 **"first to come forward in support of the British Government"**: Jackson, *The Sassoons*, 35–36.

CHAPTER TWO: EMPIRE OF THE SONS—AND OPIUM

23 **The daotai sat in his office:** Details of life in Shanghai on the eve of the arrival of the Sassoons drawn from Jeffrey N. Wasserstrom, *Global Shanghai, 1850–2010: A History in Fragments* (New York: Routledge, 2009), 1–33; James W. Hayes, "Fertile and Fortunate: Shanghai Before the Treaty Port Era," in *Journal of the Royal Asiatic Society Hong Kong Branch* 48 (2008), 175–203.

26 **David Sassoon deployed his sons:** Details of the Sassoons' early activities in Shanghai drawn from Stanley Jackson, *The Sassoons* (London: Heinemann, 1968), 31–48; Cecil Roth, *The Sassoon Dynasty* (London: Robert Hale Limited, 1941), 70–93; Maisie J. Meyer, *From the Rivers of Babylon to the Whangpoo: A Century of Sephardi Jewish Life in Shanghai* (Lanham, New York: University Press of America, 2003), 1–16; *The Sassoons*, pamphlet published in conjunction with exhibit at Ohel Leah synagogue in Hong Kong, no date, copy in author's possession; George Thirkell, *Some Queer Stories of Benjamin David Benjamin and Messrs. E. D. Sassoon & Co.* (Shanghai: Celestial Empire Office, 1888).

29 **dubbed with an Urdu word:** *Merriam-Webster*, s.v. "bund (*n.*)," www.merriam-webster.com/dictionary/bund.

29 **"hips touch hips":** Wasserstrom, *Global Shanghai*, 34.

29 **"the destiny of Shanghai":** Wasserstrom, *Global Shanghai*, 32.

30 **Applying the lessons of his father:** Jackson, *The Sassoons*, 23–24.

31 **the isolation of life in Shanghai:** Jackson, *The Sassoons*, 26–27.

32 **brutally assaulted by a "drunken freak":** Photocopy of newspaper story entitled "The Daily Press" in Hong Kong, August 30, 1861; private collection of Nathan Sassoon, Jerusalem, Israel, copy in author's possession.

32 **wrote more than 7,000 letters:** The letters, written in Judeo-Arabic dialect, are held at the Hebrew University in Jerusalem.

33 **"Silver and gold, silks, gums and spices":** Jackson, *The Sassoons*, 30.

33 **"have arrived at great wealth":** Jackson, *The Sassoons*, 39.

33 **David summoned him back to Bombay in 1862 to begin planning the family succession:** Details of the rivalry between Elias and Abdullah and the fallout from David's death drawn from Roth, *The Sassoon Dynasty*, 95–107; Jackson, *The Sassoons*, 40–48.

34 **a grand ball that featured 300 British guests:** Joan Roland, *Jewish Communities of India: Identity in a Colonial Era* (London and New York: Routledge, 2018).

35 **Elias announced that he was resigning from the family company:** Jackson, *The Sassoons*, 45–48; Joan Roland, "Baghdadi Jews in India and China in the Nineteenth Century," in *The Jews of China* 1, ed. Jonathan Goldstein (Armonk, NY: M. E. Sharpe, 1990), 141–56.

37 **"men of small capital":** Edward Le Fevour, *Western Enterprise in Late Ch'ing China: A Selective Survey of Jardine, Matheson and Company's Operations* (Cambridge, MA: Harvard East Asian Monographs, no. 26, 1968), 13. Le Fevour gives an excellent overview of Jardine's role in the opium trade that provides the basis for this section; see also Mark Nichols, "The Princely Hong: Jardine Matheson, Hong Kong, and Eastern Trade": an exhibition in Cambridge University Library, 7 May–24 July 1997. Early relations between Jardine and the Sassoons showing the Sassoons' subservient position are shown in letters held in the Jardine Matheson Archive at the Cambridge University Library, Cambridge. For example, see letter from Jardine to E. D. Sassoon & Co., May 15, 1864, criticizing delivery of "damaged opium" (JM/C14/10); see also untitled document, October 20, 1854, recounting a court judgment against the Sassoons in favor of Jardine regarding the delivery of three chests of opium (JM/F2342).

38 **For the Sassoons, legalization changed everything:** Details of the battle between Jardine and the Sassoons over the opium trade drawn from Le Fevour, *Western Enterprise in Late Ch'ing China*, 27–30; Carl Trocki, *Opium, Empire and the Global Political Economy* (London and New York: Routledge, 1999), 103–28; Bryna Goodman, *Native Place, City, and Nation: Regional Networks and Identities in Shanghai, 1853–1937* (Berkeley: University of California Press, 1995), 47–133.

39 **Finally came distribution:** Goodman, *Native Place, City, and Nation*, 68–72.

39 **The impact of all this on Jardine was swift and devastating:** Jardine ledgers for September 19, 1873, for example, show Jardine delivering just ten chests of opium to Foochow compared with forty-two from the Sassoons, and the warehouse already holding two chests from Jardine compared with 260 from the Sassoons. Ledgers held by Jardine Matheson Archive, University of Cambridge Library (JM/A8/119/3); see also Maggie Keswick, ed., *The Thistle and the Jade: A Celebration of 150 Years of Jardine, Matheson & Co* (London: Octopus Books, 1982), 79; details are also drawn from Le Fevour, *Western Enterprise in Late Ch'ing China*.

40 **the power and access that came with it:** Jackson, *The Sassoons*, 52–54.

41 **highest-ranking Chinese employee . . . had become "useless" after excessive opium smoking:** Eiichi Motono, "A Study of the Legal Status of the Compradors During the 1880s with Special Reference to the Three Civil Cases Between David Sassoon Sons & Co. and their Compradors, 1884–1887," *Acta Asiatica* 62 (February 1992).

41 **its "monstrous wealth":** Quoted in Jean Moorcroft Wilson, *Siegfried Sassoon: The Journey from the Trenches* (London and New York: Routledge, 2003), www.worldcat.org/wcpa/servlet/DCARead?standardNo=0415967139&standardNoType=1&excerpt=true.

41 **"the Chinese who smoked or imbibed opium were better behaved, quieter, and far more sensible:** Eilat Negev and Yehuda Koren, *The First Lady of Fleet Street: The Life of Rachel Beer, Crusading Heiress and Newspaper Pioneer* (New York: Bantam Books, 2011), 43.

42 **letters from brother to brother:** The correspondence of the Sassoon brothers on opium and other topics is held by the library of Hebrew University in Jerusalem. My thanks to Prof. Yaron Ben-Naeh of the university's Department of Jewish History and Contemporary Jewry and director of the Center for Research and Study of Sephardi and Oriental Jewish Heritage, for selecting several dozen letters and translating them into English from the original Judeo-Arabic. See also Yaron Ben-Naeh, "The Sassoon Family: Jewish Magnates Between East and West in the Nineteenth Century," www.eacenter.huji.ac.il/uploaded/fck/Ben-Nae_Paper.pdf.

42 **socially more broad-minded and cosmopolitan:** Edward's relations with Jews, especially Jewish businessmen including the Sassoons, is described

in Anthony Allfrey, *Edward VII and His Jewish Court* (London: Weiden-feld and Nicholson, 1991).

43 **The Sassoon brothers began romancing the heir to the British throne:** Allfrey, *Edward VII and His Jewish Court*, 48–59; Jackson, *The Sassoons*, 67–73; Roth, *The Sassoon Dynasty*, 108–88.

44 **"the Jews are the salt of smart Society":** George Washburn Smalley et al., *Society in the New Reign* (London: Unwin, 1904), 191.

44 **A British duke refused to rent his country house to Reuben Sassoon:** Documents of the Earls of Romney, 1874, 1875 (U1644/ESTAE/U1644/E115-Letters), Kent History and Library Centre, Maidstone, Kent, UK.

44 **"Hail, King of the Jews":** Letter from Dr. Evelyn Rich to Florence Oglan-der (OG/CC/2121A) held by the Isle of Wight Record Office, UK.

44 **"Will he sell his horses and scatter his Jews":** Martin Gilbert, *Churchill and the Jews* (New York: Macmillan, 2008), 5.

44 **"Indian auriferous coon":** Jackson, *The Sassoons*, 71.

45 **"We shall suffer enormous losses":** For Sassoon lobbying against the end of the opium trade, see China Association, "Circular to the General Committee," numbers 54–161 (SOAS University of London Library, CHAS /MCP/18).

46 **lamented the trail of opium:** Yangwen Zheng, *The Social Life of Opium in China* (Cambridge: Cambridge University Press, 2005), 133.

47 **profits in opium had brought the Sassoons 140 million "liang":** Zhang Zhongli and Cen Zengnian, *Shaxun Jituan Zai Jiu Zhongguo* [The Sas-soon Group in Old China] (Beijing: Renmin Chubanshe, 1985).

CHAPTER THREE: LAURA AND ELLY

50 **a name to conjure with:** Ina McCabe et al., *Diaspora Entrepreneurial Networks* (Oxford: Berg, 2005), 271.

50 **Rima Kadoorie heard about the Sassoon schools:** Details of Elly Ka-doorie's arrival in China and subsequent career are detailed in Lawrence Kadoorie, *The Kadoorie Memoir*, held by the family's archives, the Hong Kong Heritage Project. See also Dennis Way, "Names Behind the Name," manuscript in author's possession; Caroline Pluss, "Sephardic Jews in

Hong Kong: Constructing Communal Identities," in *Sino Judaica: Occasional Papers of the Sino-Judaic Institute* 4 (2003); letter from Elly Kadoorie to *Who's Who in American Jewry*, October 14, 1937, Hong Kong Heritage Project; Nigel Cameron, *Power: The Story of China Light* (Hong Kong: Oxford University Press [China], 1982), 87–98; Sarah Lazarus, "The Role of Jews in the Making of Hong Kong," *South China Morning Post Magazine*, December 13, 2014; Maisie Meyer, *Shanghai's Baghdadi Jews* (Hong Kong: Blacksmith Books, 2015), 116–27.

51 **send four of her sons to India:** Though beyond the scope of this book, the story of Elly's brother Ellis Kadoorie and his business and philanthropic activities is documented in records at the Hong Kong Heritage Project.

53 **inscribing "a barrel of disinfectant":** Lawrence Kadoorie, *The Kadoorie Memoir.*

55 **befriending the richest local businessman in Hong Kong—Robert Hotung:** Years later, Hotung would write affectionately to Elly's children that he had seen them grow up. Letter from Robert Hotung to Lawrence Kadoorie, no date but likely 1930s, held by the Hong Kong Heritage Project. See also Way, *Names.*

56 **Ellis left a house and money in trust to support a Chinese woman and her daughters:** Will of Ellis Kadoorie, "Sir Ellis Kadoorie, deceased . . . ," held by Deacons Collection, Hong Kong University Library, Hong Kong, China.

56 **Her family was part of the "cousinhood":** Details of the Mocatta family and Laura Mocatta drawn from Timothy Green, *Precious Heritage* (London: Rosendale Press, 1984), *passim*; interviews with William Mocatta.

57 **It was "very hot":** Mrs. Laura Kadoorie's Diary, Hong Kong Heritage Project; hereafter referred to as Laura Kadoorie diary.

57–58 **"At first, my mother found living in Hong Kong somewhat difficult":** Lawrence Kadoorie, *The Kadoorie Memoir.*

58 **"understand what was going on":** Interview with Lawrence Kadoorie, Hong Kong Heritage Project.

59 **"looked washed out and slightly breathless":** Pat Barr, *To China with Love: The Lives and Times of Protestant Missionaries in China, 1860–1900* (London: Secker and Warburg, 1972), 143.

59 **a pioneering cause: schools for girls:** Jonathan Sciarcon, *Educational Oases in the Desert: The Alliance Israelite Universelle's Girls' Schools in Ottoman Iraq, 1895–1915* (Albany: State University of New York Press, 2017), 87–112; See also "New Life in the East," *Jewish Chronicle*, November 26, 1909, 18.

60 **"I am quite a good sailor now":** Laura Kadoorie diary.

64 **Elly stepped outside to a small park:** Lawrence Kadoorie, *The Kadoorie Memoir*.

65 **transformed from a stockbroker to a financier:** The transformation is detailed in a PhD thesis by Yuk Chui Kong, "Jewish Merchants' Community in Shanghai: A Study of the Kadoorie Enterprise, 1890–1950," Hong Kong Baptist University, August 30, 2017.

67 **"as swarms of ants attach themselves":** David Scott, *China and the International System, 1840–1949* (New York: SUNY Press, 2008), 167.

68 **given a reception at the mansion of a senior executive of the Sassoon companies:** See "The Rise of Silas Aaron Hardoon (1851–1931) as Shanghai's Major Individual Landowner" and "Dr. Sun Yat-sen and the Jews," both in *Sino-Judaica: Occasional Papers of the Sino-Judaic Institute* 2 (1995).

69 **"The application should be refused":** Maisie J. Meyer, *From the Rivers of Babylon to the Whangpoo: A Century of Sephardi Jewish Life in Shanghai* (Lanham, NY: University Press of America, 2003), 162; see also Chiara Betta, "Marginal Westerners in Shanghai," in *New Frontiers: Imperialism's New Communities in East Asia, 1842–1953*, eds. Robert Bickers and Christian Henriot (Manchester: Manchester University Press, 2017).

69 **"worried over passports":** Laura Kadoorie diary.

71 **Wealthy Chinese began to take note of the Kadoories' efforts:** Interview with Prof Xu Xin and colleagues, Diane and Guilford Glazer Institute for Jewish and Israel Studies, Nanjing University, Nanjing, China.

72 **"kept secluded and like prisoners":** Laura Kadoorie diary.

72 **fire broke out in the mansion on Bubbling Well Road:** Newspaper articles on Laura Kadoorie's death held by Hong Kong Heritage Project, copies in author's possession.

73 **"Her virtues are all the rarer and more priceless":** "The Late Mrs. Laura Mocatta Kadoorie," *Israel's Messenger* (Shanghai), March 14, 1919.

CHAPTER FOUR: SHANGHAI RISING

77 **Shanghai, by contrast, enjoyed what most of China lacked: a stable government:** Details of Shanghai blossoming in the 1920s and 1930s and its impact on the Chinese are drawn from the excellent book by Frank Dikotter, *The Age of Openness* (Berkeley and Los Angeles: University of California Press, 2008).

79 **tips for dealing with Chinese servants:** Barbara Baker, *Shanghai: Electric and Lurid City* (Hong Kong: Oxford University Press, 1998), 20–23.

79 **"First the water-carrier to fill the tub for the daily bath":** Pat Barr, *To China with Love: The Lives and Times of Protestant Missionaries in China, 1860–1900* (London: Secker and Warburg, 1972), 142.

79 **"never took a bath by myself":** Aviva Shabi, "Baghdadi Jews in Shanghai," *The Scribe*, www.dangoor.com/72page34.html.

81 **"Almost everybody in the factory reads newspapers":** Dikotter, *The Age of Openness*, 26.

81 **Stilwell thought Shanghai looked like Philadelphia:** Stilwell's impressions of Shanghai are recounted in Barbara Tuchman, *Stilwell and the American Experience in China: 1911–1945* (New York: Random House, 1971), Kindle location 856–945 and *passim*.

81 **"never was and never will be another city like Shanghai":** Lawrence Kadoorie, *The Kadoorie Memoir*, Hong Kong Heritage Project.

82 **"In the general scramble the mother of the family was forgotten":** Letter from J. J. Patterson to W. J. Keswick, November 14, 1935, held by the Jardine Matheson Archive, Cambridge University Library, Cambridge, UK.

83 **"a bouncing ball of energy":** Nigel Cameron, *Power: The Story of China Light* (Hong Kong: Oxford University Press [China], 1982), 96.

84 **alcoholic architect who they said had built Marble Hall:** Lawrence Kadoorie, *The Kadoorie Memoir*.

85 **the most famous address in Shanghai:** Maisie Meyer, *Shanghai's Baghdadi Jews* (Hong Kong: Blacksmith Books, 2015), 119–21.

85 **"best, fanciest hotel in Asia":** Details of the history of the Kadoorie hotels including the Majestic and the Peninsula are drawn from Peter Hibbard, *Beyond Hospitality: The History of the Hongkong and Shanghai Hotels, Limited* (Singapore: Marshall Cavendish, 2010), *passim*.

87 **Elly was free to begin to expand his stock holdings:** Details of these business maneuverings are drawn from Yuk Chui Kong, "Jewish Merchants' Community in Shanghai: A Study of the Kadoorie Enterprise, 1890–1950," especially chapters 4 and 5, PhD diss., Hong Kong Baptist University, 2017, https://repository.hkbu.edu.hk/etd_oa/417.

89 **Elly had become the leader of the small Zionist movement in China:** Maisie J. Meyer, *From the Rivers of Babylon to the Whangpoo: A Century of Sephardi Jewish Life in Shanghai* (Lanham, NY: University Press of America, 2003), 171–74.

89 **Sun Yat-sen knew very little about Jews:** Details of Sun's views of Jews and dealings with Elly Kadoorie are drawn from Meron Medzini, "China, the Holocaust, and the Birth of the Jewish State," *Israel Journal of Foreign Affairs* 7, no. 1 (2013); Tom Segev, "Zionism Had a Friend in the Far East," *Haaretz* (Israel), March 1, 2013; Meyer, *From the Rivers of Babylon*, 172–74; "Dr. Sun Yat-sen and the Jews," in *Sino-Judaica: Occasional Papers of the Sino-Judaic Institute* 2 (1995); interview with Meron Medzini, former director of the Israeli Government Press Office in Jerusalem.

89 **"native Chinese make no difference between a Jew and a Christian":** Peter Kupfer, ed., *Youtai—Presence and Perception of Jews and Judaism in China* (New York: Peter Lang, 2008), 169.

90 **Sun sympathized with the plight of the Jews:** Ian Deeks, "Unlikely Assistance: How the Chinese and the Japanese Saved 20,000 Jews in Shanghai During World War II," http://history.emory.edu/home/documents/endeavors/volume1/Ians.pdf.

91 **"I didn't have much of a boyhood":** Linda Matthews, "Sir Lawrence Kadoorie Carries on the Legend of Old China Traders," *Wall Street Journal*, March 2, 1977, 1; Lawrence Kadoorie interview with Wendy Barnes, "Time to Remember," Hong Kong radio program, April 26, 1970.

92 **Elly's efforts to empower his sons:** Meyer, *From the Rivers of Babylon*, 171–80; interview with Rabbi Marvin Tokayer, who discussed the controversy with Lawrence Kadoorie.

93 **"that charming smile of his":** Letter from W. J. Keswick to J. J. Patterson, October 31, 1935, Jardine Matheson archive, University of Cambridge Library.

94 "a huge neon sign in flaming red and phosphorescent green": Mao Dun, *Midnight* (Beijing: Foreign Languages Press, 1957), 1.

94 "hermetically sealed and isolated glass case": Arthur Ransome, "The Shanghai Mind," reprinted in Ransome, *The Chinese Puzzle* (London: George Allen & Unwin, 1927), 29–30.

94 "My family lived in a bubble": Interview with Michael Kadoorie.

95 "every stone and every blade of grass" in Shanghai: Quoted in Jeffrey N. Wasserstrom, *Global Shanghai, 1850–2010: A History in Fragments* (New York: Routledge, 2009), 68.

95 the Chinese need to be "ruthless": Mao Tse-tung, "The Chinese Revolution and the Chinese Communist Party," December 1939, https://radical journal.com/essays/the_chinese_revolution_party.html.

96 march on Shanghai and retake the city: The 1927 battle for Shanghai is recounted in Harriet Sergeant, *Shanghai* (New York: Crown Publishers, 1990), 68–94.

97 "wedding of the decade": Sterling Seagrave, *The Soong Dynasty*, Kindle location 287–89.

98 Flora, announced from Bombay that she would take over the firm: Details of Flora's ascent and fall are drawn from Stanley Jackson, *The Sassoons* (London: Heinemann, 1968), 103–22.

101 Rachel Sassoon was a child: Rachel Sassoon's life is recounted in Eilat Negev and Yehuda Koren, *The First Lady of Fleet Street: The Life of Rachel Beer, Crusading Heiress and Newspaper Pioneer* (New York: Bantam, 2012), which is the source for this section and the quotations.

CHAPTER FIVE: THE IMPRESARIO

107 "unusually quick and witty, especially for a businessman": Ken Cuthbertson, *Nobody Said Not to Go: The Life, Loves, and Adventures of Emily Hahn* (New York: Faber & Faber, 1998), Kindle location 2749 (chapter 14).

109 "a war hero, crack golfer and horseman but no commercial genius": Stanley Jackson, *The Sassoons* (London: Heinemann, 1968), 202. The growing Sassoon disinterest in business is recounted on 198–202.

109 "I would either produce a genius or an idiot": Jackson, *The Sassoons*, 203.

110 Victor first traveled to Bombay, where he visited the Sassoon textile mills: Details of Victor's visit are described in Jackson, *The Sassoons*, 135–8.

110 "inevitable chorus belle on his arm": Jackson, *The Sassoons*, 135–38.

111 "If I had healthy and attractive children": Harriet Sergeant, *Shanghai: Collision Point of Cultures* (New York: Crown Publishers, 1990), 130.

112 potential leaders weren't faring much better: Jackson, *The Sassoons*, 202–3.

113 assumed that he would be a dilettante figurehead: Details of Victor's early years in India drawn from Jackson, *The Sassoons*, 200–204.

114 "I don't pretend to know anything about debating": Letter from Victor Sassoon to Yvonne FitzRoy, July 22, 1923, housed in the British Library (IOPP/ Mss Eur E312).

114 "is one to conjure with in India": Letter from Victor Sassoon to Yvonne FitzRoy, August 5 (no year), British Library (IOPP/Mss Eur E312).

115 "what must the half-educated man think": Letter from Victor Sassoon to Yvonne FitzRoy, July 22, 1923, British Library (IOPP/Mss Eur E312).

115 still spurned Victor and his wealthy family: Interview with Harvard professor Roderick MacFarquhar, whose father was a British civil servant in India in the 1920s.

116 Sassoon noticed how Silas Hardoon: Victor's initial impressions of Shanghai detailed in Jackson, *The Sassoons*, 211–12.

116 "Things never really get bad in China": Letter from Victor Sassoon to Yvonne FitzRoy, February 11, 1927, British Library (IOPP/Mss Eur E312).

116 told an Indian newspaper he was leaving: Sergeant, *Shanghai*, 131; Maisie Meyer, *Shanghai's Baghdadi Jews* (Hong Kong: Blacksmith Books, 2015), 269–70.

117 "like an Art Deco rocket ship rising from the Huangpu River": Description of the Cathay and its history drawn from Peter Hibbard, *Peace at the Cathay* (Shanghai: Earnshaw Books, 2013) and from interviews with Peter Hibbard, who graciously shared his private files with me.

118 "sharing my bed but not my bath": Sergeant, *Shanghai*, 132.

119 "smelling of must and mildew": James Hutchison, *China Hand* (New York: Lothrop, Lee and Shepard, 1936), 273, 220.

119 "Keeping trim on vegetables": Meyer, *Shanghai's Baghdadi Jews*, 273–74.

119 **Victor installed a recording booth:** Records are on display in a small exhibit off the lobby of the Cathay, now known as the Fairmont Peace Hotel, along with information on the booth and the social whirl of the hotel in the 1930s.

120 **No world cruise was complete without a stop in Shanghai:** Sergeant, *Shanghai*, 5; see also Hibbard, *Peace at the Cathay*; interview with Peter Hibbard.

121 **ignited a building boom that transformed Shanghai:** Heyward Parker James, "Victor Sassoon and the Twilight of Foreign Shanghai," M.A. thesis, 1993, Tufts University; interviews with James, who graciously shared his insights about Victor Sassoon and Shanghai.

122 **China was business:** Interview with Isaac Sassoon.

122 **included a careful color-coded system:** Sir Ellice Victor Elias Sassoon, Bart., G.B.E. papers and photographs, DeGolyer Library, Southern Methodist University, Dallas, Texas, *passim*.

123 **"The plight of the Chinese merchant":** Harold Isaacs, *The Tragedy of the Chinese Revolution* (New York: Haymarket Books, 2010), 155–56.

123 **Chiang Kai-shek dispatched his top financial officials:** Victor's frequent meetings with the Nationalists are recorded in his diaries held by the DeGolyer Library. See, for example, his entries dated January 9, 1933; January 11, 1933; January 21, 1933; January 28, 1933. See also frequent references to these and other meetings, *passim*, in his letters to Yvonne FitzRoy, held by the British Library (IOPP/Mss Eur E312).

124 **"graduates of your colleges":** Seagrave, *The Soong Dynasty*, 338.

124 **"Time does fly here":** Letter from Victor Sassoon to Yvonne FitzRoy, December 23 (no year), British Library (IOPP/Mss Eur E312).

125 **presented Victor with a "First Class Gold Medal":** Meyer, *Shanghai's Baghdadi Jews*, 277.

125 ***Fortune* did a lavish feature on the "Shanghai boom":** "The Shanghai Boom," *Fortune*, January 1935.

127 **Its commercial possibilities, Braga told Elly, were "limitless":** Beverly Howells, "Braga's Wealth of Hong Kong Stories," *South China Morning Post*, May 31, 1987. Copy of article in author's possession.

127 **turned the Cathay into a stage for parties:** Details drawn from Sergeant, *Shanghai*, 132–34.

128 **"one couldn't very well snub a man who played golf with the Prince of Wales":** Sergeant, *Shanghai*, 131.

128 **attended the races and his growing racing stables:** Meyer, *Shanghai's Baghdadi Jews*, 274.

129 **"the J. P. Morgan of China and India":** Taras Grescoe, *Shanghai Grand: Forbidden Love and International Intrigue in a Doomed World* (New York: St. Martin's Press, 2016), Kindle location 79.

129 **carefully pasted nude pictures:** See, for example, diary entry dated January 12, 1933, in Sir Ellice Victor Elias Sassoon, Bart., G.B.E. papers and photographs, DeGolyer Library.

130 **a drawer in his desk filled with diamond bracelets:** Interview with Michael Green, whose father worked for Victor Sassoon.

130 **Victor put his hand on her knee:** Interview with Patrick Cranley.

130 **an American writer named Emily Hahn:** Details of the relationship between Emily Hahn and Victor are drawn from Grescoe, *Shanghai Grand*, especially 84–92, 133–35, and 192–94; and Cuthbertson, *Nobody Said Not to Go*, especially chapters 14 and 18.

131 **"his ivory-colored face was perfectly oval":** Cuthbertson, *Nobody Said Not to Go*, chapter 15.

132 **"In the beginning he would quote Confucius":** Emily Hahn, *Mr. Pan: A Memoir* (New York: Open Road Media, 2014), Kindle location 40.

132 **"emotional complications" shuttling between Zau and Victor:** Taras Grescoe describes the relationship between Victor Sassoon and Emily Hahn in his entertaining *Shanghai Grand* (New York: St. Martin's Press, 2016). This quote is from 211.

133 **"He did me an enormous favor":** Emily Hahn, *China to Me* (New York: Open Road Media, 2016).

133 **"Even the aristocrats here, the ones I know, admit that Communism is the only way out":** Grescoe, *Shanghai Grand*, 111.

134 **being complicit in exploitation:** Grescoe, *Shanghai Grand*, 159–60.

135 **A foreigner in Shanghai "lives in a world unto himself":** Edgar Snow, "The Americans in Shanghai," *American Mercury* 20 (August 1930), 437–45.

135 **Yang Mengliang, the poor son:** Yang Mengliang, "My Days as a Waiter in the Cathay Hotel," *Yan Hunag Chun Qiu* magazine 2 (2005).

136 a Chinese customer wrote to a local newspaper complaining: Meyer, *Shanghai's Baghdadi Jews*, 271.

136 Lu Xun visited the Cathay to see a British friend: Grescoe, *Shanghai Grand*, 188.

138 "less danger than an American city on the Fourth of July": Letter from Victor Sassoon to Yvonne FitzRoy, March 6, 1932, British Library (IOPP/Mss Eur E312).

138 "treat Shanghai as theirs and everybody as their enemy": Letter from Victor Sassoon to Yvonne FitzRoy, March 6, 1932, British Library (IOPP/Mss Eur E312).

139 profitable relations with Chiang Kai-shek's Nationalist government began to sour: Details of the "banking coup" and its background are drawn from James, "Victor Sassoon and the Twilight for Foreign Shanghai"; Sterling Seagrave, *The Soong Dynasty* (New York: HarperCollins, 1985), Kindle location 341–52; Victor Sassoon diary entries dated April 25, 1935; November 4, 1935; November 7, 1945, in the collection Sir Ellice Victor Elias Sassoon, Bart., G.B.E. papers and photographs, DeGolyer Library.

139–140 consequence for the Chinese economy was catastrophic: The background of the Shanghai Banking Coup is detailed in Seagrave, *Soong Dynasty*, 323–26, 345–52; interview with Parker James.

141 future of foreign investment in Shanghai was "precarious": Joseph Chamberlain, "The Feetham Report on Shanghai," *Foreign Affairs*, October 1931.

141 "A plague on both your houses is my motto": Letter from Victor Sassoon to Yvonne FitzRoy, March 21 (no year), British Library (IOPP/ Mss Eur E312).

142 saw "dead bodies, one of a gardener and family": Letter from Victor Sassoon to Yvonne FitzRoy, March 6, 1932, British Library (IOPP/Mss Eur E312).

143 named two British citizens as Japan's enemies in China: Newspaper clipping from *Nichi Nichi Shimbun* enclosed in letter from Victor Sassoon to Yvonne Fitzroy dated December 23 (no year); British Library (IOPP/Mss Eur E312).

143 "Things are looking really serious now, and I cannot see what is to be done": Letter from Victor Sassoon to Derek Fitzgerald, January 11, 1938,

in Sir Ellice Victor Elias Sassoon, Bart., G.B.E. papers and photographs; DeGolyer Library.

CHAPTER SIX: "ME VOILA THEREFORE WALKING A TIGHTROPE"

145 **twelve-year-old Erich Reisman:** Details of Erich's story drawn from an oral history conducted by Steve Hochstadt, "Reisman, Erich, oral history interview" (1997). Shanghai Jewish Oral History Collection, https://scarab .bates.edu/shanghai_oh/11. For details of the experiences of Shanghai refugees, see also Steve Hochstadt, *Exodus to Shanghai* (New York: Palgrave Macmillan, 2012).

147 **The diplomat was Ho Feng-Shan:** Details of Ho's life and activities drawn from interview with Ho's daughter, Man-Li Ho; see also Gao Bei, *Shanghai Sanctuary: Chinese and Japanese Policy Toward European Jewish Refugees During World War II* (New York: Oxford University Press, 2013), 50–57.

148 **"natural to feel compassion and to want to help":** Glenn Sunshine, "Christians Who Changed Their World," Breakpoint, Colson Center for Christian Worldview, www.breakpoint.org/2015/09/ho-feng-shan-1901-1997.

149 **Japan's fascination with Jews:** Details of Japanese impressions of Jews before World War II and the rise of anti-Semitism in Japan are drawn from: Gao, *Shanghai Sanctuary*, 19–29; David Kranzler, *Japanese, Nazis and Jews* (New York: Yeshiva University Press, 1976).

152 **The Jews are the "true rulers of China":** This quote and quotes from Inuzuka, Japanese memos, and directives in this chapter are drawn from documents reprinted in Kranzler, *Japanese, Nazis and Jews*, 608–619; see also Gao, *Shanghai Sanctuary*, 59–126; Herman Dicker, *Wanderers and Settlers in the Far East* (New York: Twayne Publishers, 1962), 80–97.

152 **"The only race greater than the Jews":** The quote is widely cited—for example, in Sergeant, Jackson, and Roth, but is considered by some to be apocryphal.

153 **"Very sorry, we have no budget for this":** Maisie J. Meyer, *From the Rivers of Babylon to the Whangpoo: A Century of Sephardi Jewish Life in Shanghai* (Lanham, NY: University Press of America, 2003), 197.

154 "Victor, there is a war going on": Interview with Rabbi Marvin Tokayer, who was told the story by Elly's son Lawrence Kadoorie.

155 "We were trying to persuade him to support us": Interview with Prof. Maruyama Naoki.

156 given $500 to a Chinese man for "intelligence work": Diary entry for November 10, 1937, in the collection Sir Ellice Victor Elias Sassoon, Bart., G.B.E. papers and photographs, DeGolyer Library, Southern Methodist University.

156 "a very hush-hush affair": Letter from Evelyn Sassoon to Stanley Jackson, August 5, 1966. Stanley Jackson Collection, Howard Gotlieb Archival Research Center at Boston University.

156 "Japanese ambassador Ito on verge of being offensive": Diary entry for January 3, 1938, in Sir Ellice Victor Elias Sassoon, Bart., G.B.E. papers and photographs, DeGolyer Library.

157 "Can you imagine me knowing nothing": Stanley Jackson, *The Sassoons* (London: Heinemann, 1968), 253.

157 "heard lots of facts and some conjectures at our committee meetings": Details of Victor's dealings with the Japanese are drawn from Jackson, *The Sassoons*, 253–57; Meyer, *From the Rivers of Babylon*, 208–14; Maisie Meyer, *Shanghai's Baghdadi Jews* (Hong Kong: Blacksmith Books, 2015), 286–89.

157 "damn all foreigners and the world": Victor Sassoon letter to Yvonne Fitzroy, undated, British Library (IOPP/Mss Eur E312).

157 "not be long before the Japanese and the British become good friends": Lawrence Kadoorie memo to Horace Kadoorie, September 4, 1939, Hong Kong Heritage Project.

158 "Me voila therefore walking a tightrope": Letter from Victor Sassoon to Yvonne FitzRoy, undated; British Library (IOPP/Mss Eur E312).

158 "Whatever Elly gave, I'll give": Ezra Yehezkel-Shaked, "Jews, Opium, and the Kimono" (Jerusalem: Rubin Mass, 1995), 114.

158 flew to Brazil and purchased 10,000 square miles of land: Meyer, *Shanghai's Baghdadi Jews*, 282.

159 "quite impossible to absorb any large numbers of foreign refugees": The growth of the refugee population is documented in a series of reports to the Joint Distribution Committee. See, for example, M. Speelman,

"Report on Jewish Refugee Problem in Shanghai," June 21, 1939, Joint Distribution Committee archives, New York, NY; see also Meyer, *From the Rivers of Babylon*, 200–202.

160 **"'Ohel!' is right":** Letter from J. J. Patterson to W. J. Keswick, October 19, 1938, Jardine Matheson Archives, University of Cambridge.

160 **made available the first floor of one of his luxury skyscrapers:** Details of Victor's charity and support of the refugees drawn from Harriet Sergeant, *Shanghai: Collision Point of Cultures* (New York: Crown Publishers, 1990), 319–20; Victor Sassoon diary entries for March 8, 1939; April 17, 1939; April 23, 1939; June 13, 1939, in Sir Ellice Victor Elias Sassoon, Bart., G.B.E. papers and photographs, DeGolyer Library; Meyer, *Shanghai's Baghdadi Jews*, 283–6; Taras Grescoe, *Shanghai Grand* (New York: St. Martin's Press, 2016), 230–34.

161 **"God will forgive him":** Meyer, *From the Rivers of Babylon*, 212.

161 **"they were Moroccan":** Erich Reisman oral history.

162 **"wept like children":** "The Shanghai Myth," *American Hebrew and Jewish Tribune* 145, no. 20 (1939): 5.

162 **began selling his wife's gloves to other refugees:** Erich Reisman oral history.

164 **Theodore Alexander, a young man:** Oral history interview with Rabbi Theodore Alexander, United States Holocaust Museum, Accession Number: 1999.A.0122.508, RG Number: RG-50.477.0508.

168 **"I now get pilgrimages from everyone from Tokyo":** Letter from Victor Sassoon to Yvonne FitzRoy, May 3, 1939, British Library (IOPP/Mss Eur E312).

168 **The Jews, Inuzuka wrote, were like *fugu*:** Marvin Tokayer and Mary Swartz, *The Fugu Plan: The Untold Story of the Japanese and the Jews During World War II* (New York: Gefen Publishing House, 2004).

169 **the "leavings" of Europe:** Grescoe, *Shanghai Grand*, 234.

171 **no more Jews would be allowed into the city:** The events leading up to the Japanese decision to stop admitting Jewish refugees are drawn from Kranzler, *Japanese, Nazis and Jews*; Gao, *Shanghai Sanctuary*; and Meyer, *From the Rivers of Babylon*, 214–15.

171 **"German Jews from Spain joining the Chinese":** Victor Sassoon diary entry, June 22, 1939, in Sir Ellice Victor Elias Sassoon, Bart., G.B.E. papers and photographs, DeGolyer Library.

171 **"reprisals would be taken against Jews"**: "Empire Showing of Jewish Play Cancelled Here," *Israel Messenger*, undated clipping, from Joint Distribution Committee archives, copy in author's possession. Fears of growing Nazi influence in Shanghai are also recounted in Meyer, *From the Rivers of Babylon*, 205–8.

172 **"behaving just as gangsters did in America"**: Memorandum from Victor Sassoon, June 1, 1939, British Library.

172 **"mischievous Hollywood playboy"**: Meyer, *Shanghai's Baghdadi Jews*, 277.

172 **"Bad news of French asking for terms"**: Victor Sassoon diary entry, June 18, 1940, in Sir Ellice Victor Elias Sassoon, Bart., G.B.E. papers and photographs, DeGolyer Library.

173 **"This is an insult to Japan"**: Details of the meeting drawn from Jackson, *The Sassoons*, 255–56. The meeting is also recorded in Victor Sassoon diary entry from June 17, 1940.

175 **Sassoon executives called Theodore Alexander and other clerks:** Theodore Alexander oral history.

175 **Inuzuka stepped behind Victor's desk:** Interview with Rabbi Marvin Tokayer; see also letter from Henry Ford to Victor Sassoon, April 10, 1943, copy in author's possession.

CHAPTER SEVEN: WAR

177 **Lawrence Kadoorie crouched in a military rescue boat:** Details of Lawrence's actions as the Japanese invaded and captured Hong Kong drawn from Nigel Cameron, *Power: The Story of China Light* (Hong Kong: Oxford University Press [China], 1982), 139–48; Lawrence Kadoorie interview with Wendy Barnes; interviews and correspondence with members of the Kadoorie family.

179 **"the days when Kowloon went lightless by night"**: Cameron, *Power*, ix–x.

180 **"there was no means of stopping"**: Interview with Lawrence Kadoorie, Hong Kong Heritage Project.

181 **"And then, suddenly, this"**: Emily Hahn, *China to Me* (New York: Open Road Media, 2016).

181 "one cigarette, a small tin of watery rice": Judy Green and Judy Diestal, "Jews in Hong Kong," in *Encyclopedia of the Jewish Diaspora* 3 (ABC-CLIO, 2009), 1188.

182 "I'm not going to Shanghai with your father": Nicky Careem and M. A. Hopper, "The Legendary Name of Kadoorie," *Kaleidoscope* (Hong Kong) 3, no. 9 (1976): 4–20.

183 sent American Laura Margolis to Shanghai: Details of Laura Margolis's experiences in Shanghai taken from Laura Margolis, "Report of Activities in Shanghai, China, from December 8, 1941, to September, 1943," American Joint Distribution Committee Archives, New York. Margolis also recounted her experiences in a report to the American Jewish Joint Distribution Committee, "Race Against Time in Shanghai," March 1944, available online at the JDC archives, https://archives.jdc.org/wp-content/uploads/2018/06/shanghai_race-against-time-in-shanghai.pdf. See also her oral interviews with the U.S. Holocaust Museum, https://collections.ushmm.org/search/catalog/irn504643, and with a University of Wisconsin researcher, https://dc.uwm.edu/etd/548; Maisie J. Meyer, *From the Rivers of Babylon to the Whangpoo: A Century of Sephardi Jewish Life in Shanghai* (Lanham, NY: University Press of America, 2003), 214–17.

186 compose a letter to the Japanese camp commandant: Copy of letter in author's possession; details of the captivity in Hong Kong and transfer to Shanghai taken from Lawrence Kadoorie, *The Kadoorie Memoir*, and oral histories, in Hong Kong Heritage Project.

186 more than 3,000 jammed aboard: Interviews with Lawrence Kadoorie archived at Hong Kong Heritage Project.

188 "live as normally as possible": "Lady Muriel Kadoorie," Geni, accessed May 23, 2018, www.geni.com/people/Lady-Muriel-Kadoorie/6000000011181437076.

189 German members of the SS had arrived in Shanghai: Margolis, "Report of Activities in Shanghai, China"; Pan Guang, "Uniqueness and Generality: The Case of Shanghai in the Annals of the Jewish Diaspora," in *From Kaifeng to Shanghai*, ed. Roman Mallek (Sankt Augustin: Steyler Verlag, 2000); Meyer, *From the Rivers of Babylon*, 207–8; Herman Dicker, *Wanderers and Settlers in the Far East* (New York: Twayne Publishers, 1962), 112–25.

190 create a ghetto in the Hongkew neighborhood: David Kranzler, *Japanese*

Nazis and Jews: The Jewish refugee community of Shanghai, 1938–1945
(New York: Yeshiva University Press, 1976), 620–26.

191 **"He could be very mean":** Samuel Iwry, *To Wear the Dust of War: From Bialystok to Shanghai to the Promised Land, an Oral History*, ed. L.J.H. Kelley (New York: Palgrave Macmillan, 2004), 120.

192 **astonished many of the refugees:** Exhibition, Shanghai Jewish Refugee Museum, Shanghai.

192 **"a limp, a monocle and that Shanghai brand of arrogance":** Han Suyin, *Birdless Summer* (New York: G. P. Putnam's Sons, 1968). Also recounted in Taras Grescoe, *Shanghai Grand* (New York: St. Martin's Press, 2016), 295.

194 **"inclined to blame you for his miserable lot":** Letter from Henry Ford to Victor Sassoon, April 10, 1943, copy in author's possession; also quoted in Grescoe, *Shanghai Grand*, 273–74.

194 **"You can forget China":** Stanley Jackson, *The Sassoons* (London: Heinemann, 1968), 259.

196 **"last communication I received":** Ernest Heppner, *Shanghai Refuge: A Memoir of the World War II Jewish Ghetto* (Lincoln: University of Nebraska Press, 1993), 58.

197 **"We were lucky. Nobody gassed us":** Illie Wacs and Deborah Strobin, "The Liberation of the Shanghai Jewish Ghetto," *Huffington Post*, January 27, 2012, www.huffpost.com/entry/the-liberation-of-the-shanghai-jewish -ghetto_b_1236647.

197 **Ho Feng-Shan was recalled by his superior:** Interview with his daughter, Manli Ho.

198 **acknowledged that she had been too harsh:** Interview with Maisie Meyer.

198 **sent all his Jewish employees checks for three years' salary:** Theodore Alexander oral history.

198 **kept a framed photograph taken by Victor Sassoon:** Interview with Prof. Naoki Murayama, who visited the apartment and saw the photograph.

CHAPTER EIGHT: "I GAVE UP INDIA AND CHINA GAVE ME UP"

201 **At Marble Hall, Lawrence's four-year-old son, Michael, pedaled his tricycle:** Speech by Michael Kadoorie to Hong Kong Jewish History historical

meeting, Hong Kong Heritage Project. Details of activities at Marble Hall in the weeks after the American liberation of Shanghai drawn from memo from Horace Kadoorie to Lawrence Kadoorie, September 30, 1945, Hong Kong Heritage Project.

202 **hitch a ride on a British military plane:** Lawrence Kadoorie, *The Kadoorie Memoir,* Hong Kong Heritage Project.

203 **Horace left Marble Hall to go to the Shanghai Gas Co.:** Letter from Horace Kadoorie to Lawrence Kadoorie, September 23, 1945, Hong Kong Heritage Project.

206 **waiting to see "which way the wind would blow":** Lawrence Kadoorie diary entry, December 20, 1945 (Hong Kong Heritage Project).

206 **start unloading properties:** Stanley Jackson, *The Sassoons* (London: Heinemann, 1968), 267.

206 **"Unnecessary, unjustifiably stupid":** Victor Sassoon diary entries, June 10 and 12, 1948, in Sir Ellice Victor Elias Sassoon, Bart., G.B.E. papers and photographs, DeGolyer Library, Southern Methodist University.

207 **Victor entered a room filled with hundreds of grim-faced employees:** Jackson, *The Sassoons,* 268.

207 **"Conditions in Shanghai are deteriorating":** Letter from Horace Kadoorie to Henriques, November 4, 1946; Horace Kadoorie to S. E. Levy, August 8, 1946, Hong Kong Heritage Project.

209 **began spending several hours a day searching for a tombstone:** Letter from Horace Kadoorie to Lawrence Kadoorie, January 30, 1948; see also Horace to Lawrence, February 17, 1948, and Horace to Lawrence, March 16, 1948, Hong Kong Heritage Project.

209 **one of the most valuable ivory collections in the world:** Correspondence with members of the Kadoorie family.

211 **"Sir Victor's speech was excellent":** Letter from Horace Kadoorie to Lawrence Kadoorie, March 19, 1948, Hong Kong Heritage Project.

211 **"I need some summer clothes as I have nothing":** Letter from Horace Kadoorie to Lawrence Kadoorie, April 19, 1948, Hong Kong Heritage Project.

211 **"The Chinese is like a woman":** Taras Grescoe, *Shanghai Grand* (New York: St. Martin's Press, 2016), 298.

213 "I gave up India and China gave me up": Jackson, *The Sassoons*, 268.

214 Ovadia was a prisoner: Details of Ovadia's years in Shanghai under the Communists drawn from Ovadia letter to Victor Sassoon, in Stanley Jackson Collection, Howard Gotlieb Archival Research Center at Boston University. See also Jackson, *The Sassoons*, 271–74.

216 formed a union and presented demands for higher wages: Letter from David Ezekiel to Horace Kadoorie, October 19, 1950, and Ezekiel to Horace Kadoorie, January 23, 1950, Hong Kong Heritage Project.

216 The manager then slipped a message through an intermediary to Lawrence Kadoorie: Letter from S. Zenkovich to Lawrence Kadoorie, October 14, 1954, collection of Peter Hibbard.

218 "taking over many valuable properties in and around Shanghai": Letter from J. W. Morcher to Horace Kadoorie, February 28, 1950; J. W. Morcher to Mrs. H. H. Lennox, March 17, 1950. For Madame Sun's support of Jews suffering under Nazism, see "The Civilized World Against Hitlerism," *Israel's Messenger* (Shanghai), June 2, 1993, 7. For the Chinese seizure of Kadoorie properties elsewhere in Shanghai, see "Statutory Declaration by Douglas Webster," November 9, 1989, and "A Report on the Astor House in Shanghai," April 7, 1957, Hong Kong Heritage Project.

218 "a symbol of the struggle against the dead weight of imperialism": Jeffrey N. Wasserstrom, *Global Shanghai, 1850–2010: A History in Fragments* (New York: Routledge, 2009), 77.

219 "consider everything we have in Shanghai as lost": Letter from Lawrence Kadoorie to Horace Kadoorie, November 22, 1956, Hong Kong Heritage Project.

CHAPTER NINE: THE RECKONING

223 spent weeks pleading with British and American military officers: Lawrence's return to Hong Kong is described in Lawrence Kadoorie, *The Kadoorie Memoir*, Hong Kong Heritage Project.

224 Hong Kong was now the "most looted city in the world": Vaudine England, *The Quest for Noel Croucher: Hong Kong's Quiet Philanthropist* (Hong Kong: Hong Kong University Press, 1998), 159.

225 hadn't seen "so much food for many years": Descriptions of Hong Kong drawn from Lawrence Kadoorie private diary entry, December 15, 1945; letter from Lawrence Kadoorie to Muriel Kadoorie, May 4, 1945, Hong Kong Heritage Project.

225 Lawrence still had assets: Interview with Victor Fung.

227 "may become another Shanghai": Memo from Lawrence Kadoorie to Horace Kadoorie, June 7, 1946, Hong Kong Heritage Project.

227 "circumstances rose which rendered it advisable for this to be destroyed": Memo from Lawrence Kadoorie to Brigadier D. M. MacDougall, December 25, 1945, Hong Kong Heritage Project.

227 dizzying array of projects: Details drawn from memo from Lawrence Kadoorie to Horace Kadoorie, November 28, 1945; memo on committee chaired by Lawrence Kadoorie on housing, building and reconstruction, April 9, 1946; "The Harbour Ferry Services Advisory Committee—Report, September 22, 1950"; "Minutes of Meeting of Sub-Committee of Hong Kong Labor Advisory Board, November 15, 1945"; Lawrence Kadoorie private diary entry, December 16, 1945, all from Hong Kong Heritage Project; "Rents and Houses," *South China Morning Post*, July 19, 1946; "Public Invited to Air Views on Ferry Service in Questionnaire Scheme," *Hong Kong Tiger Standard*, November 24, 1950.

229 "bring in men of different backgrounds and talents": England, *Noel Croucher*, 160.

230 The Rong family, moguls of the flour and textile industries: Elisabeth Koll, "The Rong Family: A Chinese Business History," paper, Harvard Business School, 2010.

232 Jewish Star of David: The house and mosaic still exists at 186 Shaanxi Rd. N., Shanghai.

233 "Will you give us electricity if we come to Hong Kong?": Details of the arrival of the Shanghai capitalists drawn from Carles Brasó Broggi, "Shanghai Spinners: Pioneers of Hong Kong's Industrialization, 1947–1955," Industrial History of Hong Kong Group, December 25, 2018, https://industrialhistoryhk.org/shanghai-spinners-pioneers-hong-kongs -industrialization-1947-1955; Hong Kong Heritage Project, "Tai Ping Carpets—a Brief History," www.hongkongheritage.org/pages/post.aspx?

post=18; interview with members of the Kadoorie family. For the role of the textile industry and Shanghai capitalists in Hong Kong, see Wong Siu-Lun, *Emigrant Entrepreneurs: Shanghai Industrialists in Hong Kong* (London: Oxford University Press, 1989).

234–35 **"immense fear, eerily like the Jews in WWII":** Rong Yiren's visit to the Cathay Hotel drawn from Dayan Chen, *The Peace Hotel* (Shanghai: Shanghai Press, 2015), 19–50.

236 **never made a business decision:** Details of the relationship between the Kadoorie brothers drawn from interviews with David Akers-Jones, members of the Kadoorie family, William Mocatta, Leung Chik, Eileen Marsden, Michael Green, and Robert Dorfman. See also oral histories of Rita Kadoorie and Michael Kadoorie in the Hong Kong Heritage Project.

236 **spotted a new gardener:** Interview with the gardener, Leung Chik.

238 **spotted a fire that destroyed a nearby farm:** Interview with the farmer, Mr. Fu.

239 **"If that makes him happy, I am OK":** Interview with S. J. Chan.

239 **Politics fueled the urgency behind the program:** Interview with David Akers-Jones, former chief secretary and acting governor of Hong Kong. Details of Horace's activism on behalf of refugees and farmers in the New Territories drawn from letter from Horace Kadoorie to K. M. A. Barnett, July 5, 1955; draft letter from Horace Kadoorie on his frustrations with Rural Development Committee meetings, December 5, 1959; letter from Horace Kadoorie to DCC Liddington, December 14, 1970; all Hong Kong Heritage Project.

240 **Typical of the families Horace was helping were the Tsangs:** Interview with Tsang family; the activities of the KAAA are recounted on its website, www.kfbg.org/eng, and in Harry Rolnick, "The Kadoorie Experiment with Charity," *Asian Business & Industry*, November 1976.

242 **"everything about pigs except the taste":** Interview with Leung Chik.

243 **"non-involvement in political issues":** Steve Tsang, *A Modern History of Hong Kong* (London: I. B. Tauris, 2004), 158, Kindle location 3771–86.

245 **"neon-emblazoned outpost of capitalist modernity":** Mark Lambert Clifford, "Let There Be Light: China Light & Power and the Making of Modern Hong Kong," PhD thesis, University of Hong Kong, March 2019.

245 two most effective anti-Communists Asia had produced: Jonathan Swift, "It Started with a Spilled Barrel," *Reader's Digest*, no date, copy in author's possession. See also Lawrence Kadoorie memo prepared for meeting with British secretary of state Oliver Lyttleton, December 14, 1951, Hong Kong Heritage Project.

246 "no doubt that Hong Kong is run by an elite": Vaudine England, "Lord Kadoorie," *Discovery* (Hong Kong), March 1986, 58–59.

246 beat back calls to nationalize his electricity company: Leo Goodstadt, *Uneasy Partners: The Conflict Between Public Interest and Private Profit in Hong Kong* (Hong Kong: Hong Kong University Press, 2005), 176–80.

246 "squeals of the privileged": Hong Kong Public Records Office (HKRS 131/3091/48).

247 never used the return portion of his ticket: For details of Victor's life after Shanghai, see Stanley Jackson, *The Sassoons* (London: Heinemann, 1968), 275–87; interview with his wife's niece, Evelyn Cox.

249 "His world had changed so much": Interview with Evelyn Cox.

250 "Promise me you will never go to China": Interview with Evelyn Cox.

251 Shanghai itself became a target: Robert Bickers vividly describes the turmoil the Cultural Revolution brought to Shanghai in his *Out of China: How the Chinese Ended the Era of Western Domination* (Cambridge: Harvard University Press, 2017), Kindle location 322–57.

252 Cultural Revolution spread to Hong Kong: Robert Bickers and Ray Yep, eds., *May Days in Hong Kong: Riot and Emergency in 1967* (Hong Kong: Hong Kong University Press, 2009), 1–8 and *passim*.

253 blocking the street and waving flags: Oral history of Horace Kadoorie's secretary and others, Hong Kong Heritage Project.

253 convened a meeting of the family: Details of the Kadoorie response to the 1967 riots drawn from interviews and correspondence with members of the Kadoorie family.

CHAPTER TEN: THE LAST TAIPAN

258 "Apartments are lighted by a Kadoorie-controlled utility": Linda Matthews, "Sir Lawrence Kadoorie Carries on the Legend of Old China Traders," *Wall Street Journal*, March 2, 1977, 1.

258 **effectively controlled 10 percent of Hong Kong's economy:** Interviews with William Mocatta and members of the Kadoorie family.

259 **"brought down the Bamboo Curtain":** "A Businessman Philosopher," *Forbes*, December 19, 1983, 117.

259 **Beethoven's Fifth Symphony:** Lawrence Kadoorie interview with Wendy Barnes.

261 **"We would value your help":** Interview with members of the Kadoorie family; interview with Y. B. Lee. Details of maneuvers that led to the start of nuclear power talks are drawn from those interviews along with "Memo from K. M. Wilford to Sir Murray MacLehose," August 5, 1974, National Archives FCO/40/512 294929; "Project 77 Report to Board of Directors," September 30, 1977, Hong Kong Heritage Project; Y. B. Lee, "The Dawn of Daya Bay," China Light and Power internal document, October 2007, copy in author's possession.

262 **had long dreamed of selling electricity to China:** Lawrence Kadoorie, speech, March 29, 1979, Hong Kong Heritage Project; Memo to Sir Murray MacLehose, August 5, 1974, National Archives FCO 40/512/294929.

263 **venting anti-Semitic comments:** Interviews with sources who spoke with Lawrence Kadoorie at the time; interviews with members of the Kadoorie family; Frank H. H. King, *The Hongkong Bank in the Period of Development and Nationalism, 1941–1984* (Cambridge: Cambridge University Press, 1991), 684.

263 **as an old China hand:** Letter from Lawrence Kadoorie to James Callaghan, May 26, 1978, National Archives, Records of the Prime Minister's Office, Kew, UK.

264 **Lawrence then made his way to Shanghai:** Interview with members of the Kadoorie family.

264 **Lawrence was then taken to see the graves of his parents:** Interview with members of the Kadoorie family and William Mocatta.

265 **wrote to Callaghan renewing his plea for an ambitious plan to sell electricity to Guangdong:** Correspondence between Callahan and Lawrence Kadoorie and comments on Kadoorie plans from National Archives, Records of the Prime Minister's Office, Kew, UK.

267 **"remarkable octogenarian who is thought to be one of the world's richest men":** Brief for Prime Minister's Meeting with Sir Lawrence Kadoorie,

no date but likely August 1979, National Archives, Records of the Prime Minister's Office, Kew, UK.

267 "If ping pong diplomacy can bring about a rapprochement": Notes on meeting with Sir Lawrence Kadoorie, July 28, 1980, National Archives, Records of the Prime Minister's Office, Kew, UK.

267 crossed out sentences: Draft letter from the prime minister to send to Lawrence Kadoorie, no date but likely August 1979, National Archives, Records of the Prime Minister's Office, Kew, UK.

268 "could be the future of Hong Kong we are talking about": Lawrence Kadoorie notes to management group meeting, June 27–30, 1980, National Archives, Records of the Prime Minister's Office, Kew, UK.

270 "We know you are Jewish": Details of the meeting based on interviews with officials and researchers at the Shanghai Academy of Social Sciences.

270 Peter Max, the American illustrator: Liao Guangjun, "A Jewish Artist Looking for His Shanghai Amah," September 14, 2016, trans. Huang Xie'an, http://en.shisu.edu.cn/resources/features/jews-in-shanghai-1.

271 an important military connection: Interview with Meron Medzini, former director of the Israel Government Press Office in Jerusalem.

274 useful conduit to British businesses in Hong Kong: Interview with David Li.

274 Lawrence faced defeat as well: Remarks of Lord Kadoorie on British Nationalities Bill, October 20, 1981, Hong Kong Heritage Project.

276 "Humpty Dumpty took a great fall": "A Businessman Philosopher," Forbes, December 19, 1983, 116–17.

276 joked about their ages: Meeting between Deng Xiaoping and Lawrence Kadoorie based on interview and contemporaneous notes of Nai Ling, who was Kadoorie's interpreter; oral history of Nai Ling, Hong Kong Heritage Project; Y. B. Lee, "The Dawn of Daya Bay."

278 Lawrence met Pan Guang: Interview with Pan Guang.

CHAPTER ELEVEN: BACK ON THE BUND

281 "I keep my spirits up": Letter from Lawrence Kadoorie to Rabbi Marvin Tokayer.

281 "hope to see you in Daya Bay at the opening": Y. B. Lee, "The Dawn of Daya Bay," 45.

281 driven to Boulder Lodge for his usual Sunday curry lunch: Mark Hughes, "Human Dynamo Who Powered Hong Kong," *South China Morning Post*, August 26, 1993.

282 attend a reunion in San Francisco of some of the Shanghai refugees: "Shanghai Recalled as a Haven for Jews," *New York Times*, August 4, 1980; Theodore Alexander oral history; reunion program and memorabilia held by Hong Kong Heritage Project.

283 Lawrence left the raising of the children to Muriel: Oral history of Rita Kadoorie and oral history of Michael Kadoorie, Hong Kong Heritage Project; interview with Michael Kadoorie.

284 "a man of many enthusiasms . . . unfortunately business isn't one of them": Linda Matthews, "Sir Lawrence Kadoorie Carries on the Legend of Old China Traders"; see also Jonathan Friedland, "Realm of the Peer," *Far Eastern Economic Review* (July 8, 1992): 62–66.

284 deft in negotiating with and working with China's leaders: Interview with Y. B. Lee, who attended the meetings.

285 The Kadoories were ranked the tenth richest: Pei Yi Mak, Blake Schmidt, Venus Feng, Yoojung Lee, Steven Crabill, Peter Eichenbaum, Andrew Heathcote, and Tom Metcalf, "Asia's 20 Richest Families Control $450 Billion," *Bloomberg*, August 23, 2019, www.bloomberg.com/features/richest-families-in-asia.

285 expanded his alliance with the powerful Rong family: Steve Mufson, "To Chinese Firm, Access Becomes a Key Commodity," *Washington Post*, March 26 1997, A21.

285 told them he wanted to return to Shanghai and build a hotel: Interview with Clement Kwok; interview with Paul Tchen.

287 grand opening of the new Peninsula Hotel on the Bund: "Grand Opening: The Peninsula Shanghai," The Peninsula Hotels, YouTube video, March 11, 2012, www.youtube.com/watch?v=l4_GpSqQkew.

287 "Your family has always been a friend to China": Interview with members of the Kadoorie family; interview with William Mocatta; for Michael's dealing with Chinese leaders, details drawn from interview with Y. B. Lee.

295 Victor Sassoon's niece Evelyn Cox sat in the tourist bus: Interview with Evelyn Cox.

297 "this horrible rich person who lived off the poor people": Interview with Evelyn Cox.

297 "My family used to be in the drug trade": Interview with Hugh Sassoon.

298 met with China's finance minister, Lou Jiwei: Interview with James Sassoon.

Index

Jardine, Matheson & Co., xiii, 18–20, 25–28, 32, 33, 36–40, 67, 82, 84, 93, 116–17, 160, 207, 215, 231, 286, 297
Jardine, William, 37
Jazz Age, 85
Jerusalem, 4, 5, 92
Jewish refugees, xxvii–xxviii, 145, 148–49, 153, 153–73, 226
  children of, 271
  Cuba's turning away of, 183
  Evian Conference on, 159
  Ho's visas and, 148, 197
  Japan and, 155–73
  Inuzuka's "fugu" plan for, 168, 169–70
  Joint Distribution Committee and, 169, 183–85, 191, 197
  Kadoorie family and, xxvii–xxviii, 153, 164–67, 173–74, 191, 197–98, 237, 282, 288, 291
  Sassoon family and, xxvii–xxviii, 153–64, 168–73, 191, 197–98, 235, 288, 292
  in Shanghai, 145, 148–49, 153, 155–74, 182–85, 189–92, 195–98, 218, 229, 269–72
  Shanghai, reunion of, 282
  Sugihara and, 289
Jews, xxiii, xxiv–xxv, 147
  American, 150
  anti-Semitism and, xxiv, 44, 82–83, 88, 105, 116–17, 144, 150–52, 155, 160, 192, 249, 262–63
  in Babylonian Captivity, 4–5
  in Baghdad, 3–5, 7–9, 88
  Brazil as possible haven for, 158–59
  in Britain, 3, 11, 42–44, 56, 58, 60
  Chinese-inspired Judaism, 89
  in cousinhood, 56
  diaspora of, 5
  Dreyfus affair and, 103–4
  flights from oppressive rulers, 3–4
  Holocaust and, 4, 196–97; see also Jewish refugees
  Israel created, 89

Japan and, 149–52
Judaism and modern life, 5
  in Kaifeng, 89, 289
Kristallnacht and, 160, 164
  in London, 58, 60
Protocols of the Elders of Zion and, 150–51
  in Russia, 150, 155
Sabbath of, xxiii, 5, 15
"Shabbos goys" and, xxiii
Sun Yat-sen and, 89–90, 153
Zionism and, see Zionism
Jiang Qing, xv, xx, 251
Jiang Zemin, 284, 293
Jimmy's Kitchen, 134–35
Jobs, Steve, xxviii
Joint Distribution Committee, 169, 183–85, 191, 197

Kadoorie, Ellis, 56
  death of, 83
  schools opened by, 60
Kadoorie, Elly, xii, xiii–xiv, 48, 51–57, 60–63, 68–69, 72, 73, 76, 82–93, 126–27, 141, 153, 158, 159, 174, 179, 181, 225, 227, 230, 250, 267, 283, 286, 290
  alias used by, 54, 59, 88
  becomes millionaire, 65–66
  Boulder Lodge retreat built by, 127
  Braga and, 126–27, 179
  British citizenship battles of, 69, 82, 87, 88, 126, 274
  Bubbling Well Road mansion of, 72
  cancer of, 185–86, 194–95, 209
  charitable causes of, 59–60, 87, 94
  Chiang and, 97
  David Sassoon compared with, 51
  death of, 195, 209, 225, 259, 294
  in disinfectant incident, 52–53
  Elly Kadoorie & Sons, 59
  empire of, 83
  as financier, 65–66
  fire and, 72–73, 82

girls' schools built by, 59–60, 87, 94
grave and tombstone of, 209, 212, 252,
    264–65
in Hong Kong, 53–55, 57–58
hotels of, 83, 85–87
Hotung and, 55, 87–88, 127, 179
investments of, 70
Japanese companies and, 178
as Japanese prisoner, 181, 182, 185–86,
    187, 194, 209
Jewish refugees and, 153
Kadoorie Hill built by, 127
Keswick and, 82–83, 84, 93
knighthood of, 87, 126
Kowloon investment of, 126–27
Laura's marriage to, 57
Laura's meeting of, 56–57
London sojourn of, 63–64
as outsider, 83, 88
rubber crisis and, 64–66, 70
Sassoon family and, 51–53, 62, 83, 88
social barriers and, 55
sons of, 92, 294; *see also* Kadoorie,
    Horace; Kadoorie, Lawrence
stock brokerage formed by, 54
stock holdings of, 64–66, 70,
    87–88, 92
Sun Yat-sen and, 68, 89, 90, 153
Victor Sassoon's meeting with,
    153–54
World War I and, 69
Zionism and, 88–90, 92
Kadoorie, Horace, xiii, 57, 61, 66, 72, *76*,
    82, 84, 88, 91, 92, 96, 159, 160, 165,
    182, 187, 195, 202–5, 207–11,
    216–17, *222*, 236–42, 245, 253, 264,
    281, 283, 290–92, 294
Chinese refugees aided by, 236–40
Communists and, 212, 213
death of, 282, 283
departure from Shanghai, 211
as farmers' advocate, 238–43, 246,
    258, 279
Fu and, 238, 279

in Hong Kong, 211, 212, 236–42
Japan admired by, 178
Japanese arrest of, 177, 182, 183, 187
Jewish refugees aided by, 164–67,
    173–74, 237, 282
Kadoorie Agricultural Aid
    Association of, 239–43, 257,
    258, 292
Kadoorie School of, 166–67, 173, 175,
    182–84, 191, 198, 216, 270, 282, 286
Lawrence and, 226–27, 236, 239, 294
Leung Chik and, 236–38, 242, 243
Madame Sun and, 217, 218
parents' tombstone and, 209, 212, 252
Tsang family and, 240–41
Kadoorie, Laura, xii–xiii, *48*, 56–63,
    70–73, 84, 104, 160, 178, 294
in boat incident, 61–62
charity work of, 56, 59, 71, 91,
    292–94
children of, 59
death in fire, 72–73, 82, 83, 85, 294
diary of, 57, 60–63, 69–72, 78
education as cause of, 59–60, 72, 87,
    293, 294
Elly's marriage to, 57
Elly's meeting of, 56–57
funeral for, 73
grave of, 212, 252, 264–65
in Hong Kong, 57–60
London sojourn of, 63–64
travels of, 57, 60–63
women's opportunities promoted by,
    71–72
Kadoorie, Lawrence, xiii, xv, xxii, 53, 57,
    58, 61, 66, 72, *76*, 82, 84, 91–93, 165,
    167, 174, 179, 202, 204, 207, 208,
    211, 212, *222*, 245, *256*, 257–69,
    272–79, 281–84, 290–92, 294
Callaghan and, 263–64, 265, 267
colonialism as viewed by, 246
Communists and, 210–11, 216–17
death of, 282, 283, 284
Deng and, *256*, 273, 276–77, 278, 281